GREAT GOLF

Game-Changing Tips from History's Top Golfers

Edited by Danny Peary and Allen F. Richardson

Foreword by Gary Player

TRIUM
BOOK

D1057293

Mom,
Always there when it counts.
—A.F.R.

For my formidable foursome: Laura, Suzanne, Zoë, and Julianna.
—D.P.

Library of Congress Cataloging-in-Publication Data

Great golf : game changing tips from history's top golfers / edited by Danny Peary and Allen F. Richardson ; foreword by Gary Player.
    p. cm.
    ISBN 978-1-60078-672-3
    1. Golf—History—Anecdotes.   I. Peary, Danny, 1949–   II. Richardson, Allen F.
GV963.G676 2012
796.352—dc23

                                                                          2011049426

This book is available in quantity at special discounts for your group or organization. For further information, contact:

Triumph Books LLC
542 South Dearborn Street
Suite 750
Chicago, Illinois 60605
(312) 939-3330
Fax (312) 663-3557
www.triumphbooks.com

This collection is a streamlined variation on *Great Golf: 150 Years of Essential Golf Instruction from the Best Players, Teachers, and Writers of All Time,* which was published by Stewart, Tabori & Chang in 2005.

Printed in U.S.A.

ISBN: 978-1-60078-672-3

Design by Amy Carter

CONTENTS

PART ONE: PRE-SWING FUNDAMENTALS

PART TWO: THE SWING

FOREWORD

I am grateful to Danny Peary and Allen F. Richardson for asking me to contribute to their ambitious anthology. Their collection of articles, written by many of the greatest names in golf over the last 150 years and presented chronologically within the various chapters, confirms that golf instruction and golf history always have been intertwined. Similarly, golf instruction has been part of my history. I have taken instruction, given instruction, read instruction, and written instruction, all to my great benefit.

Undoubtedly, there is tremendous value in reading the essays in this large volume. It's my belief that reading is to the mind what exercise is to the body. While some golfers prefer visual stimulation in the way of video or photographic instruction, others learn more through reading. Learning the basic fundamentals and reading extensively about the game and how it is played is essential during the formative years of an aspiring golfer, and can clearly help an established golfer re-evaluate what he or she is doing. One must always be open-minded to learning more and changing, as I certainly was during my own career.

My earliest golf instruction was received from my father, who worked underground in the gold mines of South Africa. He was a good player and one day he was invited to play with the mining company executives. He asked me to join him, and I was immediately taken with the game. I was in my mid-teens when I took up golf, and my father taught me the basics. I played every chance I got. Over the years I have read most of the authors who appear in this book, but while growing up, I did not read instructional books at all. They simply were not available in South Africa at the time. However, Jock Verwey, the father of my girlfriend Vivienne (who is now my wife), was a golf coach in Johannesburg and became my instructor. Under his tutelage I began to develop into a pretty decent player and took the job as his assistant pro. The remarkable Ben Hogan and Sam Snead were the other two major influences on me as I set my sights on a professional career. I admired Hogan for his fundamentals and work ethic and Snead for his athleticism (and eventually his longevity).

As a club pro, the two things I tried to teach my pupils were patience and my now well-documented mantra, "the harder I practice, the luckier I get." Unfortunately, it's easier to get a camel through the eye of a needle than to get the average weekend golfer to practice. It is the hardest thing about being an instructor. However, I have never stopped telling aspiring golfers to practice, and that theme is common to all my books, including the one I'm working on now.

The first book that really influenced how I played was not a golf book, but Norman Vincent Peale's *The Power of Positive Thinking*, which definitely could be applied to the game and its instruction. Positive thinking in golf is a whole lot better than overthinking. I do believe too many young players, especially today, get "paralysis of analysis." I also think many young players spend too much of their practice time trying to add distance to their drives. In some places it has been written that my philosophy has been to "learn to hit the ball for distance, which always will stay with you, and then learn to golf the ball to score." But that's not my philosophy at all! Seventy percent of all shots are played from 100 yards in and so you must practice your short game with that in mind. That is my philosophy—or, at least a major part of it.

Also, as someone who changed his grip and swing early on, I have taught and written that while there are right and wrong things to do in golf, it still must be left to the individual player to find what works or feels best for him or her. This is absolutely true. As long as you have learned the essential, basic fundamentals, what your swing looks like is less important. One only has to look at Jack Nicklaus, Arnold Palmer, Lee Trevino, and me to see how "different" we look when swinging the club. However, our fundamentals are sound and that's what matters. As so many writers in this book stress: learn the fundamentals before moving on!

I believe that aspiring golfers who read this book will profit greatly from what the old masters wrote on various aspects of golf. Harry Vardon, Bobby Jones, Hogan, Snead and the others had to be, in many ways, more talented than today's young guns. Just consider the condition of the courses they played on and the equipment and ball they had to use. In fact, the views I expressed in the 1962 essay I wrote on escaping bunkers that is included in this volume, which might have been considered a breakthrough piece back then, have changed in some ways. Today's equipment—wedges with square grooves and more than 60 degrees of loft, for example—coupled with the consistency of the sand in any given week on the Tour, have made bunker play much easier than it was 43 years ago.

Unfortunately, a lot of touch, feel, and flare have been eliminated from sand play since I wrote "The Blaster."

Modern equipment, the ball, and impeccably maintained golf courses are the biggest changes that have taken place in golf in the last 20 to 40 years. The theories on how to play the game haven't evolved all that much; in the majority of cases, they have simply been—as this book's editors point out—re-examined and recycled using different language. As someone who is called the "World's Most Traveled Athlete," I honestly believe that there has been absolutely nothing new with the golf swing since I began writing instruction. However, the changes in balls, clubs, and courses have resulted in a remarkable depth of talent on the Tour.

With so many players on the Tour having essentially the same skills, now more than ever it's attitude, mental toughness, and the hunger to win that make the difference. I am pleased that this book's editors also have included two golfers with whom I've long been associated, Jack Nicklaus and Arnold Palmer, because there are no better models for young players who want to learn what it takes to win. When we competed as the so-called "Big Three," I saw just how mentally tough they were.

Great Golf is a treasure trove of essays by golf champions, as well as the teachers of champions. If you want to become a complete golfer, physically and mentally, then you are sure to find what you're looking for—just begin on page one and keep reading. I am delighted that readers will find me in this book, as one of the individuals who has tried to play a part in the history of golf instruction.

—Gary Player

PREFACE

*"I love golf, I live golf, I dream golf.
If only I could play golf."*

This old joke surely sums up the relationship most struggling golfers have with the marvelous but endlessly frustrating game. The supreme joke teller, Bob Hope, insisted he couldn't give up golf because his sweater collection would go to waste. But the rest of us consider it so enjoyable and challenging that quitting is *not* a viable option. All we want is to play better.

As golf has evolved and grown since it was first played in a remote corner of Scotland 600 years ago, all aspiring golfers have desired the same things: a reliable, repeatable swing; a fail-safe short game with a sure putting stroke; a bigger drive; and confidence. In short, we want consistency, touch, *and* power. But, intriguingly, golf always has eluded perfection, and because of that, it has generated endless debate, discussion, and a thousand theories on how best to use a set of oddly shaped clubs and one's physical and mental attributes to register a winning score. The continuing quest for the elusive formula for how to play golf correctly has spawned a corresponding industry devoted to instruction and theory.

The genesis for this book, in fact, was our own obsessive reading of golf instruction. Yes, we had purchased new equipment and spent countless hours at driving ranges and in our front and back yards making deep divots. We had taken lessons and played as much as our egos could handle. To supplement all this, we felt the need to read as much golf instruction as we could get our hands on, no matter who wrote it. We did it partly because, as sports historians, we were fascinated by the evolution of golf instruction from the mid-1800s, which coincided with the evolution of the amateur and professional game. More significantly, we hoped to use our new knowledge to upgrade our own games. But as we spent too much time trying to navigate through an endless maze of golf instruction, where there was far less good than bad and ugly material, we realized how convenient it would be if there was *one* book that included only the best lessons.

Our goal was to pull together more than 150 years of advice, knowledge, and theory and present it in its original form, as written by the pioneers and influential individuals who followed. Included are both classic essays from famous golfers and gurus and articles by them on aspects of the game for which they are *not* best known and a few forgotten or obscure pieces that deserve attention today. Each chapter in the book's four sections is arranged chronologically to show how various golfers and experts during different eras espoused past theory, refined a theory, or came up with something entirely different.

As with art, it appears that each generation of golfers has borrowed from the masters who came before them, modifying an old technique with their own dash of ingenuity, and creating something that both honors the past and is wholly their own. In many instances, the various writers from all eras basically agree on a specific premise. At other times, ideas are reconfigured or cast aside entirely and replaced by vastly different opinions. In some cases, it can be like dueling golf theorists. *Great Golf* is not meant to settle debates; rather, we hope it adds fuel to the fire, leaving to the reader the judgment of how best to proceed.

The authors of the book's 67 chapters are a veritable "who's who" of golf history, with lessons by renowned golfers who either wrote instruction or actually became instructors, such as Willie Park, Jr., Horace G. Hutchinson, Harry Vardon, J. H. Taylor, James Braid, Bobby Jones, Byron Nelson, Ben Hogan, Sam Snead, Gary Player, Jack Nicklaus, Nick Faldo, Chi Chi Rodriguez, Tom Watson, Ernie Els, and Tiger Woods; legendary teachers such as Ernest Jones, Percy Boomer, Davis Love, Jr., Bob Toski, Jim Flick, John Jacobs, Harvey Penick, Jim McLean, David Leadbetter, Hank Haney, Dave Pelz, and Butch Harmon; and great writers such as P.A. Vaile, O.B. Keeler, Alistair Cooke, and Michael Corcoran.

The names listed above are only of men, but *Great Golf* also provides a needed forum for female golfers and instructors whose contributions to the body of golf instruction have long been unfairly neglected. Celebrated players Genevieve Hecker, Cecil Leitch, Joyce Wethered, Helen Hicks, Babe Zaharias, Mickey Wright, Marlene Bauer Hagge, and Nancy Lopez; and teachers Vivien Saunders, Beverly Lewis, and Kellie Stenzel take their rightful places with their male counterparts. Indeed, we wonder how different this book would have been if the bored, male, Scottish shepherd of legend, hitting a rock with his crook, had been out in that meadow with a female companion, and they had said, *together*, "Ah, let's invent golf." Perhaps if women had been there at the beginning, the skill, creativity, and art would be even more enhanced in this best of all games, whose appeal reaches to both the heart and the mind.

—Danny Peary and Allen F. Richardson

ACKNOWLEDGMENTS

When we published the original version of *Great Golf*, our intention was to unearth (or reintroduce) and keep alive for golfers and golf historians marvelous instruction that had been written by golf legends over the previous 150-plus years. So we are thrilled that seven years later Triumph Books has embraced our collection, resurrecting and reimagining it for an entirely new readership.

For this streamlined, "best of the best" volume of essential instruction, we thank: Mitch Rogatz, president and publisher of Triumph Books, whose vision, support, and feedback were so essential in the creation and fulfillment of this project; and Tom Bast, editorial director at Triumph and champion of *Great Golf* from the start. Tom was the primary contact with our agency, RLR Associates, and the man who presented the title to Triumph's editorial board and negotiated the contract. Special thanks also must go to the two primary hands-on editors of this book: Don Gulbrandsen, Triumph's managing editor at the time, who helped shape this book in its infancy, and then shepherded it through its initial stage with his always helpful insight, unfailing support, and easy availability; likewise to Noah Amstadter, developmental editor at Triumph, who skillfully handled the second stage, for his flexibility, keen eye, and, again, easy availability. Both of you made the doing not only timely and efficient, but also fulfilling and fun. What more could we ask of an editor?

Finally, to Amy Carter, with our gratitude and admiration for her graceful, clean, and modern design; and to Nick Panos, the creative mind behind the great new cover for *Great Golf*; and Bill Ames, our crack publicist.

Again we also would like to acknowledge Gary Player for lending his words and name to *Great Golf*. During his nearly 60 years in the public eye no one has better exemplified what is great about golf. We sincerely say that it is an honor to have his name on our cover and his foreword to begin our book. Very special thanks to Gida Campbell, the media director of the Gary Player Group, for her enormous help.

We are most grateful to our agent, Scott Gould of RLR Associates, Ltd.

for finding our book a new home. Thank you Robert L. Rosen, for always being there, and everyone else at RLR, present and past, including agent Jennifer Unter, for getting this project off the ground.

We also wish to again convey our tremendous appreciation to our original editor Anne Kostick at Stewart, Tabori & Chang, and her crack team, which included copyeditor Lara Comstock. We thank Leslie Stoker, our publisher at STC, and Jessica Napp, Kate Norment, Andrea Glickson, Galen Smith, Dervla Kelly, and Kristen Latta.

We spent countless hours doing research at the USGA Library in Far Hills, New Jersey. We would have been lost if it weren't for Doug Stark, USGA Librarian and Curator of Archival Collections; Rand Jerris, the extremely knowledgeable Director of the museum and archives; and unsung heroine Patty Moran, the Archives Research Assistant whose work on our behalf was far beyond the call of duty; and Nancy E. Stulack, Registrar, Museum and Archives. We thank everyone there for their kindness. If you want to research golf, there is no better place.

Also extending invaluable help on background research and in reaching individuals were: Frank Thorp, who researched copyrights at the Library of Congress in Washington; Mark Cubbedge, Peyton Taylor, Tammy G. Smith, and Jack Peter of the World Golf Hall of Fame, Samantha Groves, the curator of the British Golf Museum in St. Andrews, Scotland; Bill Cioffoletti and Una Jones of the PGA of America; Kathy Widick and Dana Von Louda of the LPGA; and Dr. Gary Wiren, PGA Master Professional.

For their help and patience answering a multitude of questions about the game of golf and the methods of various golfers, we thank Frank A. Cisterino, PGA golf professional and former owner of Willow Creek Golf Club, Vermilion, Ohio, along with his son, Anthony D. Cisterino, the former assistant teaching pro at that facility; Beverly Lewis, European PGA teaching pro and former captain of the British PGA; George Lewis of Golfiana, PGA Master Professional, Mamaroneck, N.Y.; Chris Meadows, European PGA teaching pro, golf mentor, teacher, and friend; Chris Bleile, PGA, and Director of Golf, Sawmill Creek Golf Club, Huron, Ohio, along with Ryan Spicer, PGA and head golf professional at Sawmill; Christopher Toulson, PGA, Corporate Director of Instruction at the Jim McLean Golf Schools; the late Ned Vare, teaching pro, author, friend, and the son of Glenna Collett Vare; Cheryl Anderson, PGA and LPGA, the 2006 LPGA Teacher of the Year, the 2007 Metropolitan PGA

Section Teacher of the Year, and now the Director of Instruction, Mike Bender Golf Academy, Lake Mary, Fl.; Patrick Robertson, PGA and assistant golf professional at the Connecticut Golf Club; Boris Busljeta, PGA and certified personal coach at GolfTEC, New Rochelle, N.Y.; Angela Aulenti, PGA and LPGA, and Director of Golf, Sterling Farms Golf Club, Stamford, Ct.; Barbara Boltin, LPGA and Director of Instruction, Sterling Farms; Vance Levin, PGA and Head Professional at E. Gaynor Brennan Golf Course in Stamford, Ct. and teaching pro at Sterling Farms; and with a special thank you to Robert J. LaRosa, PGA and head golf professional at Sterling Farms, who patiently answered our endless questions on golf technique and history, no matter how tiresome and inane. We also extend very special gratitude to Tom Kokoska for his invaluable insight on the science and technology of the game; and to Chris Ajemian, Westchester County, N.Y., teaching pro, for his unique perspective and support.

When we acquired permissions for the original volume we were given exceptional treatment by a number of people on both sides of the Atlantic. For your next permissions party, we recommend you invite: Carol Christiansen, Deborah Foley, Rebecca Heisman, Alicia Torello, Caryn Burtt, Michael Greaves, Bette Graber, and Lisa Phillips of Random House; Catherine Trippett and Nicole Gross of Random House Group, London; Rose Marie Cerminaro, Jeniqua Moore, Lydia Zelaya, Marie Florio, and Nicole Albers of Simon & Schuster; Florence B. Eichin of Penguin Group (USA) Inc.; Melinda Lin-Roberts of Human Kinetics; Julie DiMarco and Bob Carney of *Golf Digest*; W.L. Pate, Jr. of the Babe Didrikson Zaharias Foundation, Inc.; Kate O'Hearn and Briar Silich of Hodder and Stoughton, Ltd.; Jack and Ann Snead; Sidney L. Matthew; Melvin Powers of Wilshire Book Company; Patty Berg and her assistant Toby Hingson; Mrs. Armen C. Boros; Martin J. Elgison, of Alston & Bird, and the family of Bobby Jones; Albert Zuckerman, Susan Ginsburg, and Emily Saladino of Writers House LLC; Grace Anderson Smith of *Time*; Faith Freeman Barbato of HarperCollins; Laura Scott of HarperCollins, England; Michelle Irwin of Golden Bear International; Jimmy Ballard and Laurie L. Ensor of J.B. Golf Enterprises; Jon M. Bradley, CPA of Weaver and Tidwell L.L.P., representing Byron Nelson; Byron Nelson; Jack Nicklaus; Ken Bowden; Patrick Shearer, Scott Plikero, and Ebony Rosa of McGraw-Hill Education; Colin Webb of Palazzo Editions Limited; David Grossberg, attorney representing Alistair Cooke; Richard Myers of Thinkandreachpar.com; Pauline

Zline of Taylor Trade Publishing; Esther Robinson of St. Martin's Press; Kellie Stenzel; Rosanna Bruno of Russell & Volkening, Inc.; MaryKate Roberts of Time Warner Book Group; Butch Harmon and his assistant Carole; Mary Kay McGuire-Willson and the family of Johnny Farrell; Bev Norwood and Jennifer Bassett of IMG: Christine Duggan of Gerald Duckworth & Co.; Gerardine Munroe: Katy Smith; Erick McClenahan of Icon Sports Management; Chi Chi Rodriguez; Ilene Tannen of Pennie and Edmonds, LLP; Tara Gavel and Lorin Anderson of GOLF Magazine; Andrew Clark of Harlequin, Mills & Boon, Ltd.; Hilary Doan of AP Watt; Mimi Ross of Henry Holt & Co.; Paul Williams and Steve Kendall of Country Life/IPC Country & Leisure Media; Carolann Workman and Walter Weintz of Workman Publishing; John Jacobs; Kathryn Bradwell of Callaway Editions; Leigh Gensler; Maria Bohman of Nick Faldo Enterprises; Peter Tummons of Metheun & Company; Scott Rowan of Triumph Books; Monique Riedel of St. Remy's Media; Julie Kacala; Gail Blackhall; Jessica Napp; Margaret L. Kaplan; and Robert Sidorsky. Thank you all for being so attentive and generous.

We are compelled to thank our authors, dead and alive, whose fascinating writing fills the pages of our book. You are the book, and we salute you.

And finally, for their unfailing support, we wish to express our heartfelt gratitude to Roy and Dawn Barnes, Joan and the late Fred Baum, John and Valerie Bell, Dr. Robert Brody, Amy Byronette, Tom Clavin, Lance and Mardi Cone, Al and Susan Daniels, Lori Delfico, and Kelly R. Johnson, Danny "Disco" Dellano, Jeanie Dooha, Susan Friedland, Cory Gann and Sharon Holt, Roy Greenberg, Wendy Hirschhorn, Philip and Mayda Idone, Cindi Kane, Joan Kokoska, Bob Kouffman, Debbie Thron, Daniel Rubinstein, Carol Summers, Mary Tiegreen, Bill Truog, and Simon and Anita Wood. And loving family members Karen Curry, Samantha Richardson, Cody Greenoe, Roberta Trosper; Gerald Peary, Amy Geller, Suzanne Rafer, Zoë Weaver Ohler, Gene Ohler, Julianna Ohler, and our dear moms, Nancy Richardson and the late Laura Peary.

Ben Hogan, who likened the "Vardon" overlapping grip to a work of art, nevertheless altered his in 1945—repositioning his little finger. The average golfer, however, should stick to the conventional position: resting the little finger of the right hand in the crease formed by the first two fingers of the left. (Hulton Archive/Getty Images)

PART ONE

PRE-SWING
FUNDAMENTALS

THERE IS NO GREATER SATISFACTION in golf than hitting the ball precisely as intended. But as the greatest players and teachers have preached for more than a century, to hit successful shots consistently, aspiring golfers must spend countless hours mastering the *pre*-swing fundamentals. Indeed, most duffers fail to improve because they don't work on their grips, setups, and pre-shot routines. In the late 1800s, golfers began experimenting with new grips that moved the club from the palms into the fingers, encouraging the hands to work together. The three grips that evolved and are still taught today were the 10-finger "baseball" grip, the interlocking grip, and, most notably, the overlapping, or "Vardon grip." Around 1900, golfers also broke away from the setup associated with the classic St. Andrews swing. Since then, instruction emphasizing the proper setup has evolved into a set of standards that applies to the width of the stance, posture, balance, alignment, and ball position in relation to the clubs being used and the desired shot. The pre-shot routine was the last of the pre-swing fundamentals to be codified in golf manuals. However, even early champions like Jim Barnes and Joyce Wethered urged golfers to *first* "visualize" their shots, and Bobby Jones stressed the importance of combining that mental aspect and a flawless setup. Decades later Jack Nicklaus also instructed to use imagination with a meticulous setup to produce consistently good shots, and many more golfers bought into the concept.

CHAPTER 1

THE GRIP

Art Is in the Eye
of the Beholder

The Grip of the Club:
Two Hands Like One

1905 • Harry Vardon

Great Britain's "Great Triumvirate" of Harry Vardon, J.H. Taylor, and James Braid dominated golf from the early 1890s to World War I. That Vardon surpassed the fame of his two rivals is due equally to his links legacy—"The Stylist" won six British Open titles and was a tremendous success touring America—and his popularization of the overlapping grip that had been pioneered by Scots Johnny Laidlay and F.A. Fairlie and was being used by Taylor and other golfers to make their hands work together. Vardon's seminal *The Complete Golfer* is still widely read because he explained his influential swing and other reasons he was his era's best all-around player, but the starting point continues to be the "Vardon grip." Although its early detractors feared it might break players' thumbs, it became the foundation for "modern golf" and remains, over 100 years later, the grip of choice.

My grip is one of my own invention. It differs materially from most others, and if I am asked to offer any excuse for it, I shall say that I adopted it only after a careful trial of all the other grips of which I had ever heard.... In my opinion it has contributed materially to the attainment of such skill as I possess. The favor which I accord to my method might be viewed with suspicion if it had been my natural or original grip, which came naturally or accidentally to me when I first began to play as a boy, so many habits that are bad being contracted at this stage and clinging to the player for the rest of his life. But this was not the case, for when I first began to play golf I grasped my club in what is generally regarded as the orthodox manner, that is to say, across the palms of both hands separately, with both thumbs right round the shaft (on the left one, at all events), and with the joins between the thumbs and first fingers showing like two Vs over the top of the shaft. This is usually described as the two-V grip, and it is the one which is taught by the majority

HARRY VARDON'S STROKESAVERS:

- Hold the club more in the fingers than the palms.
- Start by laying the club across the knuckle joint of the left forefinger.
- Place the left thumb just to the right of center on the club.
- Fold the right hand over the left thumb.
- Let the little finger of the right hand ride on the first finger of the left.

of professionals to whom the beginner appeals for first instruction in the game. Of course it is beyond question that some players achieve very fine results with this grip, but I abandoned it many years ago in favor of one that I consider to be better. My contention is that [my] grip…is sounder in theory and easier in practice, tends to make a better stroke and to secure a straighter ball, and that players who adopt it from the beginning will stand a much better chance of driving well at an early stage than if they went in for the old-fashioned two-V. My grip is an overlapping, but not an interlocking one. Modifications of it are used by many fine players, and it is coming into more general practice as its merits are understood and appreciated. I use it for all my strokes, and it is only when putting that I vary it in the least, and then the change is so slight as to be scarcely noticeable.…

I do not grasp the club across the palm of either hand. The club being taken in the left hand first, the shaft passes from the knuckle joint of the first finger across the ball of the second. The left thumb lies straight down the shaft—that is to say, it is just to the right of the center of the shaft. But the following are the significant features of the grip. The right hand is brought up so high that the palm of it covers over the left thumb, leaving very little of the latter to be seen. The first and second fingers of the right hand just reach round to the thumb of the left, and the third finger completes the overlapping process, so that the club is held in the grip as if it were in a vice. The little finger of the right hand rides on the first finger of the left. The great advantage of this grip is that both hands feel and act like one, and if, even while sitting in his chair, a player who has never tried it before will take a stick in his hands in the manner I have described, he must at once be convinced that there is a great deal in what I say for it, although, of course, if he has been accustomed to the two V's, the success of my grip cannot be guaranteed at the first trial. It needs some time to become thoroughly happy with it....

I have the strongest belief in the soundness of the grip that I have thus explained, for when it is employed both hands are acting in unison and to the utmost advantage, whereas it often happens in the two-V grip, even when practiced by the most skillful players, that in the downward swing there is a sense of the left hand doing its utmost to get through and of the right hand holding it back.

There is only one other small matter to mention in connection with the question of the grip. Some golfers imagine that if they rest the left thumb down the shaft and let the right hand press upon it there will be a considerable danger of breaking the thumb, so severe is the pressure when the stroke is being made. As a matter of fact, I have quite satisfied myself that if the thumb is kept in the same place there is not the slightest risk of anything of the kind. Also, if the thumb remains immovable, as it should, there is no possibility of the club turning in the hands as so often happens in the case of the two-V grip when the ground is hit rather hard, a pull or a slice being the usual consequence. I must be excused for treating upon these matters at such length. They are often neglected, but they are of extreme importance in laying the foundations of a good game of golf.

From *The Complete Golfer*, by Harry Vardon. Methuen & Company, London, England.

CLUB DEFINITIONS

Here are the names of now antiquated clubs with roughly their modern equivalents:

Brassy—2 Wood or 3 Wood

Spoon—3 Wood

Driving Cleek—1 Iron

Cleek—2 Iron

Mashie—5 Iron

Mashie Niblick—7 Iron

Niblick—8 Iron or 9 Iron

Evolution of the Hogan Grip

1948 · Ben Hogan

Ben Hogan's Power Golf was published in 1948, soon after the driven, introverted Texan won the U.S. Open, and a few months before his career almost ended in a nearly fatal car crash. Although less detailed and sophisticated than Hogan's 1957 instructional masterwork, *Ben Hogan's Five Lessons, The Modern Fundamentals of Golf,* it gave readers insight into how the period's most dominant (with Sam Snead and Byron Nelson) and obsessive player never stopped finding ways to improve. In the book's first chapter, the lefty who became a right-handed golfer as a boy revisited how he altered his grip to have more success, coming up with an overlapping grip that had a different finger placement than Harry Vardon's model, and, like Bobby Jones', differed from Vardon's in regard to pressure points. The result was that from 1946 until the accident in early 1949, he would win a remarkable 32 tournaments.

The grip I now use was arrived at by a series of trial-and-error experiments which began when I first took up the game. As recently as the fall of 1945, when I got out of the service, I made a radical change in my grip which I had been experimenting with whenever I got a chance to play golf while in the Army.

I had been aware for some time that if I wanted to make a comeback as a successful golfer after I was discharged from the Army I would have to make a change in my grip to correct a tendency I had always had to over-swing on the backswing....

Formerly I used a grip in which I had what might be best described as a long thumb when speaking of the position of the thumb of the left hand on the shaft. During the course of the backswing that thumb used to slide down on the shaft, and as a result I was always guilty of a certain looseness at the top of my swing which prevented me from getting the maximum of control.

In correcting this I pushed the left thumb back up on the shaft. The entire change couldn't have amounted to more than half an inch in the movement of the thumb, but it was enough to restrict my backswing so that it no longer is loose....

It took me some time to get accustomed to that new grip, but I had...it in working order when I resumed tournament play in 1945.... I've used it ever since.

The nearest publicized grip to which my grip can be compared is the overlapping grip made famous by Harry Vardon, the great English player, and adopted by so many top players in this country. Strictly speaking, however, my grip is not the same.

My grip differs from the conventional overlapping grip in the relationship between the little finger of the right hand to the index finger of the left hand and the position of my right hand on my left.

In the conventional overlapping grip the little finger of the right hand overlaps the index finger of the left hand. Whereas I have found that I am able to get a firmer grip, transmitting more power to the clubhead, by gripping the little finger of my right hand around the knob of the knuckle of the index finger of my left hand.

My grip also differs from that of other golfers in that my right hand rides higher on the outside of my left hand. This enables the two hands to act as a single unit, thus imparting considerably more hand action and consequently more clubhead speed at the moment of impact.

Getting the proper grip at the start is one of the most important steps in learning how to play golf. For that reason let us first consider the intents and purposes of the grip in relation to golf.

One reason why the grip is so important is because by means of it we telegraph our energy and our desires to the club. To do this with a maximum amount of efficiency we've got to have a grip which will permit our hands and wrists to work properly as one unit and not against each other.

BEN HOGAN'S STROKESAVERS:

- "Shorten" the left thumb, pushing it back a half inch up the club shaft.
- Grip the knuckle of the left index finger with the right little finger.
- Hold the club more in the palm of the left hand, but in the fingers of the right.
- Apply more pressure with the last three fingers of the left hand, and the two middle fingers of the right.

The idea is to have free and uniform hand action throughout the swing while still maintaining the clubface at the proper angle when it strikes the ball. The objective is to make a solid contact of the clubhead with the ball at the exact moment you are telegraphing your greatest amount of energy to the club via the grip....

As I favor my own version of the overlapping grip, naturally that's the one I'm going to talk about.... Starting with the left hand, my grip is very definitely a palm grip. The leather or rubber grip on the shaft of your club will lie diagonally across the palm of the left hand just above the callus pad.

In folding the left hand around the club the left thumb will be slightly on the right side of the shaft. As you look down on your left hand in gripping the club you should be able to see the first three finger joints on the outside of that hand. It also should be apparent to you that your left hand is well over the shaft.

In gripping with the left hand there is definitely more pressure on the last three fingers of that hand than there is on the index finger and thumb. While gripping with these three fingers you should also push down on the top of the leather or rubber grip of your club with the butt of your hand. This will assure you of a firm grip. Try it and you will get the sensation of having the club locked in that hand.

As far as the right hand is concerned my grip is definitely a finger grip. By that I mean that the club lies diagonally across the fingers of the right hand below the callus pad. When you fold the right hand over the grip on the shaft you will find that if you have gripped the club correctly there is a cup formed in the palm of the hand that will allow space enough for the left thumb. The thumb of the right hand is slightly on the left side of the shaft and not on the top.

Make sure that the right hand rides high on the left hand. The purpose of this, of course, is to mold the two hands together so that they can act as one unit and not two. The greatest pressure in the right hand is in the two middle fingers. That is because the club is well down in the fingers of the right hand with a lot of hand left over.

How to Grip

1977 • Jack Nicklaus with Ken Bowden

In the 1950s, then British Ryder Cup captain Dai Rees claimed the interlocking grip was almost passé. In America, Lloyd Mangrum and, for a time, Julius Boros were the only PGA golfers of note using the grip once employed by Francis Ouimet and Gene Sarazen. In the 1960s, only one notable new golfer on the Tour used it, but since it was emerging superstar Jack Nicklaus, the interlocking grip was legitimized once again as a viable alternative to the overlapping grip. Tom Kite, Tiger Woods, and 2011 U.S. Open champion Rory McIlroy would later use the interlocking grip, but Nicklaus is still the golfer most associated with it. In this essay written with *Golf Digest's* then editorial director Ken Bowden, Nicklaus asserted he used the interlocking grip because of his small hands, but he argued convincingly that any golfer desiring a natural, firm, easy-to-learn grip that assures the hands will work in unison should give it a try.

My grip today is the one I started with—the interlocking grip, in which the little finger of the right hand and the forefinger of the left hand intertwine. I've nothing against either the overlapping grip or the 10-finger grip, but I really can't understand why the interlocking grip is not more popular. It has, in my view, three big assets. First, it is more natural than the overlapping grip, where the hooking of the small right finger over the knuckle of the left forefinger seems to me to be an artificial linkage. Second, the interlocking grip is the easiest to learn—beginners find it much easier than the overlapping grip. Third, it automatically locks the hands together—you try pulling mine apart! However, the correct grip for you is the one that works best for you. You should experiment to discover which that is, then stick to it.

The right hand grip is primarily in the fingers, for two reasons. First, a finger grip promotes maximum "feel" or "touch." Second, a finger grip allows the right hand to whip the clubhead through the ball with a powerful slinging action. Imagine the way a baseball pitcher generates speed by grasping the ball near the end of his fingers....

Rory McIlroy won the 2011 U.S. Open by a record eight shots, making him the event's youngest winner since Bobby Jones in 1923. McIlroy—like Tiger Woods and Jack Nicklaus—is one of just a few PGA Tour golfers to employ the interlocking grip. (Andrew Redington/Getty Images)

I grip the club firmly with all my fingers, but I feel pressure particularly in specific areas of each hand. In the left hand, these pressure points are the last two fingers and the pad or butt of the hand. In the right hand, the pressure points are my thumb and index finger....

Whatever style of grip you choose, keep it as natural as possible. I believe that for most golfers the most natural grip is one in which the *back* of the left hand and the *palm* of the right hand and the *clubface* are square to the target when the player takes his address position. I grip the club this way because I know that with it, if the rest of my swing is correct, the clubface will be square to the target at impact....

*"The basic factor in all good golf is the grip.
Get it right, and all other progress follows."*

—Tommy Armour

Don't be mislead into thinking that big hands are essential for good golf. My hands are small and not particularly strong, but I still get reasonable power into my shots. I do so much more through *leverage* than hand action. I create the leverage through my arms and the club, as a result of proper body action and timing. My hands serve primarily as a connection, or hinge, between my arms and the club. As such, they transmit, rather than generate, power.

JACK NICKLAUS' STROKESAVERS:

- Intertwine the little finger of the right hand and the forefinger of the left.
- Grip more firmly with the last two fingers and pad of the left hand.
- Grip more firmly with the thumb and index finger of the right.
- Extend the left thumb down the shaft for more feel and control.

Especially if you have small hands, your left thumb can form a valuable anchor for your grip. Push the left thumb down the shaft as far as it will go—this is what the pros call a "long left thumb." You'll find this will firm up your grip and also increase your "feel" and control.

Hold the club firmly, but don't squeeze it. I think of my grip pressure as "firm but passive."

From *Jack Nicklaus' Lesson Tee*, by Jack Nicklaus with Ken Bowden, from a collection of articles in *Golf Digest*, 1972–76. Copyright © 1972, 1973, 1974, 1975, 1976, 1977, and renewed © 1992 by Golden Bear, Inc. Used by permission from Jack Nicklaus and Ken Bowden.

Toward a Stronger Grip

1993 • Harvey Penick with Bud Shrake

Harvey Penick's Little Red Book probably produced as many converts as Mao's treatise of the same name and established him as a cross between Confucius and Obi-Wan Kenobi in the golf world. A welcome mix of wise observations and reassuring advice that the gentle Texan (who died in 1995) had accumulated while teaching collegians and pros like Tom Kite, Mickey Wright, Ben Crenshaw, and Kathy Whitworth, it deservedly became a perennial best seller. Yet the famed teacher's green-covered follow-up offered as many gems, including this take on the grip. Note that Penick described how the modern player combines "feel" and "body motion" while using the slightly stronger "Vardon grip," rather than Hogan's neutral one. Many thoughtful current teachers have picked up on his suggestion that players practicing new grips should wait until they are completely comfortable before actually hitting balls.

For a number of years during Ben Hogan's prime and thereafter, many golf teachers taught the neutral grip—in which the Vs of the thumbs and forefingers point more or less toward the nose or right eye.

This was Hogan's grip, and it was the right thing for him because he was always fighting a hook. In fact, most good players tend to be hookers. This neutral grip worked well for the good players and still does.

For players who are not so good, the neutral grip encourages a slice.

Recently, some gentlemen from Tokyo came to visit me at Austin Country Club. We were sitting in the grassy patio, nibbling at hors d'oeuvres from a tray, drinking ice tea, and chatting about golf through an interpreter.

Mr. Tsuyoshi Honjo, editor in chief of *Baffy* magazine, asked if I would look at his grip. He removed his jacket, rolled up his sleeves, and placed his hands on a 7 iron that was sent out from the golf shop.

His Vs pointed straight at his nose.

"I see you have read Ben Hogan's book," I said.

"Oh yes…" he beamed. "Everyone has read Mr. Hogan's book."

Ben Crenshaw weeps after winning the 1995 Masters. Just days earlier, Crenshaw served as a pallbearer at the funeral of his coach, mentor, and friend Harvey Penick. He later said his emotions overtook him at the end of the tournament—one he was not expected to even contend in—because of Penick's death. (AP Images)

*"Hold the club with about the same amount
of pressure you would use in holding a bird,
just firm enough not to let it fly away,
but not firm enough to hurt it."*

—SAM SNEAD

"I imagine you are quite a slicer," I said.

"Oh yes…" he said, not so happily. "[I have a] very big slice."

I asked him to roll both his hands to the right until his Vs pointed at his right shoulder. I tossed a little tiny carrot off the tray, into the grass at his feet.

"Hit the carrot," I said.

We kept it up for half an hour, Mr. Tsuyoshi Honjo hitting tiny carrots off the patio grass with a 7 iron and a strong grip.

The reason I wanted him to hit the carrots instead of golf balls is that he would have no expectation about hitting carrots, and so his mind would be free to concentrate on the grip and the swing. If we had put a golf ball in front of him, he would probably get tense.…

"How does the grip feel?" I asked my Japanese visitor.

"I think I hit it much harder and farther." He smiled.

"Please practice that grip and that swing, hitting carrots or leaves or twigs, until you feel good about it," I said. "Then go to the practice range and use the grip and swing on some golf balls. I think you will be pleased.…"

In the last few years I have noticed that the golf grip is evolving back toward a stronger position. In the days of Vardon, the Vs pointed at the right shoulder.

HARVEY PENICK'S STROKESAVERS:

- The average player is better off using a stronger grip.
- Make sure the Vs point to the right shoulder.
- Practice hitting leaves, twigs—anything but a golf ball—until comfortable with a new grip.

During the era of Hogan, the Vs moved to point at the nose. Now [with such players as] Freddie Couples, Davis Love III, John Daly, and others, the grip has once again moved the Vs toward the right shoulder.

I believe this is because of all the good modern players who have learned to combine the hands-and-arms swing of the strong grip with the big muscle swing of the neutral grip.

Without a doubt, the strong grip is better for the average player. As Mr. Tsuyoshi Honjo said, a less-than-expert player soon feels he can hit the ball harder and farther with a strong grip.

TRYING TO GET EVEN ISN'T GOOD

Golf Channel teaching pro Michael Breed offers a handy tip for building the proper grip. On his popular Monday night program, *The Golf Fix*, and in his 2008 book *The Picture-Perfect Golf Swing*, Breed advised golfers to make sure the left thumb is farther down the shaft than the first knuckle of the left index finger. If the knuckle is even with, or lower than, the tip of the left thumb, it means the golfer is holding the club too much in the palm. Breed, a club pro at prestigious Sunningdale Country Club in Westchester County, New York, adds that to "hinge the club back and swing it through with power, you need to hold the club more in your fingers and less in your palm," advice that harkens back to Harry Vardon.

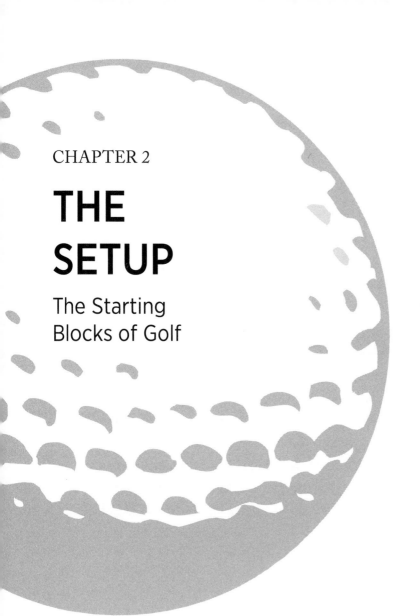

CHAPTER 2

THE
SETUP

The Starting
Blocks of Golf

Advice to Beginners—The Stance

1897 • H.J. Whigham

In the decade after golf was introduced in America, Scot H.J. Whigham helped spread its popularity, both through his play and by writing about the fundamentals for those learning the sport. The son-in-law of Charles Blair Macdonald, the first official American amateur champion, Whigham won back-to-back American Amateur titles, in 1896 and 1897, and then published America's first true instructional book. In advising on the setup, he was old-fashioned only in favoring a wide stance; otherwise, he opposed the key setup elements of the classic "St. Andrews Swing." Advocating a more modern square or slightly open stance, even weight distribution, and placing the ball nearer the left foot, Whigham offered a blueprint for hitting the high, controlled fade suitable for American courses. Anticipating Jack Nicklaus by 70 years, he also urged his readers to concentrate less on swing mechanics than the pre-swing fundamentals that are compulsory for hitting good shots.

L et the novice grasp his club…and stand square to the ball, not stooping too much, nor yet uncompromisingly rigid.…

He must take his position, then, with the ball placed rather more toward his left than his right leg, and at such a distance that he can place the head of the club comfortably behind it without stooping or stretching out the arms, and leaving as obtuse an angle as possible between the arms and the shaft of the club.

The feet should be from two to two and a half feet apart, according to height, and the right if anything advanced a trifle in front of the left.

This style has generally been referred to as driving off the right leg, as opposed to the method of driving from the left leg.… But that is in reality an abuse of language.

When the right leg is advanced so far that the weight of the body rests almost entirely upon it, the expression is perfectly correct; but that is not what is at present intended. The beginner must accustom himself to stand fairly erect,

H.J. WHIGHAM'S STROKESAVERS:

- Stand square to the ball, without stooping or going rigid.
- Place the ball forward, or closer to the left foot than the right.
- Distribute the weight evenly between both legs.
- Assume the correct stance, and the mechanics of the swing will happen naturally.

with the weight of the body equally distributed between each leg; he will then drive not from one or the other, but from both, and that is the only correct method.

In swinging back he will let the weight fall naturally upon the right foot until the top of the swing is reached. In coming forward again, the weight will follow the club, and when the drive is finished it will rest almost entirely upon the left foot.

But this must be done unconsciously. As soon as the beginner allows himself to think about changing his center of gravity his swing is sure to get out of gear. It will be quite sufficient, then, if he will stand correctly in the first place, and swing as I shall instruct him.

From *How to Play Golf*, by H.J. Whigham. Herbert S. Stone & Co., Chicago, Illinois. Copyright © 1897/1902.

"If you can afford only one lesson, tell the pro you want it on the fundamentals: the grip, the stance, and the alignment."

—Nancy Lopez

The Stance

1904 • Genevieve Hecker (Mrs. Charles T. Stout)

Slender, blue-eyed, 20-year-old Genevieve Hecker was America's first female golfing sensation, "a wonder" as one magazine portrayed her. After winning two national amateur championships, she published America's first instructional book written specifically for women—as British champ May Hezlet simultaneously published *Ladies' Golf*—with chapters taken from the magazine *Golf*. Her book was reissued recently because of its historic significance, charm, and still-valid instruction. At a time when men were formulating theories on how everyone should play the new American sport, Hecker told women to follow their own instincts because "how can a man understand the ways and moods and means which must be taken into consideration when a woman prepares to golf?" Like Whigham, she observed the stance from behind and said not to obsess over mechanics, yet she had a unique style of teaching that was at once feisty, funky, and a mix of old-fashioned femininity and feminism.

After settling the question of the proper method of gripping the club to one's entire satisfaction, the next step in order is the determining of the relation the position of the feet shall bear to the ball, and the direction it is wished that the ball should take.

This is technically called the stance, and there are almost as many ways of standing as there are of gripping the club.

The stance may be divided into three classes, which are called:

I.—Off the right foot.

II.—Off the left foot.

III.—Standing square.

The most common method is the first, and probably so because the player can see the direction in which she wishes the ball to go better, and consequently feels more confidence that it will go there.

In adopting this stance, the right foot is placed in advance of the left, the exact difference depending upon the player's fancy. In other words, if a line were drawn

GENEVIEVE HECKER'S STROKESAVERS:

- Let feel and physique dictate the width of the stance.
- Bend at the knees and let the arms hang naturally.
- Vary the stance depending on the type of shot.
- Position the ball in accordance with the chosen stance.

on the ground parallel to the line of flight, the left toe should be just touching it, while the right would be anywhere from one to ten inches over it....

In driving "off the left foot," the right foot is withdrawn in almost the same proportion as it is advanced when driving "off the right foot," and the stance is virtually the inverse of the former.

In standing square, the stance is as its name implies. Both feet are on a parallel line, and the weight of the body is equally divided between them.

The distance which the feet should be apart is another matter which must be decided by the individual and should be regulated by both feeling and physique....

The knees should be bent in the smallest degree, just so that the knee joint is not stiff, and the arms, when the clubhead rests behind the ball, are bent in an equally small degree at the elbow.

The position of the ball and its relation to the feet are most important.

When the "standing square" stance is adopted, the ball should be nearly opposite the left heel—that is, within two or three inches of the line which a right angle drawn by the feet and ball would make.

When playing "off the right foot" the ball should be more to the right, and as the foot is advanced, so proportionately should the ball be moved to the right.

When playing "off the left foot" the ball should be inversely moved to the left....

Ordinarily I place the ball and I tee about three inches to the right of my left heel, and I rest the weight of my body equally on each foot. I have found that by adopting this stance I can obtain a full, easy backward swing, and that I can swing my club in a sweeping circle much farther and straighter in the line of flight of the ball....

Never make the mistake of taking up a certain stance simply because some celebrated golfer uses it. Be a law unto yourself, for unless you stand so that you feel natural and easy and as though you were going to hit the ball exactly as you wish, you never will be able to do so. Confidence in golf is at least half the battle. If you find that some champion uses the same stance that you do, well and good. Say to yourself, he uses good judgment and is a legitimate champion, and feel well satisfied that the champion follows you, but never follow him....

The ball should be teed at whatever place the clubhead lies when it is gripped in the proper way, and then allowed to fall naturally to the ground straight in front of the player. The whole idea is to get it at such a distance that it will be directly in the line of a *natural* swing. There is a great diversity of opinion about the distance one should stand away. Some of the best drivers in the country stand so far that the toe of their club, when addressing the ball, is quite two or three inches behind the ball, while others have the ball even with the neck of the clubhead. I do not favor either of these extremes.

If the ball is too far away and the player has to *reach* for it, as it were, the whole position is quite apt to be cramped, and the swing is consequently without snap, or else, in endeavoring to have it free and easy, the player does not always "reach" the exact fraction of an inch which is necessary for the perfect performance of the shot, and a bad slice or pull results.

From *Golf for Women*, by Genevieve Hecker (Mrs. Charles T. Stout). The Baker & Taylor Co., New York, N.Y.

GET THE DISTANCE JUST RIGHT

Two-time PGA champion and Ryder Cup hero Leo Diegel offered a timeless piece of advice for how to determine if golfers are standing the correct distance from the ball. Using the right hand (fingers spread), golfers can measure the space between the left leg and the end of the club shaft. If the hand doesn't fit into the space, they are crowding the ball, and if the hand doesn't "span the gap," they are standing too far away.

Balance

1962 • Sam Snead with Al Stump

Sam Snead was 50 years old when he wrote his classic instruction book *The Education of a Golfer* with the estimable sportswriter Al Stump (of *Cobb* fame). The living legend from Hot Springs, Virginia, still hadn't won the last of his record 82 PGA tournaments and would play another 19 years on the Tour. No one had more natural talent than Snead, but that didn't mean that every facet of his game wasn't the product of countless hours of practice and analysis. True, the following excerpt in which he audaciously tells President Eisenhower to stick out his butt more and corrects "Stardust" composer Hoagy Carmichael's footwork at address is characteristically full of disarming wit. Yet in his homespun, direct fashion, Snead makes it clear that the balance he maintained during his famously graceful, rhythmic swing was possible only because he practiced, with *serious* intent, balance in his stance.

Once, when I played with President Ike Eisenhower at White Sulphur Springs, he remarked that his restricted backswing was causing him to lose sleep. "They tell me to turn, turn," said Ike, "if I want more distance off the tee."

I said nothing, and when we finished, Ike asked, "What do you think?"

"Stick your butt out more, Mr. President," I said.

Some of Ike's bodyguards were shocked, but he only blinked.

"I thought it *was* out," he said.

Well, it wasn't—not enough, anyway. The big hitting muscles are located in the back of the legs, shoulders, and in the middle back, and that's one reason your weight shouldn't be forward on the balls of your feet or toes but back through the heels. When these muscles are in full play, your rear end sticks out. Another reason is that the force of the downswing may pull the body forward, throwing the clubhead into a shank or scuff position. Ike wasn't settled back enough where he could dig in with good balance. His turn was on the short side, but some of the reason for that showed up when I spoke to his doctor. I mentioned that Ike wore glasses with small lenses, so that to keep his eyes on the ball he was forced to reduce his turn. Shifting his weight back a little and wearing larger lenses helped Ike later—or so I was told.

Stepping, rocking, and swaying are all caused by an off-balance stance. Hoagy Carmichael played "Celebrity Golf" with me, and I said, "You're taking a left step forward at the address; then on your forward press you're stepping back with the right foot. Hoagy said he wasn't. At a running of the TV film he was proven wrong. It astonished him, for he thought balance was one problem he'd licked. He was an example of a golfer who can't believe what you're telling him because he doesn't feel like he's doing a specific wrong. You must prove it to him.

Footwork, balance, is everything to me because of my life-long theory (and Ben Hogan agreed) that the more you minimize hand, wrist, and arm action, the better. I believe the body pivot launched by the feet is the *big* factor. Many golfers get too much wrist leverage into their shots, where I have as little as possible. If your pivot is good, a gradual speeding up of the clubhead as it nears

Sam Snead stressed establishing good balance to eliminate faults such as stepping, rocking, and swaying. In particular, he advised sticking one's butt out for a more balanced stance and less restricted motion— a technique shown here in a 1949 photo of Snead's famously athletic and graceful swing. (AP Images)

SAM SNEAD'S STROKESAVERS:

- Establish good balance to eliminate faults such as stepping, rocking, and swaying.

- Stick the butt out for a more balanced stance and less restricted swing—the same advice Snead once gave to President Eisenhower.

- Ease slightly more weight onto the right foot to promote a relaxed stance.

- Take a slightly closed stance—this offers more traction, essential to good balance and a good swing.

the hitting area will follow without any forehand wham or rushing of the shot with the arms.

If the head and body stay behind the ball and the hips don't move in there too far and waste power before contact, you are set up to knock the cover off it. One of the ways I get distance is in the way my knees bend into position on the downswing. And the knees can't put you into a power-hitting position unless the feet are working for you.

1. It's automatic with me that, in taking my stance, slightly more weight is placed on the right foot than the left, and I feel an easy sort of looseness from the bottom of the foot clear up to my hip socket. I'm relaxed with no chance of a hip lock.

2. I'm in a slightly closed stance—about 10 degrees on tee shots; the closed stance gives me more traction than any other.

From *The Education of a Golfer*, by Sam Snead, with Al Stump. Simon & Schuster, New York, N.Y. Copyright © 1962 by Sam Snead and Al Stump. Reprinted with the permission of Jack Snead.

The Setup, Aim and Alignment, and Ball Position

1992 • Tom Watson with Nick Seitz

Tom Watson's extraordinary playing career is well known to anyone who has watched golf over the last 40 years. He was the PGA Player of the Year six times and the PGA Player of the Decade for the 1980s, and counted among his victories two Masters, one U.S. Open, five British Opens, and several majors on the Champions Tour. Moreover, since 1977, the popular Kansan has been a playing editor for *Golf Digest*, written several excellent instructional books, and starred in his own DVDs. His instruction has been consistently smart, sound, provocative, and creative. Note that in this excerpt, in which he takes a fresh look at long-established setup theory, Watson presents the classic "railroad-tracks" image, telling readers how to square their alignment by imagining that their feet are on the inside track and the ball and target line run along the outside track. Watson also echoes Snead on posture and balance, and explains how (and why) to vary ball position for different clubs.

I almost always can predict when my 15-handicap friends are going to hit a good shot, because they will be set up well. Their posture will be good. Your posture virtually dictates how you will strike the ball.

Posture is a problem for most players, but it is probably the simplest problem to correct. Since posture directly affects your balance and the plane of your swing, it is extremely important. I advocate an elementary 1-2-3 approach to establishing good posture.

- Stand up straight, with your feet slightly wider than your shoulders. Open—toe out—your right foot about 15 degrees and your left foot about 30 degrees. This is so you can turn more away from the ball and back through it.
- Bend from the waist. Now you have created a sound spine angle and can swing down at the ball. You will want to maintain this spine angle

LPGA star Paula Creamer is well known for her good posture and alignment. Creamer's tee shot in a 2008 event above shows how pre-swing fundamentals help a golfer maintain a good spine angle and a balanced position through a powerful through-swing. (Doug Benc/Getty Images)

throughout the swing. It stabilizes you and keeps your head from bobbing up and down....

- Flex your knees and stick out your read end. This final stage balances you and puts ballast in your swing. You should almost feel as though you're sitting down. If you fall forward as you swing, you know that your butt isn't sticking out enough. Stick it out until you feel a little tension in the small of your back.

Your weight will still be toward your toes, but not too much. You're poised to move. Your lower body can work easier. You'll be able to stay down on the ball, making contact. No good athlete gets his weight back on his heels. A fast runner is on the balls of his feet....

I'd rather see you put too much weight toward your toes than err toward your heels. If you're back on your heels starting your swing, there's no way you can turn your hips correctly. You'll have to just lift the club with your arms and make a weak swing. You'll straighten up and fall back. If you fall forward, at least you can swing your arms down the line with some speed.... Your knees should be flexed enough that they are just about over your toes as you look down. Your legs will be flexible from that position....

There's another positive result of flexing the knees and setting your weight on the balls of your feet. An active lower body keeps the head quiet.... If your legs are stiff—if you have "cement" legs as I call them—and your weight is back toward your heels, your head is going to move way too much.

Your weight should be distributed about equally between your feet. I like the way Jack Nicklaus exemplifies that and also how he positions his weight toward the insides of his feet. Jack's in wonderful balance....

From [the setup posture I've described] you can let your arms hang naturally and comfortably, and that's where you'll grip the club. Your wrists will be semi-cocked already. If your left arm and the club form a straight line, your wrists are too high, and you will swing stiff-armed.

You should never feel you have to reach for the ball, even with a driver, and you should never feel cramped either. Your arms should be able to swing in front of you in a relaxed manner, and from the setup posture we've talked about they will....

COMMON SETUP FAULTS

The most frequent setup mistake I see is standing too erect. It happens typically with people who are short or who have weak legs, or both.

If you are too erect, your arms hang too close to your body, and you cannot swing them freely in front of you. Your arms might hit your legs. The club will go around behind you too soon, and you won't be able to make a full, easy turn and coil on the backswing. Your swing is dominated by the arms having to work too hard without much help. You probably will spin out.

You must have enough bend at the waist to make an easy shoulder turn. The shoulders have to stay on plane. That means you cannot stand too erect.

At the other extreme, crouching and bending over too much results in a swing that's too upright. About all you can do is stick your arms straight up in the air. The club wants to move too vertically instead of around the body.... When you are bent over too much, you are apt to lift up coming into the ball and make poor contact.

AIM AND ALIGNMENT

How you line up a golf shot pretty much determines where it will go. Aim and alignment are factors you can control before you swing, and they deserve extra care. You aim the clubface and align your body, in that order.

Aiming the clubface is like aiming a gun. If you don't aim the face accurately, you won't hit your target. I recommend the Jack Nicklaus method of spot-aiming. I don't use it completely myself, but I'm convinced it's the best way. It's like spot-bowling. Instead of concentrating on a distant target (the pins), a bowler focuses on a close-in target (a spot on the lane)....

You should start from a few yards behind the ball and pick out your intended target line. You are looking out over the ball at your target. You get a much clearer picture of the line from behind the ball than from the side, where you will address it. You'd aim a gun sighting down the barrel, right?... You have identified your target line and are still standing behind the ball. Now you want to identify an intermediate target or aiming spot just a few feet in front of the ball. It might be a light blade of grass or a leaf or a small stick. You build your aim and alignment off this spot.

Keep referring to your spot as you move into your stance from behind the ball. Aim the clubface first, then align your body. Too many people align the body first, which causes faulty aiming.... You circle into the ball from behind, checking your intermediate spot as you do. Aim the clubface squarely at your spot. Aim the bottom line of the clubface to make sure it's square.

Your right foot is roughly in position. Spread your left foot out into place, and adjust your right foot so you're comfortable. Be sure as you take your stance that you do not change the attitude of the clubface....

Look up and check to see that your clubface, your spot, and your ultimate target off in the distance are all in line. If you fear they are not, back off and start your aiming and alignment process all over again.... You have to get this part of the game right or you cannot play acceptable golf. Be brisk, but be exacting.

THE BODY IS PARALLEL LEFT

Basically your body should be aligned to your target line at address. Imagine a pair of railroad tracks. The ball and your target line are on the outside track. Your feet are lined up on the inside track. Your feet, hips, and shoulders are aligned parallel or square to the target line....

A common fault is aligning the body at the target.... If your body is aligned at the target, then your clubface almost certainly is aiming to the right of the target! Your body should be aligned somewhat left of the target, so the clubface can aim straight at it. Then you can make a natural swing without having to compensate and try to pull your shot back in the proper direction....

Your eye position is also important. It's possible to align your body accurately, but cause yourself problems when you look at your target before you start your swing, especially if you lift your head. Your eyes must be parallel like your body. If your eyes are cocked to the right of the target, that's most likely where your swing and the ball will go. If your eyes are cocked left, your swing and shot are prone to go left.

Even good players have trouble with their eye alignment.... I suspect it has something to do with a player's dominant eye, and it might make sense to get

TOM WATSON'S STROKESAVERS:

- Focus on good posture; it virtually dictates good ball striking.
- Pick an intermediate target, then aim the clubface and align the body.
- Imagine a set of railroad tracks to promote good alignment: The ball and target line run along the outside track, the feet, hips, and shoulders along the inside track.
- Keep the eyes parallel to the target line; good eye alignment is also crucial.

your eye doctor's thinking. But the point is to align your eyes the same as your feet, knees, hips, and shoulders. It's [also] helpful to swivel your head when you look at the target instead of lifting it. If you lift your head, you probably will lose your eye line....

Your overall head position is worth mentioning, too. Some amateurs sink their chins down into their chests as they line up a shot. They are defeated before they ever start to swing, because it's impossible for them to make a good turn. You want to swing your left shoulder under your chin on the backswing, and that's impossible if your chin gets in the way.

BALL POSITION

I advocate varying your ball position. The hitting zone is from the middle of the stance forward, and that's where you should put the ball. The longer the club, the farther forward you play the ball.

For a normal shot with a driver, I want the ball opposite my left heel. For a wedge it will be back almost in the center of my stance.... You move the ball back in your stance for a shorter club because you make a more descending swing. You cannot hit down on the ball effectively if it is off your left heel.

I know there are some great golf minds that advocate one standard ball position, just inside or opposite the left heel—Jack Nicklaus and Ben Hogan for two. But you have to be very athletic in your lower body to go down and get the ball. If it's in a bad lie, all the more reason to put the ball back in your stance. If

THE EYES HAVE IT

I n the classic book *How to Become a Complete Golfer,* Bob Toski and Jim Flick advised golfers to align their eyes properly, claiming many players either ignore this simple setup fundamental or do it wrong by cocking the chin at an angle that sets the eye line to the right of the target. The eye line must be parallel to the target line, and the head should be straight as the golfer addresses the ball. They added that when golfers want to sight their target, they should rotate the head to the left rather than tilting it up and down to make sure the head and eyes get back into proper alignment before the swing starts. The same advice applies to putting.

you have trouble driving your legs and shifting your weight through the shot, you almost surely shouldn't play everything off your left heel. Most older players fall into this category. I've heard that Hogan moved the ball back as he got older, and I wouldn't be surprised to see Jack do it one day....

My left foot is essentially constant for every swing, driver through wedge. I change the width of my stance and open or close my stance by adjusting my right foot.

My stance narrows and also opens as the club I am using gets shorter. With the driver, my right foot is about an inch back of my stance line and 20 degrees toed out to the right. With the wedge, my right foot is about an inch in front of my stance line and a bit less toed out. I never want my right foot perpendicular to the line. It's too hard to turn my body on the backswing.

The essential reason for changing the right foot is to promote or restrict hip turn. A shorter club requires a more vertical swing, with less body pivot and more arm swing.

You use different swings in this game. Your rhythm should stay the same, but your arc changes. Golf is difficult for a tall man because he has to swing so vertically, and the body doesn't want to. It's easier for someone my size (5'9", 160 pounds) to swing every club freely....

How far should you stand from the ball? I get this question a lot.... You'll be farther from the ball with a driver than a 5 iron, but if you set up soundly that takes care of itself. Don't reach for the ball or feel cramped.

Reprinted by permission of Pocket Books, a division of Simon & Schuster Adult Publishing Group, from *Tom Watson's Getting Back to Basics*, by Tom Watson with Nick Seitz. Copyright © 1992 by Tom Watson.

CHAPTER 3

THE PRE-SHOT ROUTINE

Like Clockwork

Visualizing the Shot

1931 • Joyce Wethered

Tall, shy Joyce Wethered succeeded rival Cecil Leitch as the queen of British golf in the early 1920s, and became perhaps the greatest female golfer in history. Bobby Jones claimed she was the best golfer he'd ever seen—men included. Three-time British Open champion Henry Cotton wondered if she was the best *ever*, period. In her articles and books, it's evident that a major reason for her success was that she was ahead of her time in believing physical play is affected by what goes on in the mind. She has been credited, wrongly, for being the first to write about "visualizing shots"—Jim Barnes and others did so years earlier—but she was responsible for fleshing out the concept. As she contended in this famous essay, good players have a better chance for a great shot if they first visualize the ball landing where they wish to hit it and rolling exactly as they want.

There is a great deal of talk about temperament. We understand that it counts for so much in competitive golf, just making the difference between the first- and second-class player, and deciding the issues that depend on the closest margins. Temperament is concerned with our thoughts, and the player has two or three hours of thinking before him while he plays a round. It is interesting to consider the nature of some of these thoughts, either while the strokes are being played or during the longer intervals that divide them.

In watching a big match the spectator can probably learn very little from the demeanor or the expression of the players; but at the time it is evident that their minds are exceptionally alert and keyed up. This is a state which can produce inspired moments, and can, at the same time, produce chaos. The part that the mind plays in imagination is extremely varied and differs with each individual. There is the time spent while the player is walking after his ball, or waiting through what may seem interminable ages while his opponent studies his putt and mediates upon the green. At these times it may be a matter of great difficulty to keep the mind still and at rest.

Joyce Wethered swings a hickory-shafted club in 1932. One of the greatest women's golfers in history, Wethered was a pioneer in emphasizing that good players have a better chance for a great shot if they first visualize the ball landing where they wish to hit it. (AP Images)

To many the mind is a racing, revolving machine that cannot be quieted when once it is roused. A few favored individuals may possibly be ignorant of these difficulties and may experience no trouble in keeping their minds evenly concentrated on the match undisturbed by what has happened or what is likely to happen presently. But I suspect that they are rare exceptions even amongst those who declare that they have no nerves. Calmness can be cultivated, and without it the technique of hitting the ball can be seriously affected. If consistent accuracy is to be expected, stroke play must be largely mechanical; the mind must be as free as possible from technical worries and able to concentrate upon visualizing what has to be done.

This personal vision of the shot is a thing which everyone experiences, and it would be of the greatest interest to be able to get behind the minds of some of the most distinguished players and see the shot as they see it. I believe it would be a different vision every time; the elevation and degree of run or backspin would vary, although probably the ball would finish in very much the same place.

By vision, I include the whole feeling of the shot as you are going to play it. Personally, I find that certain contours—for instance, in the shape of the greens—have an effect on the imagination, suggesting either a sliced or pulled shot. I must definitely allow for it or correct the feeling in the making of the stroke. The most subtle of golf architects are well aware of this force of suggestion and quite rightly make full use of the fact in order to puzzle the player and get him in two minds.

It is surprising how difficult it is sometimes to hit a straight shot at a hole where perhaps some hill or contour—not affecting in any way the actual flight or landing of the ball—makes one feel that the ball must curve in its flight also. In most cases you must play the shot as you visualize it in order to make it convincing; but there is a danger also that, if you see the shot wrong or allow the influence to overpower you, you will be led astray.

JOYCE WETHERED'S STROKESAVERS:

- Concentrate on visualizing the shot—it frees the mind from mechanics.
- Commit absolutely to the swing; waver and errors creep in.
- View difficult shots as adventures to promote success and restore confidence.

NARROW YOUR TARGET

Texan Kathy Whitworth won 88 titles, the professional record for both men and women. She said that one reason for her amazing success was her ability to narrow her target. In her 1990 book *Golf for Women*, written with Rhonda Glenn, she stated: "The smaller your target, the straighter you are going to hit the ball." Ben Hogan also subscribed to this theory, though typically he took it even further, saying if a tree was on his target line, he would pick out a single leaf as an aiming point. Other pros, when talking about short putts, urge golfers to pick out a single blade of grass hanging over the cup.

This leads to another factor. The mind is always conscious of the weakness which we know to exist in our game, and we often consciously, and sometimes unconsciously, look at an approach in a way we should avoid, simply because we want to save ourselves from the necessity of playing a shot which we distrust.

If we have a tendency to slice the ball, we are apt to see the shot drifting from left to right; we may even see it running away from us across the green. If we take our golf seriously, we shall not feel satisfied, if we allow ourselves to yield to the inclination to play the shot in this way. We must resist and counteract the tendency by visualizing the shot as being held up firmly with even a suspicion of draw in order to strengthen our resolution. The club generally follows the inclination of the mind. We must positively see the ball flying as we wish it to, and the time will come when our technical ability will triumph over the weakness which previously would have mastered us.

The first-class player, when in full practice, is certain of what he is trying to do. He knows where his ball is to pitch, what it will do when it lands, and how it will find its way to the hole side. He sees it all, and his power over the club makes the result inevitable. But should he waver and be undecided, the ball will answer the mental vacillation to which he has yielded.

On the putting green, also, the mind can be a grave source of trouble. Begin to dislike the look of a putt, and the chances of holing it at once become less. The sight of a slippery patch can weaken our determination; or a particular slope may make us feel that we are uncertain of the strength of the putt. How many putts are affected by our thoughts about them while we are waiting to play! How sensitive we are to likes or dislikes on the green!

I can recommend only one frame of mind which might help us. We can, if we wish, pretend to enjoy the shots which frighten us. We can positively make ourselves look forward to playing as many of them as possible. Instead of fearing them we can stimulate an interest in them. A delicate pitch over a bunker can be converted by a little judicious mental effort into a delightful adventure. We can assure ourselves that we enjoy using our putter, even if we feel incapable of holing a putt.

You may say that is only a method of self-deception, but if we can make ourselves believe what we wish to believe, we shall in a very short time have restored our confidence. Our pitches will then be deadly, and the 2-yarders will drop satisfactorily. There is more in the question of liking and disliking than one thinks. We all enjoy the shots we can hit successfully, and it is only a step further to approach unpleasantly doubtful shots in the same spirit.

From *The American Golfer* (September 1931), by Joyce Wethered.

Now, It's Up to You

1948 · Ben Hogan

Ben Hogan scholars in search of brilliant instruction usually go directly to his 1957 book *Ben Hogan's Five Lessons, The Modern Fundamentals of Golf.* However, to find Hogan writing about his pre-shot routine, they must go further back to his less-acclaimed first book for this very brief, but often cited excerpt. The story goes that Hogan once didn't even notice when his playing companion made a hole in one, and that's not surprising after reading here that his goal was absolute concentration before striking the ball. However, unlike Patty Berg, Hogan didn't say to concentrate solely on hitting the ball, but echoed Joyce Wethered in using a pre-shot routine to conjure up images of shots hitting their final targets. He also came up with the idea of backing off the shot if somehow he was distracted—a tactic now widely taught and used without apology by both professionals and smart amateurs.

While I am practicing I am also trying to develop my powers of concentration. I never just walk up and hit the ball. I decide in advance how I want to hit it and where I want it to go.

Try to shut out everything around you. Develop your ability to think only of how and where you want to hit the shot you are playing. If something disturbs my concentration while I am lining up a shot I start all over again.

An ability to concentrate for long periods of time while exposed to all sorts of distractions is invaluable in golf. Adopt the habit of concentrating to the exclusion of everything else while you are on the practice tee, and you will find that you are automatically following the same routine while playing a round in competition.

BEN HOGAN'S STROKESAVERS:

- Never hit the ball without first deciding how and where it will go.
- Develop the ability to concentrate and shut out distractions.
- Back off a shot when something disturbs concentration.

Naturally, on the practice tee you don't get the variety of golfing problems you get in competition, and it is more difficult to keep interested. My solution is to play each shot…as though it were part of an actual round.…

While playing an actual round, I sharpen up my concentrative powers and stimulate my interest in each shot by sizing it up as I walk up to where my ball lies. Make a habit of doing this, and you will increase your powers of concentration threefold while also speeding up your play.

From *Ben Hogan's Power Golf,* by Ben Hogan. Copyright © 1948 by A.S. Barnes and Company, Inc. Reprinted with the permission of Writers House, LLC, as agent for the Ben Hogan estate.

"Don't be in such a hurry. That little white ball isn't going to run away from you."

—Patty Berg

Addressing the Ball

1960 • Robert Tyre (Bobby) Jones, Jr.

Bobby Jones' first instructional book with material not first written for magazines or newspapers was published 30 years after he retired with a justified claim that he was the greatest golfer ever. In an eight-year amateur career, he had won 13 national championships, including golf's only Grand Slam in his final year of competition. Jones was a tremendous student of the game and continued to write brilliant, influential instruction as well as make 18 shorts teaching Hollywood celebrities, produced by Warner Bros. for a then-whopping $1 million. Back then, nobody really talked much about a "pre-shot" routine, but it's clear from this excerpt that Jones thought in those terms for himself and his pupils. He advocated a fluid, economical, and almost continuous motion leading up to the ball, a method to eliminate tension that applied both when he played and when he wrote his book, and is still valid today.

It is [essential] to standardize the approach to every shot, beginning even before taking the address position.

It is far easier to maintain a complete relaxation if one keeps continually in motion, never becoming still and set. It sounds far-fetched, I know, but I have had a few players tell me that after taking great pains in addressing the ball, they have reached the point where they simply could not take the club back. It is a manner of freezing and is well know to tournament players as a form of the "yips."

Long ago, and with no remembered intention, I standardized my approach in the following way: Having decided upon the club to use and the shot to play, I could see no reason for taking any more time in the address than was necessary to measure my distance from the ball and to line up the shot. The more I fiddled around arranging the position, the more I was beset by doubts which produced tension and strain.

I began then to approach every shot from behind the ball looking toward the hole. It was easier to get a picture of the shot and to line it up properly from this angle than from any other. Ordinarily, coming up from behind, I would stop a little short of what my final position would be, just near enough to the ball to be able to reach it comfortably. From there, the club was grounded, and I took one look toward the objective. The club gave me a sense of my distance from the ball; looking down the fairway gave me the line, while my left foot swung into position. One waggle was begun while the right foot moved back to its place. When the club returned to the ground behind the ball, there was a little forward twist of the hips and the backswing began. I felt most comfortable and played better golf when the entire movement was continuous. Whenever I hesitated or took a second waggle, I could look for trouble.

The little twist of the hips I have mentioned is a valuable aid in starting the swing smoothly, because it assists in breaking up any tension which may have crept in. Often referred to as the "forward press," it has been regarded by many as the result of a movement of the hands. In actual fact, the hands have nothing to do with it. The movement is in the legs, and its chief function is to assure a smooth start of the swing by setting the hip turn in motion. Without it,

BOBBY JONES' STROKESAVERS:

- Develop a pre-shot routine and stick to it on each shot.
- Hold off tension and indecision by staying in motion.
- Size up the shot from behind the ball, take aim when over it, and then hit.

the inclination is strong to pick up the club with the hands and arms without bringing the trunk into use.

I do not think it wise to prescribe any definite number of waggles. This depends too much upon how long is required for the player to settle into a comfortable position and obtain proper alignment. But it is important to make the movement easy, smooth, and comfortable and to form the habit of getting the thing done without too much fussing and worrying.

Pre-Shot *and* Going to the Movies

1974 • Jack Nicklaus with Ken Bowden

In the introduction to his celebrated pupil's classic book *Golf My Way*, Jack Grout testified that Jack Nicklaus became, arguably, the greatest player ever because he paid equal attention to what came before his famous swing as the swing itself. Nicklaus always stressed the critical importance of a meticulous, consistent pre-shot routine and, in this well-known essay, coauthored by noted writer-editor Ken Bowden, he, interestingly, contends that *the shot he visualizes each time determines his exact setup*; and that his mind refuses to let him swing until his setup is correct. Even more noteworthy is that he took Joyce Wethered a step further, equating his form of visualization to "Going to the Movies," a concept he made famous. Significantly, in his Hollywood spectacular it isn't enough to picture the next shot, but to picture it as a *perfect* shot—which Nicklaus accomplished more than any other golfer.

I am sometimes accused of being a slow player. Well, the truth is that I walk very fast up to the ball, make a fairly fast decision about what I want to do when I get there, but then sometimes set up to the shot slowly.

There are some good reasons for my being so methodical about my

Jack Nicklaus surveys a putt during the 1972 British Open. Nicklaus employed a meticulous, consistent pre-shot routine on every shot—from the green back to the tee. But beyond that, he also contended that the shot he visualized each time determined his exact setup, and that his mind refused to let him swing until that setup was correct. (AP Images)

setup. I think it is the single most important maneuver in golf. It is the only aspect of the swing over which you have 100 percent conscious control. If you set up correctly, there's a good chance you'll hit a reasonable shot, even if you make a mediocre swing. If you set up incorrectly, you'll hit a lousy shot even if you make the greatest swing in the world. Every time I try to deny that law by hurrying my setup, my subconscious rears up and beats me around the ears....

I feel that hitting specific shots—playing the ball to a certain place in a certain way—is 50 percent mental picture, 40 percent setup, and 10 percent swing. That's why setting up takes me so long, why I have to be so deliberate. In competition I am not simply trying to hit a *good* shot, but rather the *perfect* shot for the particular situation. I frequently fail, of course, often because I've mentally pictured the wrong shot. But unless I can set up *exactly right* in relation to the shot I have pictured, I know I have no chance of executing it as planned. Therefore, I *must* get perfectly set—it's almost a compulsion—before I can pull the trigger. My mind simply *will not let me* start the swing until I'm "right," no matter how long it takes.

I am usually the last golfer in a group to play his fairway shots. At one time, out of courtesy, I would stand by while the others played, then go to my ball and assess my shot while they waited for me. Now, as unobtrusively as possible, I walk ahead to the region of my own ball to make my decisions while the others are playing their shots. So far as is possible, I do the same thing on the putting greens. And, if you care to notice next time you're at a tournament, I also walk pretty darn fast on the golf course.

The point I'm stressing is the vital importance of the setup on every shot you hit. This includes picturing the shot, aiming and aligning the clubface and your body relative to your target, placing the ball relative to your intended swing arc, assuming your overall address posture, and mentally and physically conditioning yourself just before pulling the trigger....

JACK NICKLAUS' STROKESAVERS:

- Use a methodical, deliberate, and unhurried setup for every shot.
- Visualize a sharp, full-color picture of the perfect shot before hitting.
- Remember: An incorrect setup *always* produces a lousy shot—even with a great swing.

GOING TO THE MOVIES

I never hit a shot, even in practice, without having a very sharp, in-focus picture of it in my head. It's like a color movie. First I "see" the ball where I want it to finish, nice and white and sitting up high on the bright green grass. Then the scene quickly changes and I "see" the ball going there: its path, trajectory, and shape, even its behavior on landing. Then there's a sort of fade-out, and the next scene shows me making the kind of swing that will turn the previous images into reality. Only at the end of this short, private, Hollywood spectacular do I select a club and step up to the ball.

It may be that handicap golfers also "go to the movies" like this before most of their shots, but somehow I doubt it. Frequently those I play with in pro-ams seem to have the club at the ball and their feet planted before they start "seeing" pictures of the shot in their mind's eye. Maybe even then they see only pictures of the swing, rather than of what it's supposed to achieve. If that's true in your case, then I believe a few moments of movie-making might work some small miracles in your game. Just make sure your movies show a perfect shot. We don't want any horror films of shots flying into sand or water or out of bounds.

Abridged from *Golf My Way*, by Jack Nicklaus with Ken Bowden. Copyright © 1974, and renewed © 2002 by Jack Nicklaus. Used by permission of Simon & Schuster Adult Publishing Group. *Golf My Way* is available in an updated, expanded edition (2005).

WHAT'S THINKING GOT TO DO WITH SWINGING?

Pia Nilsson and Lynn Marriott have written three best-selling books together and coached thousands of amateur and professional golfers, including Hall of Famer Annika Sorenstam. But perhaps their most enduring concept comes from their first book, *Every Shot Must Have a Purpose* (2005). In that now-classic tome, the two Swedish instructors advised golfers to make decisions on shot selection, wind, lie, possible hazards, and any other mental or mechanical decisions they wish in what they called the "think box," or the area behind the ball. The golfer should then commit totally, step over an imaginary line to the "play box," take their grip, align their body, glance at the target, and then swing—or as they summarized it, "quit thinking and play." Their mantra for this, "decide, commit, swing," is advice that echoes back to Joyce Wethered and Bobby Jones.

Developing a Routine

1999 · Michael Corcoran

Shotmaking Techniques, a condensed volume of *The PGA Tour Complete Book of Golf,* is one of the most reader-friendly instructional books of the last 25 years. Popular golf writer Michael Corcoran (whose other books include one on the flag) clearly advances his own theory and supports it with those of numerous PGA members, and the result is an entire book that makes sense. In this excerpt Corcoran provides a recommended checklist for a solid pre-shot routine, which if it had been published 70 years earlier would have made all future writing on the subject superfluous. Also he presents former British Open champion and 2006 American Ryder Cup captain Tom Lehman discussing his own pre-shot routine, which includes finding an intermediate target and waggling the club. Significantly, Lehman points out that one's routine should never vary in *any* way, including taking the same number of clock ticks before every shot.

Without question, preparing to play the shot is more important than anything you do once the club is in motion. If the beginning is not right, there is not much chance of achieving the hoped-for end results. Chances are you have heard or read a description of a Tour player's pre-shot routine and how important it is to his game. It can be—and should be—just as important to your game. The word *routine* is used here in the purest sense—that is, a sequence of thoughts and movements that are repeated with great efficiency. The routine is significant and should not be glossed over.

The basic elements of a pre-shot routine are:

- An assessment of the lie of your ball. Is it going to interfere with clean contact?
- The selection of a target.
- Accurate determination of the yardage between your ball and the target.
- The selection of an intermediate target (from behind the ball) to aid in aiming the clubface.
- The setting of your body into place (or alignment and posture).

MICHAEL CORCORAN AND TOM LEHMAN'S STROKESAVERS:

- Focus on only one key swing thought.
- Always take the same amount of time on the pre-shot routine.
- Make the routine second nature, like breathing.
- Step back and start over if something doesn't feel right.

- A single key swing thought—for example, "Take the club away low and slow." You should have only one swing thought as you prepare to play a shot. Tour players often say things such as "I wasn't really thinking about anything when I played that shot," because they concentrate on choosing the right club and getting aimed properly. After that, they trust their swings to get the job done.
- A practice swing that matches the swing you would like to make when actually playing the shot.
- A visualization of the shot as you expect it to fly. "Seeing" the shot before it is played is a hallmark of almost every great player.

TOM LEHMAN: WAGGLING THE CLUB MAKES IT EASIER TO START YOUR SWING

"I think the most important thing about my pre-shot routine is that it always takes the same amount of time. I think if someone were to time me on every shot over the course of a season, there would be a variation of no more than one second—which means the same number of waggles, the same number of looks at the target, etc.

"You should be completely comfortable with your routine. It should be second nature so that you're not even conscious of how you do it. I couldn't tell you exactly what I go through to play a shot. It's one of those things like, 'How do I breathe?' I know it's the same every time, because I've done it so many times that I just know I'm doing it right.

"If I don't do my routine correctly, I'm aware of it because I've done it thousands and thousands of times. There's an immediate feedback that says, 'Hey, this isn't right!' At that point you should always step back and start over. Everyday players seem reluctant to do this, but on Tour the players don't hesitate to back off if something doesn't feel right.

"I start from behind the ball, and I take a couple of practice swings and visualize the ball in flight. When I walk up to the ball, I take a little half swing and then get over the ball and shuffle around until I feel comfortable. I waggle the club a few times and look at the target and then I swing.

"When my wife is watching me play, she says she knows exactly when I'm about to hit the ball because my last waggle is always a little bigger than the others. I never come to a complete stop between that final waggle and the start of my swing. I've always found that if I get to a point where I'm totally static—where I'm not moving at all—that the chances of my hitting a good shot are dramatically decreased.

"If you watch any athlete who is good at something—someone shooting free throws or getting ready to steal a base—they're always wiggling their hands or bouncing the ball or looking at the basket. They bend their knees, they breathe, they shrug their shoulders—they do something so that they don't become totally frozen. I think it's because it's easier to get a big motion going if you already have a little motion going. I know I take the big waggle, make a little forward press with my hands, and away I go. It's just my way of initiating my swing without coming to a dead stop."

From *The PGA Tour Complete Book of Golf*, by Michael Corcoran. Henry Holt and Company. Reissued in condensed form as *Shotmaking Techniques*. Copyright © 1999 by Mountain Lion, Inc. Used by permission of Michael Corcoran.

A KING AND HIS COURSE

Arnold Palmer was known for his late rallies, but everything he did beforehand paved the way for his thrilling finishes. In *Go For Broke, My Philosophy of Winning Golf* (1973), he suggested learning about all 18 holes of a golf course before playing the first hole. He wrote: "It's like going on a trip: you usually buy a road map, choose your routes, know where the shortcuts are, know whether going off the expressway is going to be rewarding in some way.... You just don't start driving aimlessly on a road.... Similarly with a golf course: you just don't start hitting a ball aimlessly around it. You look at its 'map' and you see what it has to offer: where the birdies are, where the dangers are, how one hole is related to another, where the shortcuts are...what you can do to make the course bend to your philosophy."

Brittany Lincicome tees off during the 2011 LPGA ShopRite Classic, which she captured with a final round 66 for a one-stroke victory. One of the longest hitters on the LPGA tour, Lincicome uses her whole body to generate power. Note the unwinding of the hips and how she is facing the target at the end of her swing. (AP Images)

PART TWO

THE SWING

IN 1857, H.B. FARNIE WROTE that driving the ball was the most "dashing and fascinating" part of golf, *and* its "principle difficulty." That central paradox is still true today. The swing lies at the heart of the game, and yet constitutes its central mystery. Ever since that legendary ancient shepherd first hit a rock with his crook, golf theorists have offered numerous and conflicting ideas on the best way to swing a golf club, with some teachers emphasizing feel and others mechanics. As the swing evolved from the "handsy" St. Andrews method of the early Scots to the big-muscle power swings of Tiger Woods and Michelle Wie, the disagreement only intensified. At the same time, golf instructors broke down the swing into individual components, such as the swing plane and "delayed hit," and then asked golfers to practice each before blending them into one continuous, athletic motion. Traditional instruction also split the swing into the backswing and through-swing, and then told the golfer to reconnect them—although in the best swings these two elements may overlap. But the main arguments remained over what to emphasize in teaching the swing, as well as to whom. For the average golfer to "dig the thing out of the dirt," as Ben Hogan called it, "feeling" the clubhead with the hands, or "small muscles," is recommended. For the better golfer, relying on the big muscles of the torso and legs may be the way to go. However, the best golfers might strive for an ideal "mix."

CHAPTER 4

SWING THEORY

From Gadflys and Gardeners to Gurus

Elementary Instruction

1890 • Horace G. Hutchinson

The famous British golf writer Bernard Darwin (grandson of Charles) once said that Horace Hutchinson might have disappeared from the pages of time—dismissed as yet another upper-class dilettante—had his youth not coincided with the beginning of interest in golf in England. Hutchinson embraced the new game, winning two British Amateur championships and then staking out his own library section by writing 16 books on various aspects of golf. Despite a rather stiff upper lip, Hutchinson possessed a deft touch in his instructional writing, making the difficult and complex "Scottish game" comprehensible to aristocrat and commoner alike. Although his prose may seem slightly archaic today, including this essay from an early book, many of his swing concepts are refreshingly modern and useful. Asserting that the golfer must think about *swinging through the ball*, rather than "hitting at" it, Hutchinson's idea anticipated Bobby Jones and such diverse current instructors as David Leadbetter and Jim Flick.

Above everything, the golfing drive is a swing, and not a hit. These are very short and simple words, and contain a truth universally admitted—universally, almost, forgotten.... The ball is to be met by the clubhead at a certain point in the swing, and swept away; it is not to be *hit at*. The word "hit" ought to be a misnomer for the stroke....

But what precisely is the difference, it may be asked, between a hit and a sweep or swing? Just this: that the former is delivered with a jerk and with tightened muscles, and the latter is a motion whose speed is gained by gradual, not jerky, acceleration, with the muscles flexible. This...does not in the least preclude the application of great strength and great effort to the swing; it only precludes their misapplication....

The upward swing should be slow and even, the downward swing even and swift. But though the upward swing should be slow, it should...be a swing and not a lift.... Encouraging and accelerating the speed of this swinging thing at the end of the club means hard driving, in its true sense—above all, accelerating

HORACE G. HUTCHINSON'S STROKESAVERS:

- Sweep the ball off the tee; don't hit *at it*.
- Allow the swing to accelerate gradually and smoothly until well through the ball.
- Let the club do the work.

the pace to its utmost at the moment that the clubhead meets the ball. But directly we begin to force the swing out of its harmony—to over-accelerate the pace—from that instant it loses the true character of a swing and becomes a hit, a jerk—and this is "pressing."

Let the club swing *itself* through. Let it do its work itself, and it will do it well. Interfere with it, and it will be quite adequately avenged.

From *The Badminton Library: Golf*, by Horace G. Hutchinson. Longmans, Green, and Co., London, England.

"The 'click' of a solid wood shot soaring down the fairway is well worth all the hours of practice."

—JIMMY DEMARET

The Styles of Champions—
Walter Hagen

1923 • O.B. Keeler

Walter Hagen ripped into golf balls with a swing that mirrored his flamboyant personality. As stylish as was Hagen's lifestyle—he said he never wanted to be a millionaire, but wanted to live like one—he also walked the walk when he played. This is clear in this article by O.B. Keeler, the *Atlanta Journal* writer who became Boswell to Hagen's early rival, Bobby Jones. Using an unusually wide stance for stability, "Sir Walter" displayed a bigger-than-life swing that drew admiration from galleries, while intimidating opponents. Remarkably, his lower body made the transition into the downswing before his upper body completed the backswing. This move by the man in knickers and a tie was ultramodern—Jim McLean contends only the *best* players ever master this exquisitely sophisticated power move. When Hagen's shots were wild it was only because the whippy, wooden shafts of his day couldn't handle the surge.

The first impression you get of Hagen's golfing style is that it is free, slashing and of enormous power.... Watching him tear into a golf ball for a full shot, with the tremendous drive of his right side carrying all his weight far forward onto his left foot, it is impossible to escape an impression of bulk; the vast power of the man seems to dilate him; the action is expansive....

Hagen's swing is neither upright nor flat, but is nearer the former. He takes the club back smoothly to a position just dipping past the horizontal; a full swing, it would be called these days, though far short of the "St. Andrews swing" of a generation ago. The left arm all through the stroke, until the ball is gone, is rigidly straight; but that is a characteristic of all first-class players, practically; only Harry Vardon, the Old Master, eases the backswing at the top by a slight bend of the left elbow, and he brings it out straight again early in the downswing.

At the top of the swing, Hagen's right leg is rigidly braced and his weight seems to have moved back on to it, but the left foot is gripping the ground firmly; the foundation is solid all through the stroke. Once the downswing is underway, Hagen does not hesitate to shoot the left hip into a leading position, and at impact his right heel is well off the ground—his weight coming through with a rush as his right side goes driving on. But his…head remains still, the pivot of the swing, until the ball has gone and the rush of his right side fairly yanks it from its position…. He finishes the stroke with his right shoulder the nearest portion of his anatomy to the objective, and his weight is so far forward that a photograph of his finish looks as if he were running after the ball.

This is his big shot, and it is a grand effort and an impressive one. He is one of the greatest wood-club players of our generation.…

From *The American Golfer* (May 19, 1923), by O.B. Keeler.

WALTER HAGEN'S STROKESAVERS:

- Widen the stance for a firm foundation—this promotes a good slash at the ball.
- Keep the left arm straight in the backswing.
- At the top: use the right leg as a brace, but keep the left foot planted.
- Drive off the right side until all the weight shifts to the left foot.

KEEPING A LEVEL HEAD

Seymour Dunn, an early swing theorist, counted Jim Barnes, Walter Hagen, and Gene Sarazen among his adherents, and first wrote about the swing plane in 1922–almost 40 years before Ben Hogan. But the Scottish expatriate is perhaps best remembered for a simple tip that is still taught today. Dunn told golfers to take an address position near a wall, and then lean their heads against those walls while practicing the pivot, or body turn. The idea is to keep centered during the exercise. The Golf Channel's Martin Hall, Jim McLean, and countless other instructors teach the modern version of this drill. McLean, who attributes his version to Paul Runyan, tells golfers to take a pillow and put it against the wall and lean the head into it, keeping it in place as they take an imaginary swing.

The Swing Technique

1946 • Ernest Jones

Before becoming the most famous instructor of his time, Ernest Jones was forced to rethink his own swing after losing part of his right leg during World War I. He came up with the mantra he'd preach for 40 years and that would be the title of his 1952 book *Swing the Clubhead*. Armed with his trademark props—a pocketknife and a handkerchief—the English expatriate lectured at $5 a pop to professional champions and seemingly hopeless amateurs in a loft space in Manhattan—the precursor to today's widely popular Chelsea Piers. Jones popularized the idea of the swing as a pendulum-like action, while readily dismissing those who would emphasize body and brawn over *feel*. In this excerpt from his popular first book, Jones insisted that if the hands and fingers lead the club, the body (and mind) naturally will follow—a swing philosophy that still inspires prominent instructors such as Manuel de la Torre, Bob Toski, and Jim Flick.

One of my duties as professional was to teach others to play. From my first effort, I realized that I had not the slightest idea of how to go about it.... I read books by the leading professionals, and many others besides, but I am frank to confess that, with a single exception, these, instead of helping me, merely added to my confusion, because of their many contradictions.

There was among these a volume, *The Art of Golf*, by Sir Walter Simpson, published in 1887, which proved very helpful because it set me to thinking along a line entirely different from anything I had encountered up to this time. It pointed out, among other things, that in golf "there is one categorical imperative, 'Hit the Ball,' but there are no minor absolutes."

I think "Swing the Clubhead" is preferable to "Hit the Ball," because there are more ways than one of hitting it.... And I claim nothing new or revolutionary in "Swing the Clubhead," because the identical term "swing" is used to designate the player's effort to wield the club, whether it bears any resemblance to a real swing or not. Yet I am convinced that very few players indeed can explain satisfactorily just what is meant by swinging the clubhead, and further that few high-handicap players really swing in making a stroke....

The longer I teach golf, the more I realize how very little the average golfer understands by what he or she refers to as "my swing." The term, of course, relates to the action of moving a golf club in striking the ball. But just what is implied in referring to the action as a swing is to most golfers a field wholly unexplored....

"The vital thing about a hole is that it should either be more difficult than it looks or look more difficult than it is. It must never be what it looks."

—SIR WALTER SIMPSON,
THE ART OF GOLF, 1887

Learning to swing the clubhead is the one essential to laying the foundation on which is built all permanent, consistent development of skill in playing this ancient game...[and] there is only one thing that you are allowed to use in hitting the ball—the clubhead. To hit the ball effectively with the clubhead, you must move the clubhead in a manner which will develop the greatest force in striking the ball. The greatest force you can develop with a given amount of power is centrifugal in nature, that is, it is achieved by swinging. There is no need to enter here into a study of physics to establish that fact. [Even] in the

ERNEST JONES' STROKESAVERS:

- Swing with the hands, and let the body respond to that motion.
- Develop *feel* for the clubhead, imagining it's a weight on the end of a string.
- Keep the wrists flexible to insure rhythmic motion.
- Think of the swing—felt through the fingers and hands—as a pendulum.

Canadian swing guru Sean Foley dabbles in kinesiology, geometry, and Eastern philosophy to enhance his teaching skills. But in 2010, his main area of study became Tiger Woods. Fearlessly stepping into shoes emptied by Butch Harmon and Hank Haney, Foley accepted the challenge of restoring Tiger's once-ferociously intimidating game—then hit hard by a long layoff due to scandal and injury. According to *Golf Digest*, which named Foley to their "Best Young Teachers" list that year—Foley was age 36 and Woods 34 in 2010—the instructor had his star pupil doing drills familiar to any range rat: swinging with a golf glove under the right armpit, hitting balls barefoot, and walking through a shot by stepping forward with the right foot. Foley, whose 2011 DVD was entitled *The Next Generation: Once a Generation, Everything Changes—Own the Future*, later provided the magazine with his basic teaching tenets, which again, wouldn't surprise anyone rising from a ripping-good 20-year slumber: work on better posture, swing with a towel under the arms, increase hip turn, keep the club shaft ahead of the ball at impact, and finish taller.

time of David and Goliath men realized the value of using a swinging action to develop maximum force.

Further, there is only one medium through which you can transmit to the clubhead the power which you possess. That medium is your hands.... Various parts of your anatomy function in the action of playing a golf stroke, but what the rest of the body does is wholly responsive to the initiating action of swinging the clubhead through the use of the hands and fingers....

Moving a weight back and forth on the end of a string…is possibly the simplest demonstration of a swinging action. A pocket knife attached to the corner of a handkerchief serves the same purpose. Since the handkerchief is flexible, it cannot transmit power through leverage.... When the knife is swung through approximately half a circle…the handkerchief is drawn taut, because a swinging action is always an expanding action, with the weight exerting an outward pull…and this condition will prevail whether the swing be short or long.

[Now, if I swing] a club along with the handkerchief, executing a swing through approximately half a circle…the handkerchief in its movement serves as a check on whether there is an actual swing of the clubhead. If I push or pull on the shaft of the club, it may still be moved through a similar arc, but the movement of the knife and the handkerchief will not coincide.

The action [described] is, of course, that of a pendulum. Its fundamental and distinguishing characteristic is the same whether the pendulum is swung through a small arc or a large one.... Flexibility in the wrists makes it possible for the golfer both to extend the arc of the swing and to bring about a change in direction without disturbing the rhythmic action characteristic of swinging. A sense of feel of what is being done with the clubhead takes care of this.... [And] the sensation, felt in the hands, of what is being done with the clubhead, is the guide by which conscious effort should be directed. All other physical actions on the part of the body should follow as responsive movement.

From *Swinging into Golf*, by Ernest Jones and Innis Brown. Copyright © 1946 by Robert M. McBride & Company. Revised from the book published by Whittlesey House, a division of the McGraw-Hill Book Company, Inc. Copyright © 1937 by the McGraw-Hill Book Company, Inc.

The Force-Center

1946 • Percy Boomer

Like his father, Percy Boomer was a village schoolmaster who golfed as a hobby. But after winning three European championships in the 1920s and having his dad's former students Harry Vardon and Ted Ray seek his counsel, Boomer decided it was time for a career change. For the next 30 years, mostly in France, Boomer taught golf royalty, true royalty, and commoner alike. His only book, *On Learning Golf* (for which the Duke of Windsor wrote the foreword), remains in print and is considered a classic. Modern golfers will recognize a number of phrases in this excerpt—such as "muscle memory" and "connection" in the swing—which Boomer either coined or popularized. But perhaps his most significant contribution was providing the historic link from the Ernest Jones school to the more modern "big muscle" theorists by arguing that the clubhead shouldn't swing the body, the body should swing the clubhead.

I think that few experienced golfers will disagree with the dictum of that great teacher Ernest Jones that our strivings to attain a good swing will have been largely in vain unless at the end we have learned "to feel our clubhead."

Now this is a difficult thing to feel and an exceedingly difficult thing to teach a pupil to feel, though I have often succeeded in teaching it. The real difficulty is that you cannot teach it by teaching skill in the physical movements of the swing—yet this physical skill is a basic necessity before the feel can be induced. So we have to build up the swing and then seek for "the feel of the clubhead" somewhere in its cycle....

Incidentally, I should hate to tell you how long I had played golf before I did really feel that the club had a head to it!... In some great players this feel is so pronounced that you can actually see them seeking it and using it. Walter Hagen approaching and on a tee was a lovely example of this and so today is Henry Cotton—no other modern player gives so strong an impression of the clubhead feel as does Cotton in his drive....

Now after years of study of this matter of clubhead feel, I came to a very conscious conclusion about it, and it was this conclusion which enabled me to be quite exceptionally successful in imparting clubhead feel to my pupils. Here it is: we do not feel our clubhead with our hands; we feel it with our bodies.

What I mean is that, though the hands, being the "railhead" of our feel, do of course play an important part, yet the feel does not stay in them—the hands (and arms of course, though less consciously) *transmit this feel to the body* to the central organization of our golf mechanism. And arising from this the most common mistake we make in trying to feel the clubhead is to look for the feeling of it in our hands instead of at the center.

This matter of feel at the center is so important that I have coined a name for its seat, for where it is felt. I call it the "force-center." I cannot give you an exact anatomical definition of where the force-center *is*, because its position varies with different shots. As the shot (and the swing) become *longer*, so the force-center rises; as they become shorter, the position of the force-center drops. Yet there is always the feeling that we swing from a center, wherever that center may be. And where it is, there also must be the feel of the clubhead....

This is obviously a difficult feel to fix, and the best way I have found is by making the pupil stand in [an] imaginary barrel.... Swinging in this barrel gives him the feeling of keeping his hips up; at the same time he must now *stretch down* (even when his hands are up chest high). Because the body is braced, there will no longer by any tendency for the knees to sag in toward one another; they will roll round at a constant height as he pivots, and this is a very essential feel in the backswing....

PERCY BOOMER'S STROKESAVERS:

- Feel the clubhead with the *body*, not with the hands.
- Swing from the center of the body—the *force-center* as Boomer called it.
- Imagine swinging in a barrel; the body should pivot, rather than sway.
- Develop *muscle memory* for the correct swing movement.

The good swing is based on a pivot with the minimum of to-and-fro movement. Both hips and shoulders are held up and braced, and they move in the same circular path—except that the turn of the body slightly inclines the shoulders as they go round. Now if you stand before an imaginary ball, holding an imaginary club, with your arms stretched down but held lightly (with little tension, I mean) as if you were ready to play a shot, and then turn first right and then left, rather briskly and getting the movement from the knees, calves, and feet, you will begin to feel the pull on your arms from the force-center. *The power is largely produced by the feet and legs, but it is the force-center (somewhere in the pit of the back) which collects it and is responsible for its transfer to the arms and then out to the clubhead.*

Now take a mashie and do very short swings to and fro with it. Soon you will begin to detect the *center* which you will feel controls both the setting up of power and the guiding of the club. Do not break the wrists or lift the clubhead during this experiment. The hands do nothing but keep the club straight out in front of you; let the arms feel supple and yet pushed down as the clubhead is down, while all the time you are moving to and fro from the legs. You begin to feel connected right through, from legs to center and from center to clubhead. Though you make this experiment first with a mashie (that being an easy club to feel), the full drive is simply a big edition of the same movement and must be just as connected.

What I think you will find different in this braced pivot movement as compared with an uncontrolled swing is this: as your hips turn without sag, you will feel you are getting more power and getting it in a different way. You develop rotary power, largely from the legs. This is what I want you to feel, because, when you feel it, you may know that you have got your nether regions well fixed in space....

So I have told you how to build up a force-center, and that when you have built it up, you should be able to feel the clubhead in it. You will be able to do this only if there is no break in the connections between the clubhead and the force-center, but one of these connections—the arms—is the most liable to disconnection of any in the whole swing.

At first glance this would seem easy enough to control, because the arms should work in exact relation to the shoulders and chest. The thorax and biceps should become one in movement. But things do not work out this way, because we do inherently—and in spite of ourselves—consider golf as being played with the arms. So we *use* our arms, ever so little it may be but enough to make us disconnected. Now this is a fine and most delicate point in which lies most of the difference between a good, a very good, and a superlative golfer. It is by the management of the arms that championships are won and lost.

For it is no use to have built up perfect connections to bring coordination to the whole body throughout the whole swing if we then break the connection at a vital point by allowing our arms to work independently of our chest and shoulders. They must be not independent but reactive. The body in the swing must be a unity....

GENERATE REAL PUNCH

In the 1959 book *Golf Magazine's Pro Pointers and Stroke Savers*, three-time Masters winner Jimmy Demaret answered questions sent in by golfers with problems. A 20-handicapper asked the colorful Texan, who was as famous for his flamboyant attire as his 31 PGA titles, how he could use his wrists to get more distance on his shots. Demaret replied: "Forget about your wrists. 'Wrist-action' is strictly duffer talk." Demaret went on to explain that real power is generated from the ground up, through the legs and arms, and then transmitted to the clubhead by the hands. "This is the way a fighter generates punch," he added, "and it is the way a golfer should generate distance. I suggest you erase the thought of the 'wrist' from your mind and concentrate instead on using your hands."

I must remind you again, because it is fundamental to this book, that *learning by a sense of feel* is something quite different to learning by the intellect. Intellectual memory may be of use in learning golf, but it is never paramount. What is paramount is what I have called muscular memory, a memory for the right *feeling* of a movement which enables the muscles to repeat that movement time after time, without directions from brain or will.

From *On Learning Golf*, by Percy Boomer. Copyright © 1942, 1946, by Percy Boomer. Used by permission of Alfred A. Knopf, a division of Random House, Inc.

The Trouble with Women

1962 • Mickey Wright with Joan Flynn Dreyspool

Mickey Wright retired at the age of 34 with little left to accomplish in golf after 82 wins and 13 major championships. But it was the pressure of being Mickey Wright that led to the decision. While playing in 30 tournaments a year—sponsors often threatened to cancel if she didn't show—and promoting the women's game fulltime as the LPGA president, the articulate but somewhat shy protégé of Hall of Famer Louise Suggs finally had to step back. In this excerpt, the former Stanford psychology major talked about her admiration for the extroverted and hard-hitting Babe Zaharias. To Wright, Zaharias (like Suggs and Patty Berg) was an exception that proved the rule: other female players, often self-conscious about exhibiting "nonfeminine" play, didn't hit the ball hard enough to leave their imprint—or divot—on the earth. Today's long-hitters like Yani Tseng, Brittany Lincicome, and Michelle Wie, who play with controlled aggression, apparently got Wright's message.

O n the golf course, we women are definitely The Weaker Sex.
It's muscles, not mentality. From a standpoint of pure physical strength we cannot compete with men. The lady pros, pitted against the male pros, cannot overtake the 50-yard difference in a driver and two-club length difference in an iron shot.

Someone once explained it to me this way. A human muscle is like a rope of fibers that contract. A woman's muscle is a comparatively little rope, and a man's muscle is a bigger rope with stronger contractual power.

All humans have two kinds of muscles, the voluntary which execute movements prompted by the will and the involuntary which perform independently of will. We recruit the voluntary muscles for the golf swing. They have to work when we tell them to, and if we don't put them to work, they'll just be there doing nothing.

To compensate for this lack of strength, a woman golfer should have no wasted motion in her swing so she can utilize all those voluntary muscles to their maximum efficiency.

Good women golfers do. This is why I believe a woman can learn more from a good woman golfer. I believe, too, that if a woman understands more the whys and wherefores of the basic mechanics of a swing she can capitalize on that knowledge.

Apart from our comparative lack of strength, I think too many women golfers possess an even greater weakness on the golf course. *Women don't hit the ball as hard as they can.*

Too many women are so concerned that they won't look graceful swinging hard at the ball that they end up with a most ungraceful powder puff caricature of a swing, looping, lunging, limp.

A psychiatrist and a golf addict, who liked to relate the two, cornered me once after a tournament to expound his theories, Freudian, of course.

"Do you know why women are afraid to take a divot?" he said to me so menacingly that if I were on a couch I would have slid down.

"Are they?" I said, completely intimidated.

"Are they!" he challenged. "I'll say they are! Women are afraid to take a divot because they don't want to damage the earth."

I'm no psychiatrist, but I am a golfer and a woman.

MICKEY WRIGHT'S STROKESAVERS:

- Hone the most efficient swing possible—women can't afford wasted motion.
- Don't be afraid to hit the ball harder, and take a divot with the irons.
- Use lighter clubs, and whippier shafts, for better feel and clubhead speed.
- Replace long irons with woods—they're easier to hit and add loft.

Jimmy Ballard's star ascended in the 1980s when two of his pupils, Hal Sutton and Curtis Strange, became stars. Established as an original thinker and vital link in the development of "big muscle" theory by his groundbreaking 1981 book, Ballard taught the "triangle-center" drill, which flows directly from Percy Boomer's theories of "the force-center." "Take a driver and grip down on the shaft until the butt of the club touches the middle of the chest about an inch up on the sternum," he wrote in *How to Perfect Your Golf Swing.* "Keeping the butt of the club touching center, swing the triangle of arms, hands and club back and through, waist high to waist high... this insures that the large muscles of the legs and torso initially control the arms and hands." The drill is a staple of teaching pros around the world.

Dr. Freud isn't to blame, but the women are. Too many don't hit the ball hard enough to leave the imprint of their swing on the turf, let alone know when or why they should take a divot.

The late Mildred "Babe" Didrikson Zaharias was the strongest woman I ever knew. An Olympic star in javelin, hurdles, and high jump at the age of 18, she was also the greatest woman athlete of [the last] or any century.

Golf was the Babe's greatest love, and she succeeded in it despite the fact she didn't take it up until she was 19. Analytically, Babe's swing was not the best. She didn't transfer her weight properly to the right side, but she offset that by her magnificent power and coordination, her gentle touch around the greens, her putting prowess and her supreme confidence in her ability to perform. No shot was too tough for her to try. She was a great scrambler—and champion.

Babe hit the ball as hard as she could every time, with all that superb muscular power behind it. Not content with that, she practiced, practiced, practiced, especially on her short game and putting.

Even for her, there were no miracles in golf. She knew she couldn't wish herself into a good game. She worked at it and tried to understand how to get the most of each shot.

The Babe was something unto herself, as far as I was concerned. I could keep up with her and out-hit her, but the Babe was the Babe with her glorious history of sports. Today, I am consistently the longest hitter among the women pros.... But, I frequently say to myself, if hitting the ball long were the only secret of good golf, why don't I win every tournament?

I don't. I win often, more often than most, but it is my swing, plus my savvy, plus my strategy, plus my short game that puts me in the winner's circle. I can out-hit many men, much to their embarrassment, for suddenly they are pitting their masculinity against my femininity; their strength against mine. That's foolish. They aren't competing with my strength; they're competing with the efficiency of my swing....

Women worry too much about the wrong things in golf. Some of their golfing values are false. When I swing a club, I am not consciously aware of my hands or my hips or my head or how I look swinging, factors which give other women undue—and hampering—concern.

For instance, a woman doesn't have to swing a heavy club to get better results. Most women, especially beginners, should use lighter clubs with whippy shafts which have greater flexibility and are designed as a substitute for strength to facilitate feel of the clubhead and allow for more clubhead speed at the hit. I use a lightweight men's club...[with a stiff shaft] but I am a pro.

Women should rely upon their woods more, without fear of being criticized. We're after results, and whatever club will put us where we want to be is the club to use.

A wood doesn't have to be swung as fast to loft a ball. A long iron, a 2 or 3, commands great expertness in the hit...but if a 5 wood is easier to hit, then hit it.

It's how we get there, not what we use to get there, that's important.

"The right way to play golf is to go up and hit the bloody thing."

—GEORGE DUNCAN,
1920 BRITISH OPEN WINNER
AND RYDER CUP CAPTAIN

The Modern Swing: How It All Began

1976 • Byron Nelson with Larry Dennis

Modest to a fault, Byron Nelson did not assess his considerable impact on the game until years after retirement. But as the record shows, the moniker *Lord* Byron is more than apt. In an era when most pros were still wielding hickory-shafted clubs, the young Nelson embraced the future, in the form of steel-shafted weapons, and redesigned his own swing to cope with the new technology. In doing so, he not only "invented" the modern swing, but also provided the prototype for a flurry of new theories about how the swing worked. Nelson completed the transition, started by Harry Vardon, from the flat swing of the St. Andrews school. He provided the bridge to the modern era by relying less on the hands and more on the body. In this excerpt— written with former *Golf Digest* associate editor Larry Dennis—Nelson describes the great leap forward.

All I was trying to do was find a better way to swing so I could make a living at the game. I found a better way and, as a result, I've been credited by most experts with developing the modern way to play golf. But I sure wasn't thinking about that at the time.

I started playing golf in 1925, when I was 13 years old and a caddie at Glen Garden Country Club in Forth Worth, Texas....

Back in those early days I had the typical old caddie swing. The hickory shafts I used then in my iron clubs had a lot of torque, or twist, in them. So you had to roll the clubface open on the backswing, then roll it closed coming through the shot. If you didn't, the force of your swing would leave the face open when you struck the ball. Naturally, you had to swing flatter, because you couldn't roll the clubface open and swing upright at the same time, the way we do today.

So the swing was loose and flat. "Turn in a barrel" we called it. There wasn't the foot and leg action you see today. The feet were kept pretty flat, and coming through we would hit against a straight left leg and side, kind of throwing the clubface into the ball to get it square again.

Byron Nelson, shown here at the 1936 L.A. Open, was one of the first golfers to use steel-shafted clubs, a move that compelled him to redesign his swing to maximize the new technology. The change undoubtedly contributed to his 11 straight wins in 1945—golf's unassailable record. (AP Images)

That swing worked pretty well with the irons. But all this time I was using steel-shafted woods and was hooking them something terrible. I never could figure out why. Then, about 1930, I got my first set of steel-shafted irons, and I began hooking with them as badly as I had with my woods.

I realized finally that the reason I was hooking was because the shaft didn't have as much torque, but my hands were still opening and closing as much as ever—*pronating* and *supinating* are the technical terms for this. I was rolling the steel-shafted club closed too quickly, and this was causing me to hook the ball.

When I discovered what was happening, I decided not to roll my hands so much. But I was still using that old caddie swing—low and around the shoulders. And I couldn't play as consistently. I'd play a 67 or 68, and all of a sudden I'd shoot 75 or 76 or 77. I didn't know where the clubhead was or what it was doing. I couldn't hit the ball as far, either, and I didn't like that at all.

Everybody else was in the same boat at the time, and nobody knew exactly what to do, but I kept on thinking. I decided that if I were going to take the club back without any pronation, then I'd have to start swinging more upright. So I began taking my hands back higher. But I was still using my feet and legs in the old way—which is to say not much at all—and that didn't work very well.

BYRON NELSON'S STROKESAVERS:

- Think straight back, straight through.
- Power into the ball with a steady head and active use of the legs and feet.
- Hold the clubhead square as long as possible at the bottom of the swing.
- Control the swing with the left side, and keep the left hand square to the target.

Then I decided I had to learn to take the club straight back. When I got to the top of the backswing, I felt as if I would just let it fall, with my feet and legs helping to carry it straight back through the ball and keeping it on line toward the target. This would eliminate the hook that was troubling me.

About that time I also developed the idea that I had to keep my head still, and with that discovery everything began to fall into place. Keep my head still...take the club

Alex Morrison's "left-side dominant" theories influenced several generations of golfers and their teachers—from Byron Nelson to Jack Grout, the Golden Bear's mentor. Morrison, a flamboyant Los Angeles club pro, told players to keep their chin pointed behind the ball through impact—a tip still resurrected by golf magazines. Doing so, of course, keeps the head behind the ball, and is a better swing thought than the old admonition to "keep the head down," or "keep your eye on the ball," ancient advice that often led golfers to freeze up and contributed to any number of errant shots. Morrison was a favorite of Hollywood celebrities such as Charlie Chaplin, Douglas Fairbanks, Bob Hope, and Bing Crosby. In turn, they helped him become a pioneer in filming the golf swing and using that as an instructional tool.

right straight back through the ball…keep my feet and legs very active, leading the club and helping me carry it through the hitting area…keep the legs going straight through toward the target instead of doing any twisting…just back and through.

I started making this change in my swing in 1930, when I was 18 years old, but it sure didn't happen all at once. I hit a lot of golf balls trying to make it work. One thing that helped me was practicing against the Texas wind. Keeping the ball down against the wind helped me learn to take the club straight back and straight through. I also think my pronounced leg drive developed from trying to keep the ball low against the wind. I was trying to swing through the ball with as shallow an arc as possible at the bottom and keep the club going down the target line as long as I could. You need strong leg action to do that.…

I think I was the first player to make the complete change from the old way of swinging to the modern method we use today. Of course, the older players weren't making many changes, even with the steel shafts. They had played their way for so long that they probably were afraid to. As we get older, we tend to resist change.

But I feel the younger players did start to copy me. Most people, I guess, like to copy somebody who is successful, and after a while I began to have pretty good success with that swing.

I turned professional in November 1932, went to Texarkana, and played in a little $500 tournament.… I finished third and won $75. I was 20 years old by then.

The next spring they hired me as the pro at Texarkana Country Club. There was so little money in the tournaments in those days that you had to make your living at a club. In fact, the only time I ever stayed on tour full time was in 1945 until the day I quit in August 1946....

I began playing in tournaments right away, though. In 1933 I tried to play in two or three without any money and ended up hitchhiking back home from California. I returned to the winter tour that fall, but in the summer of 1934 I played in only a few local tournaments. By then I had made enough of a reputation so that I was invited to the second Masters tournament....

So I kept working on this theory of keeping the face of the club square with the back of the left hand, just as though I was trying to hit the ball with the back of that hand.

I felt I was controlling the swing from the left side. But I knew I was getting some power from the right side, not early in the swing but late. That was something that just kind of happened. I wouldn't recommend that anyone deliberately try to hit with the right side, because if you do you'll be in trouble. Even though I felt I pushed off the right foot, I don't believe you should think about this, because you'll do it too much ahead of time. The right-side power builds up because of the proper use of the feet and legs. When you move to the right in the backswing and then back to the left you automatically generate the proper use of the right side.

Finally, in 1937, I had developed this style of play to my satisfaction.... I also started winning consistently that year. I won the Masters and three other tournaments, and I played on the Ryder Cup team. I never tried to change anything in my swing from that time on....

The modern players have carried the improvements in the swing even further, I feel. They tie the whole swing together better than I did. They combine the use of their feet and legs with the whole turn of their bodies.

They stand reasonably close to the ball—closer than we did in my time—and they push the club straight back. Even if some of them break their wrists immediately, they hold it, and by the turn of their shoulders they carry the club high into the air. They make a big shoulder turn, but they don't let their hips turn as much as their shoulders. As a group, the players today get their hands much higher on the backswing than I did. Over the years they have developed a longer, fuller arc, a fuller extension going back and coming through. And they do it more smoothly.

As a result, they hit the ball harder and farther, yet they hit it amazingly straight. They do this because they have such good control of the left side. I don't know a good player out there today who doesn't control his swing with the left side. They also keep the club more on line with the target during the swing, and they keep their heads very still.

From *Shape Your Swing the Modern Way*, by Byron Nelson with Larry Dennis. Published 1976 by Golf Digest, Inc. Reprinted with permission of Byron Nelson, individually, and Byron Nelson, Trustee, of the Byron Nelson Revocable Trust.

Feeling Your Hands

1988 • Bob Toski and Davis Love, Jr. with Robert Carney

Bob Toski and Davis Love, Jr. sometimes taught together, penned a book together, and entered *Golf* magazine's World Golf Teachers Hall of Fame together in 1999. Toski, the first living inductee, was briefly a 118-pound pro prior to spending the last 40 years teaching 100,000 pupils, writing books and articles, and dispensing tips on television (originally NBC) and videos. A student of Harvey Penick, Love—the father of PGA star Davis Love III—also became a revered instructor before dying in plane crash at age 53, in the same year as the publication of his book with Toski. The renowned duo expected golfers to learn how the various parts of the body should feel during the swing; and in this excerpt they paid tribute to "small-muscle" theory, quoting mutual influences Seymour Dunn and Ernest Jones on how golfers should use their hands to generate clubhead speed and let the body follow their lead.

"Some players might as well stick their hands in their pockets," said the great golf instructor Seymour Dunn, "for all the use they make of them." The hands start the clubhead moving, keep it on its natural path, and sustain its centrifugal motion.

The hands, Dunn said, are the leaders of the swing. And that surprises most golfers. You see them on the practice range struggling to lift the club with their arms or pull it with their shoulders or help it along with their legs and trunk.

They twist and turn and slap and hit, clutching the club in a grip so tight their hands lose all of their natural power....

If that shoe fits you, here's some good news: the golf swing is easier than you thought, much easier when you master the movement of the hands.... First, because your hands generate clubhead speed. Second, because your hands impose the greatest influence on the face of the club. Third, because your hands lead your arms in creating clubhead path. And finally, because they control the amount of tension in your swing. (If your hands are tight, your forearms become tight, your shoulders become tight, and so on.) In short, your hands are the boss. They control the speed at which you can swing and therefore the distance you can hit the ball. They control the accuracy with which you hit it....

Following Ernest Jones' example, swing a pen knife at the end of a kerchief. As you...learn the movements of the hands during the swing, try to duplicate that free-swinging motion.... Through your hands [you] let the club swing.

You'll note that we have not yet used the word "release" in [regards to] hand motion. In the golf swing, release means the rotation of the hands, wrists, and forearms from their position on the backswing, back to a square position at impact, to their position on the follow-through. Some books spend a great deal of time talking about release...release will occur naturally when your hands and forearms are working in tandem.

Here's an exercise by master teacher Paul Runyan, the former PGA champion, that promotes efficient hand, wrist, and forearm coordination. It will also increase your hand and, therefore, clubhead speed. You can do it while you're

BOB TOSKI AND DAVIS LOVE, JR.'S STROKESAVERS:

- Master the correct hand movements to master the swing.
- Drill: place both hands in front of the body, left palm inward, right facing away. Now flip them back and forth as fast as possible—note how soft hands are quick hands.
- Drill: hold a club between the thumb and forefinger and let it swing—feel how it slows down on the way up and picks up speed on the way down.
- Drill: swing a club at waist level like a baseball bat, gradually lowering it to ground level—this ingrains the feel of keeping the club path even and smooth.

FEET TOGETHER NOW

Bobby Jones is generally credited with creating perhaps the most commonly taught drill to this day for enhancing a golfer's ball-striking ability. Jones hit hundreds of practice shots with his feet close together to instill the proper feeling for timing, balance, and the correct swing path. If the golfer tries to swing too hard, he or she will not be able to stay poised and will, literally, fall over. According to more modern pros, the drill also teaches connection, forcing the golfer to match his upper torso to his arms and shoulders in the swing.

watching TV. Stand up and put your left hand in front of you, palm facing toward you. Now flip the palm as fast as you can so that it faces away from your leg. Repeat it again and again, keeping your hand, wrist, and forearm as loose and flexible as you can. Then do it with your right hand and arm, starting with the palm facing away from you and flipping back toward you. Now place both hands in their starting positions, move them together to your right and swing them back to your left, flipping the palms as quickly as you can as you go.... Repeat the movement over and over, starting slowly and increasing the speed of the "flip" of the wrists. Without touching a club, you've learned the correct movement of hands, wrists, and forearms during the swing. You've also learned that the "softer" your hands, the faster they flip. Which begins to explain why tight grip pressure decreases, not increases, clubhead speed. Stiff hands and wrists are slow hands and wrists.

Also great for "release" is the Baseball Drill, especially if you tend to slice the ball. Grip your club normally and begin to swing it at waist level the way you would a baseball bat. Gradually bend forward and lower the club to ground level, still thinking of a "level" swing. We've seldom seen a player who could slice the ball while trying to swing level....

FEELING THE CLUBHEAD

Hold a club between your thumb and forefinger and let it swing. Feel the weight of the clubhead, notice how it slows down on the way up, picks up speed on the way down.

HAND MOVEMENTS DURING THE SWING

Hitchhike Drill: with no club, make a full turn and swing your left hand back from an imaginary address position until it points at your right shoulder. Then swing it down and across your body until it points at your left shoulder. Do it again and again in a swing-like motion, observing the movement of your hand.

The Pivot

1990 • David Leadbetter with John Huggan

Born in England but raised in Zimbabwe, David Leadbetter dropped out of business school to follow the dodgy path of aspiring golf pro. He never made it as a player, but he quickly found a niche, spending the next 30 years building an international empire of golf schools, churning out best-selling books and DVDs, and tutoring top professionals. His childhood friend Nick Price was an early client, but it was the complete "makeover" he gave Nick Faldo in the 1980s, resulting in Faldo winning the first of an eventual six majors, that established Leadbetter's reputation. In this excerpt, Leadbetter took yet another step in the evolution of "big muscle" theory by advocating a pivot around two "axis points" and relegating the hands and wrists to mere followers. For such advice from the influential instructor, pros like Ernie Els and Michelle Wie and thousands of hackers pay top dollar.

L earning the pivot motion of the body is [a key] step toward building an athletic golf swing.… Without making a good pivot you can never fully control the swinging motion of the club.

WHAT IS A PIVOT?

The dictionary defines a pivot as a "movement around a fixed point." This is a fair description of the athletic swing except that, as we shall discuss, the transfer of your weight from its original static position at address to your right side and back to your left side is around two axis points rather than one....

WHAT THE PIVOT DOES

Your pivot motion provides three vital ingredients in your athletic swing:

- A coiling and stretching effect where your torso is wound up and loaded like a spring ready to unwind;
- A transfer of your body weight from one side to the other;
- Consistent tempo or speed.

That, in a nutshell, is what your pivot motion is all about. A clear concept of how and what your body does will put you well on your way to becoming an athletic swinger.

For now, understanding the pivot action does not require you to use a club, not in the conventional sense anyway. You will need one only when working through some of the drills. This [excerpt] describes the movement of your body—nothing more. *You must know what your body does during your swing before learning the roles played by your arms, hands, and club.* Indeed, it is my experience that most golfers feel the benefits of a proper pivot more quickly when the club and perhaps more importantly, the ball, are removed from the equation....

CONCENTRATED EXECUTION

A major force in the growth of women's golf as a player and instructor, Patty Berg contended that to hit a good shot the golfer must do one thing: focus on properly striking the ball. The only way to cut down on errors made under stress is to concentrate. In her seminal book *Golf* (1941), she advised, "Isolate each step of your golf game so that every shot becomes a separate unit within itself. Then devote your entire mental process to the proper execution of that particular shot, with no thought of what the results may be. If you are utterly oblivious of what goes on about you, then you are concentrating correctly."

Youngsters who start the game at an early age learn by imitation. Give them the opportunity to see some good, athletic swings and it is likely that their body motions will be fairly athletic in turn. However, it is my contention that most golfers never totally understand what constitutes a correct body pivot. As a result, they play all their lives with swings requiring constant patching, giving no thought to its inner workings....

CENTRIFUGAL FORCE

The term "centrifugal force" is used increasingly by teachers when discussing the golf swing. But I have found that only a few golfers really know either what it means, or what it does.

It is a force created away from the center of your swing. Transmitting from your body out through your arms and hands, it creates leverage, width of arc, and clubhead lag. In turn, they create clubhead speed and maintain the club on a steady orbit or arc.

DAVID LEADBETTER'S STROKESAVERS:

- Develop an "athletic" swing by pivoting around two axis points—the transfer of weight from one side of the body to the other.
- Make the pivotal motion of the torso the engine room of a good swing.
- Allow the arms and hands to react to *body* movements—they are followers, not leaders.
- Harness the centrifugal force generated by body motion—like a discus thrower building power by coiling his or her body—using the hands and arms as conductors of torso-created power.

So how do we harness this important force found in the swings of all good ball-strikers? Simply, it is the *efficient coiling and uncoiling of your torso in a rotary or circular motion which maximizes centrifugal force.* Think of it this way: holding a piece of string with a weight on the end, begin to spin your wrist in an anti-clockwise direction. As long as your arm stays steady, the weight moves into a constant orbit. The quicker you spin your wrist, the faster the weight moves. The weight, though, will always be moving much faster than your wrist—the centrifugal force created will see to that.

Coach David Leadbetter looks on as Michelle Wie takes a shot during a practice round prior to the 2010 LPGA Championship. Leadbetter advocates a pivot around two "axis points," relegating the hands and wrists to mere followers. (Scott Halleran/Getty Images)

This centrifugal force or outward pulling of the string is maintained by the movement of your wrist. It is that which keeps the weight in orbit. If your wrist moves out of its original position, the weight moves out of orbit. Your golf swing displays identical characteristics. If your body does not move correctly, the club will not move on the correct plane or orbit. It will also lose speed. That means shots lacking in both distance and direction.

In the same way, the relationship between body and club during the golf swing is very much like a pair of ice skaters. I'm sure you've seen this on television; the lead skater (representing the body in the golf swing) is the hub around which his partner rotates. He revolves quite slowly while the female skater (representing the clubhead) is moving at a tremendous speed. This is a perfect example of how centrifugal force can be built up around a relatively slow moving axis and transferred to another, much faster object. [In other words]…the dog must wag the tail.

Your golf swing starts from the address position, where the club is virtually static. It then gathers speed as it changes direction and culminates in a whip-like action through the ball. This acceleration stems from the turning or pivotal motion of your torso—the power base or engine room of every athletic swing. That is how centrifugal force is maximized. Through the motion of your body, power is built up; power that flows through your arms and hands into the clubhead. The impression that the power in your golf swing stems from the motion of your hands and arms is a false one. Just like a discus thrower who builds up power through the coiling motion of his or her body, you use your hands and arms merely as conductors of your torso-created power.

That is not to say your hands and arms play no part in your golf swing. They most certainly do. Even the most efficient pivot motion could not generate a great deal of clubhead speed operating alone. But there is a definite chain of command—your hands and arms must react to, not dominate, the movement of your body.

It should be clear to you that maximizing the centrifugal force in the clubhead requires a certain amount of physical ability. That is why it is very difficult to play golf well with a bad back. A lack of mobility or flexibility in your back reduces the rotary motion of your spine and cuts the supply of power to your arms, hands, and club. When forced to take over the task of moving the clubhead, they are less effective.

As proof of how important your body motion is, try hitting some balls when sitting on a stool, your feet off the ground. To hit the ball any distance is all but impossible because the only source of power is the swinging motion of your arms. Remember: *the power base in every athletic golf swing is the turning motion of your body—your pivot.*

As you work on your pivot motion, realize that you do not rotate around only one fixed axis point, your head. Imagine a line drawn down the inside of your right shoulder, through your right hip joint and past the inner part of your right thigh into the ground. Now imagine the same line traveling down the left side of your body. These are the two axis points around which every athletic swinger rotates, back and through.

Rotating around your right axis point, then your left, will encourage what I call a "turning weight transfer" in both directions. Your body weight, from a fairly even start at address, moves to your right heel on your backswing and toward your left heel on your downswing. It is quite normal for your head, especially on the backswing, to move a little laterally as you turn. It should certainly be free to swivel. Keeping your head overly still can only restrict your motion around your two axis points.

An incorrect rotation around your two axis points can, in fact, lead to a so-called "reverse pivot." This occurs when, on your backswing, your weight does not move around your right axis point, but hangs on your left side. On the downswing, that translates to your weight moving onto your right side instead of your left. By severely reducing the ability of your body to correctly control your hands and arms, this causes all manner of bad shots.

Although your pivot motion should not include any pauses or breaks in motion…for the sake of clarity, [I can describe it as]…three pieces:

- Your backswing or pivot motion to the right;
- The transition from backswing to downswing as the body changes direction;
- Your downswing or pivot motion to the left

This, I feel, is the best way for you to attain a clear understanding of the complete motion.

From *The Golf Swing*, by David Leadbetter with John Huggan. Copyright © 1990 by David Leadbetter. Reprinted by permission of HarperCollins Publishers, Ltd. and The Stephen Greene Press, an imprint of Penguin Group (USA), Inc.

The Pendulum-Like Swing

1997 • Jim Flick with Greg Waggoner

For over a half century, Jim Flick has built a reputation as one of the country's top teachers through frequent magazine articles, television appearances, and as the principle instructor for a variety of national golf schools. Focusing on how to swing the clubhead and the pendulum-like nature of the swing, he has taught golf as a game of *feel*, rather than mechanics. If that sounds vaguely familiar, it might be because of his long association with Bob Toski, with whom he wrote the popular book *How to Become a Complete Golfer*—and their mutual admiration for past masters Ernest Jones and Seymour Dunn. But Flick is hardly a throwback. While a stickler for the fundamentals, he decries the "big muscle" approach for the average, slice-bound hacker. He believes in clearing the mind of competing theories and focusing on natural movement—*playing* the game, rather than *working* at it. Of course, he also admits using a slightly different approach when counseling accomplished PGA Tour pros—over 200 at last count, including Tom Lehman and Jack Nicklaus.

The first time I talk to students about the pendulum-like swing I see a lot of skepticism in their eyes. Some of it disappears after our first short-game session because the stroke for the basic chip and pitch shots is certainly pendulum-like, and the square contact "feels" right. But the unspoken—and sometimes spoken—reaction is, "Okay. A pendulum's fine, but I'm not going to hit my ball far enough."

And I have to convince you that you will.

The term is "pendulum-like," as in similar (but not identical) to a pendulum. Unlike a true pendulum on a grandfather clock, of course, the golf swing doesn't keep going back and forth, through the same arc indefinitely. But if we examine the properties of how a pendulum swings and then liken it to golf motion, you'll see a lot of similarities.

For most golfers, the pendulum-like swing is the simplest, quickest way to achieve consistent repetition of motion—the much coveted, much pursued, always elusive Repeating Swing.

Attach a golf ball to a string, let it hang from a fixed point, get it swinging, and—presto!—a demonstration pendulum. Question No. 1: is there any acceleration? The answer is yes: pendulums accelerate as long as they're swinging down. There is a bottom point—actually, in physics I believe it's called the zero point—where there is no more acceleration. But that is also the point where you've got *maximum* velocity.

How good is that? You've got your clubhead picking up speed, picking up speed, then hitting maximum speed at contact. That would actually be an optimum transfer of energy.

Next, almost always, comes a question that—*invariably*—sends one of my teaching colleagues, Martin Hall, up the wall, off the charts, and into orbit: "If the pendulum stops picking up speed, that means I have to make sure to accelerate and follow through, right?"

Now, everyone has his hot-button issue. Mine is "One-Piece Takeaway." For Martin…the thing that drives him craziest is "accelerate and follow-through."

Listen to him on the subject:

> I can't think of anything worse to try to do with a golf club in your hands than "accelerate and follow-through."
>
> Does the swing accelerate? Yes. What's making it accelerate? Gravity. Let me repeat: it's accelerating because of the pull of gravity.
>
> Now, is there a follow-through? Of course, there is. Why? Because of the swing, because of momentum.

JIM FLICK'S STROKESAVERS:

- Develop that elusive "repeating swing" by using a simple pendulum-like motion.
- Assume good posture and light grip pressure to facilitate the action.
- Allow the weight of the clubhead, gravity, and centrifugal force to do the work.
- Avoid conscious effort, such as *trying* to "accelerate and follow through"—gravity creates acceleration, which generates momentum for the follow-through.

So with the pendulum-like swing, we have acceleration, and we have follow-through as a consequence of momentum. If you think "accelerate and follow-through" when you swing, then you are going to try to help momentum.

Believe me, momentum doesn't need any help.

Martin's right. There is a follow-through in the golf swing, but it's caused by momentum, not a conscious effort. If you go into the golf swing thinking about accelerating at impact to create a big follow-through, you'll undermine the principal of the pendulum-like swing, inevitably cause your muscles to tense up, and almost certainly disrupt the swing's arc with the midpoint increase in effort, thereby reducing the likelihood of a square club face at impact.

Not only that, but you will really annoy Martin Hall.

NOT ONE, BUT TWO

There are actually two pendulums at work. The first is formed by the hands and wrists cocking, uncocking, and recocking. The second is created by the forearms and upper arms swinging from the shoulder sockets.

My former colleague from *Golf Digest* school days Peter Kostis called them the first swing and the second swing. I think of them as two pendulums.

What permits the two pendulums to work together is the combination of the weight in the clubhead, centrifugal force, the good old law of gravity—and the golfer. These pendulums supply about 80 percent of the distance in your golf shot—provided the swinging elements of your body drive the turning elements and not vice versa.

If your grip pressure is too tight, the weight at the end of the club is restricted from doing its job.

If you try consciously to turn your shoulders and shift your weight, you destroy the natural harmony of those two pendulums.

If you try to accelerate at impact and follow-through, well you know what happens there.

But if your posture is good, and your grip pressure—fingers secure, arms relaxed—is correct, you give those two pendulums a chance to work in harmony.

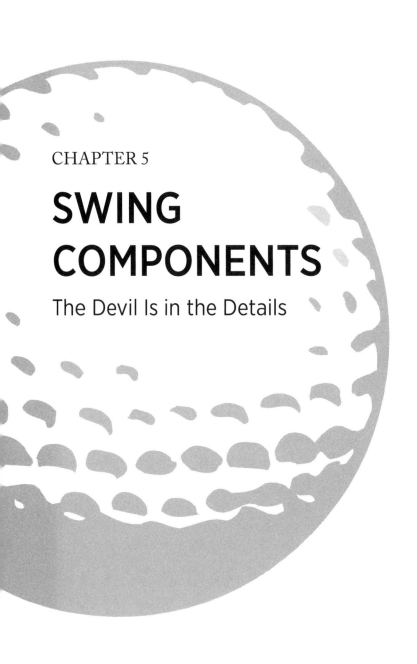

CHAPTER 5

SWING COMPONENTS

The Devil Is in the Details

The Delayed Hit

1919 • James M. Barnes

"Long Jim" Barnes stood 6'4" and towered over his more famous rivals, like Walter Hagen and Gene Sarazen, and consistently outhit them. Capitalizing on his victories in the first two PGA Championships, Barnes (who would later capture U.S. and British Opens) published the landmark book *Picture Analysis of Golf Strokes*. With full-page, stop-action photographs of his swing at various stages—and a minimum of explanatory text—it was a "How to Do It" alternative to teaching manuals that featured long, descriptive, and often hyperbolic prose, and presaged today's instructional DVDs. Barnes' book would be important if just for a photograph of his seemingly delicate wrists, freezing the moment *before* they snap the clubhead into the ball. This concrete image of the "delayed-hit" launched more theories than Helen did warships—the most common being: if golfers can maintain that power angle, they can increase power and distance.

DRIVER OR BRASSY

In starting the downward swing of the club the body begins to turn, and in unison with it the left wrist starts the clubhead. The left arm remains straight and pulls the club down simultaneously with the body turn. The right elbow comes in close to the body, still retaining the same bent position as at the top of the swing.

THE DOWNWARD SWING

The hands continue to drop with the turn of the body until the arms are about vertical by the time the club is horizontal. The right elbow is still bent and well in to the body, and the right wrist is still bent as far back as it can go.

Both feet are flat and firm on the ground.

WHERE THE REAL HITTING BEGINS

The body turn has reached a point almost the same as at the address. Although the left arm is almost straight down, the right hand has made as yet but little effort, but is now in position to begin its real work. The right wrist has retained practically the same bent position as at the top of the swing.

JIM BARNES' STROKESAVERS:

- Hold the angle of the right wrist until just before impact.
- Whip the clubhead through the ball with the right hand.
- Keep the left arm straight and pulling hard throughout this action.
- Throw the clubhead out after the ball with both the right and left arms extended.

From this point the right hand does the hitting—gets the head of the club through—while the left arm is pulling straight through with all the strength at its command.

The pressure is [now] taken off the right heel and transferred inwardly to the ball of the foot and toes. The principal difference [as the swing nears impact] is in the position of the right wrist [which now starts to move forward].

[At the moment just before impact] the left arm is still straight and pulling hard, while the right hand is whipping the clubhead through. The thumb and forefinger of the right hand are playing a very prominent part in the work.

It is interesting to note...where the maximum speed of the clubhead occurs.... [As] the clubhead itself is just above the left foot...the shaft is almost unbelievably bent from the speed which is imparted to it. At this point the speed of the swing is reaching its maximum and results mainly from the whip of the right wrist.

THE IMPACT WITH THE BALL

All the muscular movements which make up the stroke reach their climax at this point.... The body, arms, and hands [are] at maximum effort and in perfect unison.

For many years the question of how long the ball remains on the head of the club after the impact has been written about and discussed. [Photography at 1/1500 of a second now] answers that question. The ball is...in contact with [the clubface] for a distance about equal to the width of the clubhead.

While the left arm is practically straight throughout the whole swing, the right arm does not become straight until just as the ball is leaving the clubhead....

The clubhead has been thrown out after the ball, which action keeps both arms straight out from this point until practically the finish of the stroke.

The Swing Plane

1957 • Ben Hogan with Herbert Warren Wind

Ben Hogan tirelessly sought new angles to explore and explain golf, so it's not surprising that he invented the most famous geometric image in instruction history: the swing plane as a pane of glass, extending from the ball to the shoulders. Hogan believed his concept could help golfers find that elusive "slot" at the top of the backswing so that the clubhead is primed for an ideal downswing. Moreover, he thought it might satisfy golf's enduring quest for a consistent swing. As he explained in this excerpt from *Ben Hogan's Five Lessons, The Modern Fundamentals of Golf*, the golfer's goal is to keep the club parallel to or just below this imaginary pane. Dropping the arms too far below it, Hogan contended, would produce an overly flat swing and result in a vicious hook, while going too high—and "breaking" the glass—would result in a nasty slice.

O ver the period I've been in golf, oceans of words have been devoted to the arc of the swing, but only the merest trickle to the plane. This is unfortunate, for in the dynamics of the golf swing the plane is extremely important, far more important than the arc.

What precisely is this plane? To begin with, there are two planes in the golf swing, the plane of the backswing and the plane of the downswing.... The plane of the backswing...is most simply described as an angle of inclination running from the ball to the shoulders. The pitch of the angle is determined by two factors: the height of the individual's shoulders and the distance he stands from the ball at address.

On the backswing, the plane serves the golfer as sort of a three-dimensional road map. *His shoulders should rotate on this plane, continuously inclined at the same angle (with the ball) they established at address.* En route from address to the top of the backswing, *the arms and hands (and the club) should also remain on this same angle of inclination as they swing back.* (Use your left arm as your guide.) When your shoulders, arms, and hands follow the appointed route the plane sets up, it insures you that your upper body and arms will be correctly inter-aligned when they reach that crucial point where the backswing ends and the downswing begins. Then, when the downswing is inaugurated by the hips and the turning hips unwind the upper part of the body, the shoulders and then the arms and then the hands flow easily and powerfully into the swing. In other words, by staying on the backswing plane, the player pre-groups his forces so that each component is correctly geared to work with the other components on the downswing....

There is no such thing as an absolute and standard plane for all golfers. The correct angle for each person's plane depends on how he is built. A fellow whose legs are proportionally shorter than his arms, for example, necessarily creates a shallow angle for his plane. At the other extreme, a man whose legs are proportionately longer than his arms sets up a very steep angle for himself. Neither plane, let me repeat, is incorrect. Technically, it is wrong to term the man who properly swings on a shallow plane a "flat swinger," or the man who properly swings on a steep plane an "upright swinger," simply because their planes happen to be flatter or more upright than the plane of the man of more average proportions. However, if any golfer permits his arms and his club to drop well below his established plane, then, whether he normally possesses a shallow or steep or an average plane, he would be swinging too flat. Similarly, if he hoists his club above the line of this plane, he would be swinging too upright.

Perhaps the best way to visualize what the plane is and how it influences the swing is to imagine that, as the player stands before the ball at address, his head sticks out through a hole in an immense pane of glass that rests on his shoulders as it inclines upward from the ball. *If he executes his backswing properly, as his arms are approaching hip level, they should be parallel with the plane and they should remain parallel with the plane, just beneath the glass, till they reach the top of the backswing. At the top of his backswing, his left arm should be extended at the exact same angle (to the ball) as the glass.* Actually, his left arm would brush against the

Ben Hogan, shown here in 1955, saw the swing plane as an imaginary pane of glass, extending from the ball to the shoulders. He emphasized that the swing should stay even with, or just below, that pane on the backswing and that golfers should strive to get the left arm on the same angle as the glass at the top. (Yale Joel/Time & Life Pictures/Getty Images)

glass. As for his shoulders, as they turn on the backswing, the top of the shoulders will continuously be brushing against the glass.

As golf faults go, it is not too injurious if your club and arms travel on a plane a little flatter than the ideal one. *However, you are heading for disaster if you thrust your arms up above the plane so that they would shatter the pane of glass.* Poor golfers make this error at any and all stages of the backswing, but it occurs most commonly when they are nearing the top of the backswing. Then, when their hands are about shoulder high, they suddenly lift their arms almost vertically toward the sky—crash goes the glass…and their shot. They conclude the backswing on an entirely different and far more upright plane, with their hands and forearms and elbows pretzeled all over the place. Hopelessly out of position, they struggle to right themselves on the downswing. Invariably, they can't and they miss-hit the ball in every conceivable way and in all directions. There are quite a few fairly talented golfers who also make this mistake of looping their arms above the plane as they approach the top of the backswing. It explains their frequent erratic spells. They cannot groove their compensations, and they make errors on both sides of the fairway....

BEN HOGAN'S STROKESAVERS:

- Imagine a pane of glass extending from the ball to the shoulders—depending on a golfer's build, this is his or her swing plane.
- Stay even with, or just below, that pane on the backswing.
- Strive to get the left arm on the same angle as the glass at the top—finding this "slot" almost guarantees a good downswing.

Try to visualize your proper plane and to keep your arms traveling on that plane as you swing the club back. Quite a few of my friends have told me that once they got the idea of the plane in their heads, it worked wonders for them. Like nothing else, it got them out of their old bad habits and made the correct movements come so naturally they could hardly believe it.

I can believe it. I really never felt that my own backswing was satisfactorily grooved, or could be satisfactorily grooved, until I began to base my backswing on this concept of the plane. Up to that point—this was in 1938—I had been struggling along with a backswing that was a lot less uniform and, consequently, a lot less dependable than I wanted it to be. I began to wonder whether or not I could find a set "slot" for the club to hit at the top of the backswing. Then, if I could swing the club into the slot on every swing—well, that would solve my problem of inconsistency.

I began to think more and more about the golfer's plane. After some experimentation, I found to my enormous relief that, if I swung back along this plane, my club would, in effect, be traveling up a set slot *throughout* my backswing, on swing after swing. I practiced swinging on this plane and started to gain confidence that my backswing was reliable. It helped my whole swing, my whole game, my whole attitude. I can honestly say that for the first time I then began to think that I could develop into a golfer of true championship caliber.

Swing Concepts:
Timing and Tempo
1989 • Beverly Lewis

Beverly Lewis, a former playing pro, became one of Britain's foremost golf theorists and was until recently a monthly columnist for and only woman on the teaching panel of the major U.K. publication *Golf World*. In her spare time from giving lessons, doing golf commentary for the BBC, and serving a two-year stint as the first female captain of the British PGA, she wrote outstanding instructional books that take a blended approach to "big muscle" versus "small muscle" theory—with a special emphasis on the needs of women players. Golfers, like baseball hitters, are always talking of timing and tempo, but as Mark Twain said about the weather, few do anything about it. In this excerpt, Lewis does, going where remarkably few have in the last 150 years. After defining the terms, and showing their interrelationship, she tells readers how to find their personal tempo and offers drills to hone their timing.

TIMING

You have probably realized by now that golf necessitates using all the body's muscles. However, muscles do not all work most efficiently at the same pace. So there has to be a compromise where the faster muscles, such as those in the hands and arms, work only at a pace that accommodates the larger muscles, such as those in the back and thighs. Beginners sometimes think that the ball

Davis Love III learned a drill from his father Davis Love, Jr. for keeping his swing smooth and unhurried, even with a driver, and yet producing long hits. Love takes his big club and tries to swing in "slow motion"—the way sprinters practice at half speed—aiming first at a target only 100 yards away on the range. Then he goes for 150, 200, and so forth. The drill instills the proper timing and tempo so that when the full tee shot is hit, it is unhurried and brings the clubhead squarely to the ball along the proper swing path. Love has consistently ranked among the longest hitters on the PGA Tour.

can be hit farther by swinging their arms faster, but this reduces the contribution that the back and shoulders can make, and the swing is denied power and direction. Similarly, if the downswing is rushed, the thigh muscles do not have time to work, and the tautness experienced at the top of the swing is dissipated. Some golfers try to copy top professionals who accentuate their leg action, but because they do not possess the same strength of hand action as the professional, the outcome is usually a thin or cut shot. Correct timing of the golf swing calls for a balance of pace between muscles which takes time and practice to achieve. Beginners need to concentrate on making what seem to be very mechanical movements, and until such time as they acquire a little more fluency they must just accept that they will hit their share of poor shots.

For the more experienced player, who perhaps feels that she swings the club quite well but without due reward, here are two simple guides to analyzing and correcting timing.

If your shots tend to fade and slice, or you thin quite a few, then your leg action is too strong for your hand and arm action. You must concentrate on a stronger arm swing, practicing hitting balls with your feet together until the strike improves.

If your shots draw or hook, and you hit a lot of fat shots, then your leg action is not lively enough. You should put more emphasis on *pulling* with your left arm, and moving your left knee more emphatically from the top of the swing. With your arms hanging in front of you, take a club and hold either end of the shaft horizontally with your feet shoulder-width apart. Now take a swing, and you should find that your legs work more fluently.

Remember that you swing the golf club about 20 feet in an arc before you strike the ball. If you are half an inch or one degree out, you have hit a less than perfect shot. As your strength increases so the timing of your swing may alter slightly, so don't be too hard on yourself. By paying a little more attention to the timing of your swing, you may get closer to that perfect strike.

TEMPO

Timing and tempo are very much interrelated in the swing. Timing is the sequence in which different parts of the body move. Tempo is the pace at which all this movement takes place, and has a direct bearing on the timing of the swing. So, what is the correct tempo for you, and how do you find it? It has been said that your tempo reflects your character, that a person who is always dashing about will swing the club quickly, and vice versa. To some extent this may be true, but the overriding factor, whatever your character, is clubhead control.

It is self-defeating to swing the clubhead faster than you can control it, no matter whether you are by nature the tortoise or the hare. But what you are trying to achieve is a golf *swing*, and to that end there must be a certain degree of pace, or else all sense of rhythm is lost.

The pace of the backswing will have a direct affect on the pace of the downswing and, as already mentioned, this is likely to change as your swing and strength develop. I have to advise many more male players to slow down their swing than I have to ask to speed it up. With the extra strength men possess in their hands and arms, they are often guilty of making short, quick backswings without turning their shoulders.

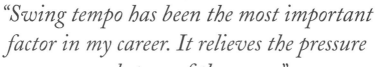

"Swing tempo has been the most important factor in my career. It relieves the pressure and stress of the game."

—Nick Faldo

This is naturally not such a common error in women, but for them a quick backswing will result often in a long backswing, where control is lost. On the other hand, I have found women players who I believe swing the club too slowly. They seem to *take* the club back instead of swinging it back. They fail to create any rhythm in the swing, which leads to a very uncoordinated downswing, and (they) usually lack leg action.

The backswing not only positions the club, it serves to create the pace and rhythm. Golf teachers spend a lot of time trying to get a pupil into a good position at the top of the swing. You might ask, if this position is so important, why don't we start from this point? Well, we don't because a good backswing helps to create good rhythm and tempo.

HOW TO FIND YOUR BEST TEMPO

Take a 6 iron and hit some shots from good lies at your normal pace, noting distance and accuracy. Now hit a similar amount of shots with first of all a faster and then a slower tempo, and again note where the balls land. From this you may be surprised to find that, by swinging at what feels to be three-quarters of your normal pace, you have hit the balls farther and straighter. On the other hand, a slightly faster tempo may reveal that your control of the clubhead is now good enough for you to put a little more speed into the swing. Of course, you may already swing at your optimum tempo. Whatever the outcome it is always an interesting exercise to return to from time to time.

You may also benefit from making a few swings without the club, by just interlocking your two hands. You will find it easier to make a smoother unhurried swing without the club or ball to distract you.

Here is one last example of good timing and tempo, to which I'm sure many of you can relate. Imagine a shot from the fairway that has to carry a hazard and for which you need a good 3 wood. To be safe you decide to lay up short

BEVERLY LEWIS' STROKESAVERS:

- Develop good timing by blending the action of the faster small muscles and slower large ones.
- Practice hitting balls with the feet together for a stronger arm swing.
- Hold a club on either end with the arms dangling in front, then take a swing to get the legs moving more fluently.
- Find the best tempo by swinging at normal speed, then at a faster and slower pace.
- Interlock the hands, then practice making a smooth, unhurried swing without a club or ball.

of the hazard, so you select a 6 iron and make a smooth, unhurried swing. To your surprise, the ball zooms off into the distance and lands in or very near the hazard, and you wish you had been more courageous and hit the 3 wood. This has happened because during the swing you relaxed and made what felt like a three-quarter-paced and length swing. In fact, you achieved perfect timing and tempo. Had you used the 3 wood, you might have tried to thrash the ball, resulting in poor timing and tempo and a bad shot.

Keep this example in your mind when you play and see if, with improved timing and tempo, the mechanics of your swing take a turn for the better. Top class golfers are always searching for good rhythm. Even for them it is something that can be perfect one day and gone the next, so don't worry if this happens to you, just keep persevering.…

What women lack in strength, they can compensate for with good timing and tempo. I have played many pro-ams with men who are usually quite surprised just how far I can hit the ball, with seemingly little effort. I would expect to hit a 5 iron shot about 155 yards (I am 5'3" tall, and weigh only about 125 pounds). I enhance my sound technique by concentrating on maintaining good timing and tempo, which results in maximum clubhead speed at impact.

From *Golf for Women*, by Beverly Lewis. Gallery Books, an imprint of W.H. Smith Publishers, Inc. Copyright © 1989 Sackville Books, Ltd. Reprinted with the permission of Beverly Lewis.

Tiger Woods hits a shot on the practice ground prior to the start of the 2007 U.S. Open at Oakmont as his then-coach, Hank Haney, looks on. Haney contended that Hogan had it wrong about the swing plane, and Woods successfully bought into that concept for almost a decade. (David Cannon/Getty Images)

Your Swing Plane—
The Foundation

1999 • Hank Haney with John Huggan

A bit of a cowboy, renowned instructor and *Golf Digest* contributor Hank Haney runs golf schools in four states, including the Hank Haney Golf Ranch, which is located on a converted horse farm in Texas. Even the title of Haney's first book carries a certain Texas swagger: *The Only Golf Lesson You'll Ever Need.* As this chapter's title attests, Haney has made the swing plane the foundation of his teaching. Significantly, he has taken Ben Hogan to task for insisting that the golfer stay on only one plane during the swing: Haney says if you follow Hogan's advice, you'll "hurt yourself and your game." In the perfect swing, Haney argues, the club actually passes through several planes, but always stays parallel to the *plane angle*, an imaginary line formed by the clubshaft at address. Ideally, you will reproduce that angle at impact.

S winging on the correct plane is the most difficult thing in golf because it is the most important thing. In fact, the swing plane isn't just the most important thing, it is the only thing.

Now, that's a pretty powerful statement when you consider that golf is ultimately supposed to be about posting the lowest score you can. But you can't do that consistently if you can't hit at least semi-decent shots.

Which is where the swing plane comes in. Let me explain.

In golf, you don't hit the ball. The way you stand to a shot doesn't hit the ball. The way you hold the club doesn't hit the ball. Your swing doesn't even hit the ball. No, only one thing hits the ball: the golf club. And the only things influencing that collision and the flight of the resulting shot are the angles on which the club is swinging into the ball. Specifically, the angle of the clubface and the angle of the shaft. So, to my mind, the swing plane is everything in that it is the one thing that has a direct bearing on the way in which club meets ball and therefore how the ball flies....

Of course, you don't swing every club on the same plane. As the club in your hand changes, so does the plane of your swing. The longer the clubshaft gets, the farther you have to stand from the ball, so the flatter your plane will be. For example, if you have a wedge in your hands, you want a little more of a descending blow so you will automatically stand closer to the ball and swing on a more upright plane than you would with a 5 iron. But your thoughts and your feelings don't change. The length and lie of the club makes any changes for you.

The swing plane is the cornerstone of my teaching and, it must be said, perhaps the most misunderstood aspect of the golf swing. It has been explained many times in print, most notably and memorably by Ben Hogan in his book, *The Modern Fundamentals of Golf*, but I don't believe it has ever been explained correctly. Hence all the confusion.

LET ME EXPLAIN

Everything you do in your golf swing has one basic aim—sending the ball to the target. Easier said than done, of course. Achieving such a goal on a consistent basis requires that you get a few things right.

A straight, solidly hit shot results when the golf club moves along the proper path, when the angle of the clubhead's approach into the impact area is correct and when the clubface is square, or squaring, as it contacts the ball. Thus, the key to any golf swing is the plane on which the club moves from address to impact. In reality, it is the only thing that matters.

As with so many other aspects of golf, there are three possibilities when it comes to swing plane. Your club is either on plane, too upright (above the plane), or too flat (below the plane).… Every golfer has [his or her] own swing

HANK HANEY'S STROKESAVERS:

- Understand that there is more than one plane in the perfect golf swing, but only one plane angle–Hogan's image of a pane of glass was wrong.

- The plane angle is dictated by the angle at which the clubshaft lies at address. Swing the club along that angle from start to finish.

- Strive to reproduce the plane angle at impact–doing so signals perfection.

Tommy Armour created perhaps the most famous and useful tip in the history of golf instruction when he came up with "pause at the top," a technique he used himself to become a deadly skillful iron player. Realizing that many golfers often hurry the start of the downswing, and thus botch their shots in a variety of ways, Armour was looking for an image that would force them to move more slowly into the transition from backswing to downswing. Whether there is actually a "pause" or not, the idea is to wait for the lower body to start the downswing, rather than using the hands first and thus coming over the top.

plane. Everyone is built differently and has different length arms, heights, setups—so each person has a swing plane unique to them.

WHAT DETERMINES THE SWING PLANE

The perfect swing plane for you is largely determined by your posture at address, the length of your arms, your height, and what percentage of that height is made up by your back versus your legs.

Having said that, swing planes of short and tall individuals are usually not that much different. They do vary some, but the real key is that you swing on your swing plane. The plane of someone else's swing is of no concern to you. In other words, everyone has a swing plane but there is no one swing plane for everyone. In general, tall people stand closer to the ball and have more upright swing planes. Those who are shorter tend to stand farther from the ball and have flatter swing planes. Look at, say, Jeff Sluman and Nick Faldo, and you'll see what I mean.

The swing plane is nothing new. As I said, it was the basis for Ben Hogan's *Modern Fundamentals* [1957]. In fact, in order to explain his swing plane philosophy, he created what may be the most famous and enduring image in golf instruction—the pane of glass angled through his shoulders and down to the ground. Hogan's theory was that you should swing the club below and parallel to the glass from address to the end of your follow-through. And that is how countless golfers have tried to swing on plane ever since.

Hogan produced a great image, but unfortunately he was wrong in this assertion. There is more than one plane in the perfect golf swing, but only one plane angle.

THE PLANE ANGLE

The plane of your swing is dictated by the angle at which the clubshaft lies at address, provided your clubs are fit correctly. Ideally, you want to reproduce that angle at impact. That would be perfection. And the best, easiest, and most repeatable way to achieve that—as you'd expect—is to swing the club on the plane angle from start to finish.

Notice I'm saying that the club swings on the same plane angle, not the same plane. If you remember nothing else from this chapter, take that sentence home with you. The most important thing to understand about the swing plane and swinging on plane is that although there is one plane angle—the angle at which you set the clubshaft at address—the club must travel through more than one plane throughout the swing.

At first glance that can seem confusing. But it isn't. Here's how it works. The club starts back along the original angle of the shaft. You swing back along that plane. Then the club swings up and is above but parallel to the original angle of the shaft. So it is passing through different planes.

"I found that the club most always moves in a circle making an angle of 45 degrees with the horizon. I found that in bringing down the club ye most turn your body as far about toward the left following the swing of the club as it had been turned before toward the right hand."

—Thomas Kincaid,
The Book of the Old Edinburgh Club (1687)

CONGRUENT ANGLES/DIFFERENT PLANES

As you move the golf club back it consistently goes up and in, the plane of your swing constantly changing as it does so. What doesn't change is the relationship between all those planes and the original angle of the clubshaft at address. They are always parallel.

Then, as you swing down, the club passes through those same planes on the way back to the ball…all the while maintaining that parallel relationship.

It's up through the planes on the backswing, down through the same planes on downswing, and up again on the same planes on the follow-through. Achieve that and the angle of the clubshaft at impact will be the same as it was at address. That is the perfect swing, one which should produce a little draw. Unfortunately, most people don't follow that path or produce that ball-flight. Most golfers have a bunch of different loops in their swings and a seemingly infinite number of different shots.

Those parallel angles are called congruent angles. In other words, they are numerically the same angle but have different points of origin as the club moves back and through. Therefore, the clubshaft does not always point to the target-line at all stages of the swing, as some teachers have argued in the past.

As for Hogan's pane of glass, Ben's idea is doomed from the start. Because your arms have a slight droop in them as they hang down in address, you never actually swing the club on the plane established by this imaginary pane of glass. It would be physically impossible. So, don't try it. You'll hurt yourself and your game.

CHAPTER 6

THE
BACKSWING

Winding Up the Spring

Slow Back—The Line of the Clubhead in the Upward Swing

1905 • Harry Vardon

The father of modern golf—in whose honor a trophy is awarded annually to the PGA golfer with the lowest stroke average—not only popularized the still-dominant overlapping grip but also developed a swing that changed the game. In *The Complete Golfer*, which includes numerous photographs of Vardon in action, he furthered the democratization of the sport, saying that he was trying to help "improving golfers of all degrees of skill"—and presumably, on all rungs of Britain's social ladder. This excerpt begins with a familiar maxim, as Vardon suggested players take the club back slowly. But then he staked out new ground. Rather than urging his followers to then sweep the club around their body in the old St. Andrews style, Vardon told them to continue taking it back along the target line—the same move taught by swing teachers today and put into practice by all good golfers.

A s a first juncture, it may be stated that the club should be drawn back rather more slowly than you intend to bring it down again. "Slow back" is a golfing maxim that is both old and wise. The club should begin to gain speed when the upward swing is about half made, and the increase should be gradual until the top is reached, but it should never be so fast that control of the club is to any extent lost at the turning-point.

The head of the club should be taken back fairly straight from the ball…for the first six inches, and after that, any tendency to sweep it round sharply to the back should be avoided. Keep it very close to the straight line until it is halfway up. The old St. Andrews style of driving largely consisted in this sudden sweep round, but the modern method appears to be easier and productive of better results.

The [golfer's] head should be kept virtually motionless from the time of the address until the ball has been sent away and is well on its flight. The least deviation from this rule means a proportionate danger of disaster. When a drive has been badly foozled, the readiest and most usual explanation is that the eye has been taken off the ball, and the wise old men who have been watching shake their heads solemnly, and utter that parrot-cry of the links, "Keep your eye on the ball."

Certainly this is a good and necessary rule so far as it goes; but I do not believe that one drive in a hundred is missed because the eye has not been kept on the ball. On the other hand, I believe that one of the most fruitful causes of failure with the tee shot is the moving of the head. Until the ball has gone, it should, as I say, be as nearly perfectly still as possible, and I would have written that it should not be moved to the extent of a sixteenth of an inch, but for the fact that it is not human to be so still, and golf is always inclined to the human side.

When the head has been kept quite still and the club has reached the top of the upward swing, the eyes should be looking over the middle of the left shoulder, the left one being dead over the center of that shoulder. Most players at one time or another, and the best of them when they are a little off their game, fall into every trap that the evil spirits of golf lay for them, and unconsciously experience a tendency to lift the head for five or six inches away from the ball while the upward swing is being taken. This is often what is imagined to be taking the eye off the ball....

The left wrist [should finish] the upward swing underneath the shaft.... In order to satisfy himself properly...the golfer should test himself at the top of the swing by holding the club firmly in the position which it has reached, and then drop the right hand from the grip.... If he then finds that the maker's name on the head of the club is horizontal, he will know that he has been doing the right thing with his wrists, while if it is vertical the wrist action has been altogether wrong.

During the upward swing the arms should be gradually let out in the enjoyment of perfect ease and freedom (without being spread-eagled away from the body)....

In the upward movement of the club the body must pivot from the waist alone, and there must be no swaying, not even to the extent of an inch. When the player sways in his drive, the stroke he makes is a body stroke pure and simple. The body is trying to do the work the arms should do, and in these circumstances it is impossible to get much power into the stroke...whilst once more the old enemies, the slice and pull, will come out from their hiding places with their mocking grin at the unhappy golfer.

Harry Vardon was among the first to move from the "St. Andrews Swing" to the more modern, upright action that is still favored today. Vardon moved the ball forward, opened his stance, and swung the club straight back from the tee to produce a high fade. (Courtesy of the USGA)

The movements of the feet and legs are important. In addressing the ball you stand with both feet flat and securely placed on the ground, the weight equally divided between them, and the legs so slightly bent at the knee joints as to make the bending scarcely noticeable. This position is maintained during the upward movement of the club until the arms begin to pull at the body. The easiest and most natural thing to do then, and the one which suggests itself, is to raise the heel of the left foot and begin to pivot on the left toe, which allows the arms to proceed with their uplifting process without let or hindrance. Do not begin to pivot on this left toe ostentatiously, or because you feel you ought to do so, but only when you know the time has come and you want to, and do it only to such an extent that the club can reach the full extent of the swing without any difficulty....

HARRY VARDON'S STROKESAVERS:

- Set up with the weight evenly distributed and the knees flexed.
- Start the backswing slowly, taking the clubhead straight back from the ball.
- Keep the head virtually motionless throughout.
- Check to see if the left wrist is under the shaft at the top of the backswing.

To the man who has never driven a good ball in his life this process must seem very tedious. All these things to attend to, and something less than a second in which to attend to them! It only indicates how much there is in this wonderful game—more by far than any of us suspect or shall ever discover. But the time comes, and it should come speedily, when they are all accomplished without any effort, and indeed, to a great extent, unconsciously. The upward swing is everything. If it is bad and faulty, the downward swing will be wrong, and the ball will not be properly driven. If it is perfect, there is a splendid prospect of a long and straight drive, carrying any hazard that may lie before the tee. That is why so very much emphasis must be laid on getting this upward swing perfect, and why comparatively little attention need be paid to the downward swing, even though it is really the effective part of the stroke.

From *The Complete Golfer*, by Harry Vardon. Methuen & Company, London, England.

The Backswing

circa 1930 • Robert Tyre (Bobby) Jones, Jr.

In the 1966 book *Bobby Jones on Golf,* Jones and *Golf* magazine's Charles Price reworked Jones' articles from the years before and after his retirement in 1930. In this excerpt, golf's first matinee idol advanced several ideas modern readers will recognize. Jones, the last great golfer to use hickory-shafted clubs, had a swing that was by necessity "handsy," but, like today's pros, employed a fully integrated body turn and relied on exquisite rhythm. Jones asserted that the left side of the body dominated the action, and that the left arm should be kept straight in the backswing—concepts that evolved into the "one-piece takeaway." He also advanced the notion that the upper body "coiled" like a spring against the resistance of the legs. In effect, these ideas led to Byron Nelson's invention of the modern swing and opened new avenues that theorists from Ben Hogan to Butch Harmon would explore.

THE PURPOSE OF THE BACKSWING

It is often urged that a person playing golf who worries about how to take the club back, how to start it down, and what to do at this stage and at that, ultimately loses sight of the only important thing he has to do—to hit the ball. We, who write on the game and those who attempt to teach it, are told often enough that we should give more attention to the contact stage and less to the details of the preparatory movements....

The backswing has for its purpose the establishment of a perfectly balanced, powerful position at the top of the swing from which the correct actions of the down-stroke can flow rhythmically without the need for interference or correction. In the end, on the basis of consistent reproduction of the successful action, the preparatory movements become just as important as the actual hitting—the entire swing, a sequence of correct positions, following naturally and comfortably one after the other....

ORIGINATING THE BACKSWING

The moderate flatness of the swing that I like must result from a correct body turn, and not from manipulation of the club by the hands and wrists. Many players begin the backswing with a sudden pronation of the left wrist that whips the club sharply around the legs, opening the face very quickly. This is just as bad as a swing straight back, carrying the arms away from the player's body.

The initial movement of the club away from the ball should result from forces originating in the left side. The real takeoff is from the left foot, starting the movement of the body. The hands and arms very soon pick it up, but the proper order at the very beginning is body, arms, and lastly clubhead. It is always easier to continue a motion than to begin it; this order has the virtue of originating the hip-turn; it goes a long way toward assuring a proper windup of the hips during the backswing....

ARGUMENTS FOR A LONG BACKSWING

One of the characteristics of the true swing, and the one that most often escapes the inexpert player, is the ample sweep of the backward windup. The average golfer, partly because he is unfamiliar with the movements that will accommodate a long backswing, and partly because he does not trust himself to go so far, almost always favors a short, hacking stroke. Quickly back and quickly down, employing a sudden acceleration almost amounting to a jerk, there is scarcely any chance of obtaining power or accuracy.

The most usual argument in favor of a backswing of good length is that it allows a longer arc and more time to attain the maximum clubhead speed at the instant of contact. But there are others of less equal force. It is certain that the more gradual acceleration made possible by the longer backswing is bound to make the swing much smoother and less likely to be yanked out of its groove; also, it is certain that it makes it possible to attain an equal speed with less sudden effort and therefore less likelihood of introducing contrary forces detracting from the power of the stroke....

If we liken the backswing of a golf club to the extension of a coil spring, or the stretching of a rubber band, I think we shall not be very far off the mark. The greater the extension or stretching, the greater the force of the return. In the golf swing, every inch added to the backward windup, up to the limit at which the balance of the body can be easily maintained, represents additional stored energy available to increase the power of the downswing. It may be possible for a player with a comparatively short windup to make up this difference by an extraordinary hitting effort, but he will never be able to do so without more than a proportionate loss in smoothness and precision....

THE POSITION AT THE TOP

There is no part of the golf swing that consists of one simple movement. The whole thing is a process of blending, correlating, and harmonizing simple movements until smooth, rhythmic motion is achieved. When actually swinging a club, there is no way to complete the body turn and wrist movement separately, having done with one before the other is commenced....

BOBBY JONES' STROKESAVERS:

- In the backswing, blend body and wrist action in a smooth, rhythmic move.
- Start with a body turn, not a lift of the hands and wrists.
- Keep the left arm straight, or at least well extended.
- Recognize that the longer the backswing, the more power is built up—it's like stretching a rubber band.

THE STRAIGHT LEFT ARM

Good form in any physical activity must be valued in terms of efficiency. The efficiency of a thermal engine, for example, is measured by the ratio of the work done by the engine to the heat energy supplied to it. The efficiency of a golf stroke must be measured, in the same way, by the ratio of the work done on the ball to the amount of physical energy used up in the swinging. The expert golfer drives far with little apparent effort because of the high rate of efficiency of his performance. The duffer, though he strains himself to the utmost, falls far behind because so much of the energy expended goes to waste.

A high rate of efficiency, and hence good form, in golf, depends upon three things: the development of the greatest possible clubhead speed at contact with whatever energy or power the player can supply; the achievement of a precisely accurate contact between club and ball, directing the blow along the line upon which it is intended that the ball shall travel; and consistency in performing approximately according to these standards.

Although these are obvious generalities, it is helpful to do a little thinking along these lines in order to appreciate the importance to a golfer of a proper use of his left arm. For it is in this particular that all duffers are most appallingly deficient, and here, too, that the better players most often go astray.

For some persons, a straight left arm is a physical impossibility. So let us say that an extended left arm is one of the prime requisites of good form. In many ways, it contributes to clubhead speed, accurate contact, and consistency of performance—the three components of the efficiency rate.

Just now we are interested chiefly in the backswing. The backward movement is merely the means of storing up power to be used in the hitting—but to increase the amount of this stored-up energy is of first importance. We have seen that the beginning was made in the hips in order to assure that the windup of the body would at least be started. When this has progressed a short distance, we began to force the club back with the left arm.

Now with the club having completed about half of its backward travel, the left arm has become almost straight, and is pushing the club as far back as it can comfortably go. The arc of the swing is thus made wide so that the space and time for adding speed to the clubhead coming down will be as great as possible.

The player who allows his left arm to bend perceptibly is sacrificing width of arc and power. His swing, because it is not as wide as it could be, is that much away from the ideal of efficiency that he could make it.

There is nothing in the straight left arm that, of itself, increases the power of the swing. It is a part of a sound method for those who are able to keep it straight, because it is the factor which definitely limits the arc of the backswing. Consequently, when the arm is straight, this arc is as wide as it can be made, and the swing can then be more easily repeated time after time in the same groove....

At that, few players keep the left arm rigidly straight during the backswing. I like to have the feeling of pushing the club back with the left arm because this assures that it will be reasonably extended, but the arm does not become completely straight until it is stretched out by the beginning of the reverse turn of the hips, back toward the ball, while the club is completing its backward movement....

The important thing, so far as the left arm is concerned, is that it should not collapse in the act of hitting. In the motion pictures of Harry Vardon, made when the great Englishman had passed his 60th birthday, a bend of almost 90 degrees could be seen in the left elbow at the top of the swing. Yet as soon as the hip-turn had stretched out the left side, this arm became straight and remained so until after the ball had been struck. The bend at the top, then, is by no means fatal if the succeeding movements are performed correctly.

What will help most is complete relaxation. Timing and rhythm can make up a lot in power. By all means, swing the club freely, both backward and forward, and avoid the tightening a short backswing must produce.

The First Part of the Swing

1957 • Ben Hogan with Herbert Warren Wind

Ben Hogan won nine majors, including a career Grand Slam, had 64 PGA Tour victories overall, and wrote instruction to explain why he was so good. In this classic lesson from his second book, he described what many golfers consider the ideal backswing model (except, possibly, for the notion of the hands starting the sequence). Hogan's key concept was to inhibit the movement of the hips, thereby building dynamic tension between the upper and lower parts of the body in order to unleash a powerful downswing. Hogan also provided the still defining image of how to "finish" the backswing, advising golfers to wait until they feel their left shoulders come under their chins. As this piece makes obvious, Hogan was a true technocrat of the game.

[M]astering a proper backswing] requires some instinct, a sense of organization, some thought, and a fair control of muscular action. It is, however, much less involved than this makes it appear. Learning the backswing actually consists of getting a few movements clear in your mind and then learning to execute them. This is where the golf shot begins to be played.

The first point about the backswing (and the swing in general) I want to

BEN HOGAN'S STROKESAVERS:

- Think of the backswing as a unified, continuous chain of actions.
- Follow this order of movement: hands, arms, shoulders, hips.
- Get it right, and the back will face the target, and the right knee will remain flexed and stable at the top of the backswing.

emphasize is this: if his body, legs, and arms are properly positioned and poised to begin with, any golfer with average physical equipment can learn to execute the proper movements. This is why you must build on a correct grip and stance, for the golf swing is an accumulative thing. All the actions are linked together....

The backswing is...initiated by the almost simultaneous movement of the hands, arms, and shoulders.... The golf swing is, in principle, a continuous chain of actions. Like the component parts of the engine of an automobile, the component parts of the swing fuse together and work together in a purposeful sequence. As each component performs its part of the operation, it sets up the proper operation of the other components with which it is connected. I bring this up at this particular point, for if a golfer clearly grasps the interrelationship of the hands, arms, shoulders, and hips, he will play good golf—he can't help but play good golf.

On the backswing, the order of movement goes like this: hands, arms, shoulders, hips.... On the backswing, the hands, arms, and shoulders start to move almost simultaneously. *Actually, the hands start the clubhead back a split second before the arms start back. And the arms begin their movement a split second before the shoulders begin to turn. As a golfer acquires feel and rhythm through practice, the hands, arms, and shoulders will instinctively tie in on this split-second schedule.* The main point for the novice is to know that they do start back so closely together that their action is unified.

On the backswing, the shoulders are always ahead of the hips as they turn. The shoulders should start turning immediately. The hips do not. *Just before your hands reach hip level, the shoulders, as they turn, automatically start pulling the hips around. As the hips begin to turn, they pull the left leg in to the right.* Now let us examine these actions in closer detail.

THE SHOULDERS

You want to turn the shoulders as far around as they'll go. (Your head, of course, remains stationary.) When you have turned your shoulders all the way, your back should face squarely toward your target…. Most golfers think that they make a full shoulder turn going back and they would challenge you if you claimed they didn't, but the truth is that few golfers really complete their shoulder turn. They stop turning when the shoulders are about halfway around; then, in order to get the clubhead all the way back, they break the left arm. This is really a false backswing. It isn't any backswing at all. A golfer can't have control of the club or start down into the ball with any power or speed unless his left arm is straight to begin with. When he bends his left arm, he actually performs only a half swing, and he forfeits half his potential power. More than this, he then is led into making many exhausting extra movements that accomplish nothing for him.

An excellent way to check that you are making a full shoulder turn is this: *when you finish your backswing, your chin should be hitting against the top of your left shoulder.* Just where the chin contacts the shoulder depends on the individual golfer's physical proportions. In my own case, it's about an inch from the end of the shoulder. My golf shirts have a worn-down spot at this particular point.

THE HIPS

Turning the hips too soon is an error countless golfers make, and it's a serious error. It destroys your chance of obtaining the power a correctly integrated

SHAKING HANDS WITH ROYALTY

Glenna Collett Vare, "The Queen of American Golf," won eight international championships in the 1920s. In *Golf for Young Players*, she devised a drill to teach women the proper weight shift in the backswing. Advising them to stand before a mirror, she told them to put their hands on their hips, and then turn to look at something beside them. "Your hips have made a turn such as they will make in a full swing of golf," she wrote, "and the whole scheme of balance, or equilibrium, are then felt and understood." A modern variation, taught by such diverse instructors as Bob Toski and Butch Harmon, is for the golfer to imagine turning to shake hands with or hand the golf club to a person standing to the right.

swing gives you. As you begin the backswing, you must restrain your hips from moving until the turn of the shoulders starts to pull the hips around.

Some prominent golfers advocate taking a big turn with the hips. I don't go along with this. If the hips are turned too far around, then you can create no tension in the muscles between the hips and the shoulders. A golfer wants to have this tension; he wants the midsection of his body to be tightened up, for this tension is the key to the whole downswing.… It is so important to have this torsion, this stretching of the muscles, that results from turning your shoulders as far as they can go and retarding the hips. It's the difference in the amount of turn between the shoulders and hips that sets up this muscular tension. If the hips were turned as much as the shoulders, there'd be no tightening up at all.

THE LEGS

When the hips enter the swing, as they are turned they pull the left leg in. The left knee breaks in to the right, the left foot rolls in to the right on the inside part of the sole, and what weight there is on the left leg rides on the inside ball of the foot. *Let me caution you against lifting the left heel too high off the ground on the backswing. If the heel stays on the ground—fine. If it comes up an inch off the ground—fine.* No higher than that, though—it will only lead to faulty balance and other undesirable complications.

The body and the legs move the feet. *Let them move the feet.* As regards the left heel, how much the left knee breaks in on the backswing determines how much the heel comes up. I never worry about the left heel. Whether it comes off the ground a half inch or a quarter of an inch or remains on the ground as a result of my body and leg action on the backswing—this is of no importance at all. I pay no attention to it.

As regards the right leg, it should maintain the same position it had at address, the same angle in relation to the ground, throughout the backswing. That is one of the checks the average golfer should make when he's warming up and when he's on the course. When you have a stable right leg and the right knee remains pointed in a bit, it prevents the leg from sagging and swaying out to the right and carrying the body along with it.

From *Ben Hogan's Five Lessons, The Modern Fundamentals of Golf,* by Ben Hogan with Herbert Warren Wind. Golf Digest/Tennis, Inc., a New York Times Company. Distributed by Pocket Books, a division of Simon & Schuster Adult Publishing Group. Copyright © 1957 by Ben Hogan. Reprinted with the permission of Writers House, LLC, as agent for the Ben Hogan estate.

Nicklaus: 22 Years at Hard Labor

1972 • Alistair Cooke

Alistair Cooke, the one-time U.S. correspondent for England's *Guardian* and host of *Masterpiece Theater*, was a man of letters and a man of the links. Among his writings on golf was this sharp examination of how Jack Nicklaus, who had just captured his 13th of an eventual 18 majors, developed his distinct backswing under the tutelage of his inspirational long-time mentor Jack Grout. Cooke viewed Grout as strict but smart enough to recognize this pupil was capable of adding creativity to the basics. There's no mention of Nicklaus' famous flying elbow, but Cooke suspected young golfers already would flame out trying to emulate the powerful, exaggerated body turn and enormously wide arc Nicklaus employed to trigger a vicious, leg-driven through-swing. Content that his pupil was fundamentally sound, Grout didn't make Nicklaus temper his tendency to swing for the fences, confirming that *great* golfers have unique styles that can't always be imitated.

Jack Nicklaus, 22, of Columbus, Ohio, is the best golfer in the world, and he means to improve. That, in brief, is what sets him apart from the other giants of the game, and perhaps from the giants of most other games also. He first picked up a golf club when he was 10 and for the past 22 years has been laboring over his game, in the flesh by day and in the mind by night. He is certainly the most cerebral golfer since Ben Hogan, whose "Fundamentals of Modern Golf" is practically an advanced text on human anatomy and aerodynamics. And he is the coolest, the least fooled, analyst of his own game since "the immortal one" of golf, Robert Tyre Jones Jr., who, since he is now dead, is more immortal than ever.

"The golf swing for me," Nicklaus told Herbert Warren Wind, his Boswell in the best golfing biography that has appeared so far, "is a source of never-ending fascination. On the one hand, the swings of all the outstanding golfers are decidedly individual but, on the other, the champions all execute approximately the same moves at the critical stages of the swing.... There is still a lot about the swing we don't know and probably never will…. In any event, scarcely a day goes by when I don't find myself thinking about the golf swing."

Jack William Nicklaus (pronounced Nick-lus, not Nick-louse) is the great-grandson of an immigrant boilermaker from Alsace-Lorraine and the son of a prosperous Columbus, Ohio, pharmacist whose hobbies were Ohio State football, golf, fishing, and telling his son of the miracles of St. Robert Tyre Jones, Jr. Jack was born in 1940, the year of Dunkirk and the Fall of France, when the British were plowing up their golf courses and planting land mines against the anticipated Nazi invasion….

He had started to toddle, and hack, around a golf course after his father injured his ankle badly, prompting the doctor to suggest that henceforth, Father Nicklaus forgo volleyball and take to gentler exercise, "the sort of movement you get when walking on soft ground." Father turned to golf but found himself something of a lagging invalid to his regular partners, so he haled in his 10-year-old son as a walking companion. The youngster got his first set of cut down golf clubs just as the Scioto golf club, to which Father Nicklaus belonged, acquired a new pro, Jack Grout, then a taut, tanned 42-year-old. Nicklaus to this day has had no other teacher except himself, who is probably the more exacting of the two.

So on a Friday morning in June 1950, the golden bear cub lined up on the practice tee with 50 other youngsters. It is clear from the record that the perfectionist strain in the Nicklaus character at once took over to refine the normal, rollicking ambition of small boys to bang out rockets. The first time he played nine holes, he had a creditable 51…. He supplemented the Friday morning regimental drill with private lessons from Grout. The knobbly-jointed stripling began to develop a golf swing….

If there was any luck in the time and place of his initiation, it was in having Grout newly arrived at Scioto. Grout was a teacher with some firm convictions, one of which, however, was that every golfer is an individual. This runs counter to the insistence of many young pros—and most of the textbooks—that every pupil must be broken in to the mold of a favorite dogma. For instance, 998 golfers in 1,000 use the Vardon grip, which has the little finger of the right hand resting on top of the cleft between the first and second fingers of the left. The 999th manages, don't ask me why, with a "baseball" grip, the two hands completely separated. Nicklaus was the 1,000th oddity who was more comfortable interlocking or hooking the little finger of the right hand securely around the forefinger of the left. Nicklaus, indeed the big bear of the broad beam and the 27-inch thighs, has small hands so surprisingly weak in their grip that he swears he has often asked his wife, a girl svelte to the point of fragility, to unscrew pickle jars for him. Grout let him stay with this eccentricity, and he uses it today.

But Grout's tolerance of idiosyncrasy had severe limits. He insisted from the start on two fundamentals. Since they apply to every golfer, young and old, they may help us all, if only we can absorb them well enough to let them pass over into what Ben Hogan memorably called "the muscle memory." Nicklaus avows that his game is rooted in these two fundamentals.

JACK NICKLAUS' STROKESAVERS:

- Keep the head steady.
- Roll the left ankle inward for balance.
- Swing for the fences if all systems are go.

The first is that "the head must be kept still" throughout the swing. Nicklaus figures it took him at least two years to master this simplicity, sometimes under the duress of having Grout's assistant hold on the hair of Snow White's head to make him, in J.H. Taylor's fine phrase, "play beneath himself." Anyone who has ever had his head gripped while trying to repeat a serviceable swing will have quickly learned the painful truth that we are all "natural" jumping jacks. I once had an easygoing friend, a cheerful hacker who refused to take any lessons on the down-to-earth assertion that "I simply try to be a pendulum." Unfortunately, the human body is constructed with marvelous ingenuity, not to be a pendulum….

The second fundamental which Nicklaus maintains gave his game its early solidity was Grout's insistence that "the key to balance is rolling the ankles inward," the left toward the right on the backswing, the right in to the left on the downswing. Here…the picture in the mind has been painted many different ways. Some talk of keeping the left heel down while "bracing the right leg." Jones hit off a sharp poetic image when he said that golf is played "between the knees." Nicklaus more recently said, "If you go over beyond your right instep on the backswing, if you relax the pressure there, you are dead." And George

Heron, the little 80-year-old Scot who as a boy made clubs for Vardon, is still telling pupils down in St. Augustine, Florida, "A knock-kneed man is going to be a better golfer than a bow-legged one."

Well, on these two fundamentals alone, Nicklaus calculated he spent four or five years, in the meantime working through the range of clubs for hours on end on the practice tee. He says today "whenever anything goes wrong," he goes out and hits a thousand balls "flat-footed," neither lifting his heels nor moving his ankles, as a drastic way of restoring his sense of balance....

"I want the sensation that I've turned my upper body over my right leg with my back to the target."

—KARRIE WEBB

There was a third fundamental taught to the young Nicklaus which decidedly does not apply to golfers of all ages and which, in Grout's day, was condemned for golfers of any age. The general practice was to force youngsters to resist the urge to go for distance and to teach them precision first. Grout felt that a boy should begin at once to stretch and develop the back muscles that would let him take the club as high, and as far behind, as a straight left arm would allow. The longer the arc of the club on the backswing, and the more acute the angle between the clubshaft and the left arm as the hands come down and go ahead of the ball: this, not the blacksmith's mighty muscle, is the secret of distance. Nicklaus achieves it with a vast arc at the top of the backswing, his left shoulder bulging beneath and almost beyond the set of his chin while his left arm and hands are poking into the stratosphere. I have walked along with him even on practice rounds when only a lynx could follow the trajectory from the clubhead through the sky.

It is a sight whose result produces flattering gasps from the crowd around the tees. It has nothing to do with Hercules and everything to do with centrifugal force. Nonetheless, it is an act which most of us over 40 had better not try to emulate, unless an ambulance is on call....

From *The New York Times Magazine* (July 9, 1972), by Alistair Cooke. Reprinted by permission of the estate of Alistair Cooke.

Drill: Clip the Tee Going Back
and Drill: Put a Brace
Behind the Right Knee

1999 • Butch Harmon

Claude "Butch" Harmon is the reigning monarch from a royal family of golf instructors, which included his late brother Dick, and their father Claude, the 1948 Masters champion and a legendary club pro and teaching professional. Butch is best known for shepherding Tiger Woods through his career Grand Slam, but his work with other superstars and hot 30-somethings like Aussie Adam Scott and American Nick Watney assures he will remain at the top of the teacher rankings. His popularity is partly due to his ability to tailor his lessons to each pupil rather than preaching a fixed philosophy. The first part of this *Golf Digest* excerpt tells golfers how to master the crucial initial step in the takeaway, a lesson that echoes Harry Vardon and Bobby Jones, yet is pure "Butch." In the second part, Harmon offers a tip for a backswing fault—straightening the right knee—that is often overlooked.

MISTAKE: POOR TAKEAWAY

There are two faults you can make in the takeaway. You can pick the club up or you can pull it back inside.

When you pick the club up, your left shoulder drops. You tilt but don't really turn your shoulders. You hang on your left side, reverse pivot, and either top the ball or chunk it.

When you take the club back inside, your left arm goes out away from your body, and halfway back it's above your right arm. The club goes behind your body, and you have to loop it up and over on the downswing, causing slices or pulls.

A GOOD TAKEAWAY

When your club is halfway back, the shaft should be exactly in line with your toes, and your right arm is slightly higher than your left.

BUTCH HARMON'S STROKESAVERS:

- Take the club back low and slow in the backswing, with a one-piece takeaway.
- Ingrain this idea by placing a tee behind the ball—then try to clip it on the takeaway.
- To maintain right knee flex—and thus power—have a friend hold a club against the back of the knee during the backswing.
- Alternatively, stick a shaft in the ground at a 45-degree angle so the top contacts the right knee.

DRILL: CLIP THE TEE GOING BACK

I believe strongly in a one-piece takeaway. That means that until your hands are waist high, you maintain the triangle formed by your arms and shoulders at address. It helps to think about taking the club back low and slow. Here's a good drill: place a tee about a grip-length behind the ball, then try to clip the tee on your takeaway. That will help you learn a low one-piece takeaway.

MISTAKE: THE STRAIGHT KNEE

Many amateurs straighten or even lock the right knee immediately as they start their backswing. That causes their hips and shoulders to turn the same amount, so they aren't building any coil for power. They end up throwing the club over the top to get back to the ball, which further reduces power and leads to slices or pulls.

Instead, maintain the flex of your right knee throughout the swing. This encourages the shoulders to turn more than the hips, storing power. On the downswing you'll be more on plane and can release the club later for a more powerful hit.

DRILL: PUT A BRACE BEHIND THE RIGHT KNEE

Knee flex is something Tiger Woods and I have worked on for years. He has perfect posture at address and tries to maintain the posture of his right leg all the way back in the swing.

If you tend to straighten your right leg on the backswing, try the drill...in which a partner pushes a club into the back of your right knee as you swing. If you're by yourself, bury the head of your wedge in the ground so the shaft is angled at 45 degrees upward, place a headcover over the grip end, then back your knee up to it before you swing.

Phil Mickelson and his coach, Butch Harmon, share a moment after the final round of the 2010 Masters, which Mickelson won to take his third Green Jacket. Harmon, who is consistently named by his peers as a top instructor, also tutors Natalie Gulbis, Aussie star Adam Scott, and "Generation Now" stand-outs Dustin Johnson and Nick Watney. (Streeter Lecka/Getty Images)

CHAPTER 7

THE THROUGH-SWING

SWING

The Moment of Truth

The Downward Swing and Finishing the Stroke

1906 • James Braid

James Braid, the lone Scotsman in the "Great Triumvirate," won his first British Open at Muirfield in 1901, besting Harry Vardon and J.H. Taylor by a comfortable margin despite hitting his opening drive out of bounds. A clutch putter and a hard hitter off the tee, he was 31 when he won that first major, but he rattled off four more Open Championships before turning 41. Braid was famous for his "sudden, furious" downswing, which Horace Hutchinson memorably likened to a "divine fury." In an initially successful but now obscure British pamphlet that was soon reissued in America by Spalding, Braid counseled the golfer to view the downswing as a sweep through the ball, rather than a "hit" at it. He also offered a valuable tip that is standard in today's teaching cannon: if you hold the finish it will help establish balance, or what Braid delightfully called "this pleasant position."

THE DOWNWARD SWING

The chief thing to bear in mind [about the downward swing] is that there must be…no attempt to *hit* the ball, which must be simply swept from the tee and carried forward in the even and rapid swing of the club. The drive in golf differs from almost every other stroke in every game in which the propulsion of a ball is the object. In the ordinary sense of the word, implying a sudden and sharp impact, it is not a "hit" when it is properly done. When the ball is so "hit," and the club stops very soon afterward, the result is that very little length comparatively will be obtained, and that, moreover, there will be a very small amount of control over the direction of the ball.

While it is, of course, in the highest degree necessary that the ball shall be taken in exactly the right place on the club and in the right manner, this will have to be done by the proper regulation of all the other parts of the swing, and any effort to direct the club on it in a particular manner just as the ball is being reached cannot be attended by success. If the ball is taken by the toe or heel of the club, or is topped, or if the club gets too much under it, the remedy for these faults is not to be found in a more deliberate directing of the club on the ball just as the two are about to come into contact, but in the better and more exact regulation of the swing the whole way through up to this point. Something may be wrong with the stance, the body may have swayed, the head may have been allowed to move, or the movement of the wrists and arms may have been wrong and not according to the standard directions as I have just laid them down. The object of these remarks is merely to emphasize again in the best place that the dispatching of the ball from the tee by the driver in the downward swing is merely an incident of the whole business. The player, in making the down movement, must not be so particular to see while doing it that he hits the ball properly as that he makes the swing properly and finishes it well, for—and this signifies the truth of what I have been saying—the success for the drive is not only made by what has gone before, but it is also due largely to the course taken by the club after the ball has been hit.

"I'm a great believer in the benefits of a balanced, poised finish."

—Ernie Els

On the whole the player will be, and must be, far less conscious of all the details of his action in the downswing than when he was taking the club upward. Having brought the club with the utmost care and thought and attention to detail to the top point, there is only one more thing to do, and that is to finish off the swing and get the ball away as rapidly as possible. It is only after the ball has gone that

JAMES BRAID'S STROKESAVERS:

- Sweep the ball from the tee and carry the club forward.
- Make sure the position at impact mimics that of address.
- Hold the finish.

Three-time British Open champion Henry Cotton, one of the great "hands" players, told pupils to hit an old tire with a 7 iron to build up strength in their hands and wrists and develop a feel for the correct impact position. The modern equivalent is the "impact bag," developed by PGA Master Professional Dr. Gary Wiren. Sold by most golf outlets as a swing training aid, the bright yellow bag is a plastic sack one fills with rags. In an accompanying DVD, Wiren tells clients to hit without fear of injury, and he demonstrates how resistance naturally stops the club in the ideal position. After a few hits, the golfer can then step away and swing at will, confident they have a better sense of the "moment of truth."

consciousness will begin to fully assert itself and enable the player to give thought to the manner of finishing. In time, and when the man is on his game, the whole thing, from start to finish, should be to a certain extent mechanical....

When the ball has been swept from the tee the arms should to a certain extent be flung out after it, and they should be carried through well clear of the body until they come to a natural and easy stop and not a forced one, just about shoulder-high but some distance from the shoulder. When this is done the club will have passed the perpendicular and will have traveled a distance toward the back, which varies in the case of different players. Some men go in for rather exaggerated finishes, and carry the club so far through that it comes almost back to their right heel, but I cannot see that there is any advantage in this process, so long as the finish is fully executed up to the point I have indicated. When the arms get well through, and the hands finish high up in the place I have indicated, the player will find that he experiences a sense of completeness and satisfaction, even of exhilaration, which will be denied to him if his drive is nipped. It is a very pleasant thing when, having followed well through and finished the stroke properly, the ball is watched speeding onward on the proper line and with just the right angle of flight to make it travel well.

It is appropriate to mention at this point just a word of warning about style. When you have followed through and finished the stroke properly, get into the habit of retaining this pleasant position until the ball has pretty well run its length and the time has come for your opponent to take his place on the tee, or, if he has already driven, for you both to be moving on....

As a final injunction, one would again urge the importance of keeping the body perfectly steady not only during the upward swing, as already emphasized, but during the downward swing until the ball has gone, and the head all this time should be perfectly motionless with the eyes glued on to the back of the ball. If the body keeps to its original position and turns from the waist, and the head remains still, it should be found that at the top of the swing the eyes are looking over the left shoulder which will be in a direct line between the head and the ball.

From *Golf Guide and How to Play Golf,* by James Braid. Copyright © 1906 by the British Sports Publishing Company, Ltd., London, England.

Analyzing the Downswing

1931 • Helen Hicks

In 1931, 20-year-old Helen Hicks won the U.S. Women's Amateur title, ending Glenna Collett Vare's three-year run. As a member of the first Curtis Cup team a year later, she, Vare, Patty Berg, and Virginia Van Wie led the Americans over a formidable British team that included Joyce Wethered and Enid Wilson. But it was Hicks' unprecedented act in 1934—when she became the first notable American female golfer to turn pro—that secured her place in history. In addition to continuing competitive play, Hicks became the first woman to tour the country giving clinics and promoting equipment after signing an endorsement contract with Wilson Sporting Goods. In this magazine article, "Hard-hitting Helen" also broke new ground as one of the first "left-side" theorists, arguing that rather than the hands and arms, the unwinding of the hips triggers the downswing. Ben Hogan and countless others would adopt this as gospel.

The downswing is one of the very important factors in golf because it is during this phase of the swing that the clubhead comes in contact with the ball; and it seems to me the main idea of the game is to "hit the ball." In order to write about the "downswing" we must start from the beginning of the objective, that is to say, at the top of the backswing. I favor the hands being held high which will assure one of a more full and rhythmic swing, instead of being flat, caused by the hands being too far around the shoulder at the top of the swing. One hears so much about the "straight left arm." Alright— the left arm should be straight, nearing, and at the point of contact with the clubhead and the ball. But if one tries to keep the left arm too straight at the top of the swing, one will find that it is very tense and rigid; therefore, this arm should be slightly bent, to feel relaxed, but also feel "all powerful." The left wrist should be cocked or bent under the shaft. The right arm should be in a position somewhat resembling that of a waiter carrying a tray. I mention this as it is the tendency of many players to let this elbow point skyward....

After a careful and intensive study of the golf swing, I feel that what I am about to say (though it may prove contrary to popular theories) is undoubtedly correct. Heretofore, the general belief has been that the first movement from the top of the backswing is the starting of the arms toward the ball. However, up to this time very little consideration has been given to the movement of the body and I feel that in the correct shifting of the body lies the secret of timing and power.

While the left wrist and forearm should feel the power and control of the club, the initial effort at the beginning of the downward swing is caused by the necessity of getting the body, or the "right side" out of the way, so that the arms and club may have a free and uninterrupted passage on the way to the ball. The body action is a lateral motion of the hips, often referred to as the forward shift, and has

HELEN HICKS' STROKESAVERS:

- Start the through-swing with a lateral shift of the hips toward the target.
- This *body* move is the secret to timing and power in the downswing.
- Get this move right, and the left heel will replant and the left arm straighten.
- Extend the arms through impact.
- Imagine the clubhead flying toward the hole.

Helen Hicks, the first notable American female golfer to turn pro, was an early "left-side" theorist, arguing that rather than the hands and arms, the unwinding of the hips should trigger the downswing. (J. Gaiger/Topical Press Agency/Getty Images)

laid the foundation for the now well-known axiom of golf—"hitting against the left side." The left heel, by reason of this shift, has now come back to the ground and the right knee begins to twist inward toward the ball. The left arm, which up to this point may have been slightly bent or relaxed, now begins to straighten and become taut. This is the beginning of the arm and wrist work, and it must never come into action before "the shift" has taken the right side out of the way....

Many golfers have the mistaken idea that a great deal of effort must be made before the ball is reached. This is not so. The real hit in golf is made between the ball and the hole, not between the top of the backswing and the ball. The latter is a common error—the cause of wasted effort and many missed shots.

THE MAGIC MOVE

Harvey Penick said that there was no one "magic move" in golf, but spent a lifetime teaching a basic swing key that would enable the golfer to hit the ball as if by "magic." At the start of the downswing, he advised, golfers should shift their weight back to the left foot and drop the right elbow back down to the side, explaining that this was one move, not two.

After the ball has been hit, the great thing to bear in mind is to keep the clubhead traveling toward the hole. That is why I have stressed that great care and effort should be made to keep the left arm in front as long as possible. This will, if applied correctly, assure one of greater distance and accuracy and will also be the beginning of the last and one of the important parts of the swing—the follow-through. Personally, I always try to picture the clubhead going out for the hole. This practically assures me of a straight left arm at the moment of impact and prevents the clubhead from leaving the correct arc of the swing. The finish of the follow-through is almost a duplicate of the top of the backswing—the difference being that at the finish of the swing the left arm is bent with the elbow toward the ground, while the right arm is more or less straight. The correct follow-through not only helps to carry out the fundamentals of the downswing but it adds a certain amount of grace and ease to the finish.…

From *Golf Illustrated* (February 1931), by Helen Hicks.

The Art of Hitting with the Hands
1953 • Tommy Armour

Born in Edinburgh, Tommy Armour emigrated to America to make his fortune playing golf. Boasting a killer instinct, a way with irons, and the ability to play the toughest courses well, the "Silver Scot" won a U.S. Open at Oakmont and a British Open at Carnoustie. Eventually cashing in on 26 wins in the 1920s and 1930s, he became a highly paid instructor. Sitting in a director's chair under a large umbrella, the impeccably groomed Armour dispensed advice in posh venues from New York to Florida. Central to his philosophy was a singular attack on standard orthodoxy of the day—that the left side dominates the swing. He insisted that it is more natural for right-handed golfers to rely on their dominant side, urging them to "whack like hell with the right hand." Controversy over this idea continues to this day—which Armour doubtless would have relished.

The great hitters in golf are those who move their hands faster than those whose distance and precision are inferior. That also is the case in sports other than golf. A fighter accomplishes knockouts by having his fists move with devastating speed. Ruth's home run record was set during seasons when the liveliness of the ball varied, but because The Babe's hands moved faster than those of any other batter, he was supreme as a long hitter. When Jimmy Thomson was consistently the longest driver in golf, motion pictures showed his hands moving at amazing speed.

To let you in on one of the great secrets of good golf, which really isn't a secret at all, one golfer gets more distance because he uses his hands for power, while the other fellow is trying to get distance by using his body.

The long hitter gets his body in position so his hands can work most effectively.

The science of hitting in golf is a matter of a formula involving velocity and mass. The mass of the clubs varies only very few ounces, but the velocity of the hits differs tremendously among golfers. From the scientific viewpoint, a volume could be written about the physics of golf, but the practical application of such information would be limited since hitting a golf ball is more of an art than a science. It's the human element that makes the performance an art.

What misleads people into thinking that swinging and hitting are different is principally a matter of the player's temperament. Macdonald Smith and Byron Nelson have been generally identified as swingers because of the graceful appearance of their actions. Hagen and Sarazen were labeled hitters because their common characteristic was to wield their clubs with what appeared to be violent and impetuous slashing.

TOMMY ARMOUR'S STROKESAVERS:

- Use the speed of the hands—not the body—to hit the ball for distance.
- Believe this: the notion that golf is a left-handed game is as ruinous as the old maxim "keep your eye on the ball."
- Use the left side as a guide, but whack the hell out of the ball with the right hand.
- Hit briskly with the right hand on short shots as well, keeping the body steady.

But, all four of them—and every other great player—had the clubhead coming in with all the speed they could command while retaining steady balance of their bodies.

Hitting the ball a long way isn't a matter of size or weight of the player. It depends on effective use of the hands, rather than on trying to throw the weight of the body into the shot or even, within reasonable limits, lengthening the backswing in the belief that a longer backswing will enable one to accelerate clubhead speed more and get the clubhead moving at maximum speed at contact with the ball....

[In short:] Hold the club firmly with the last three fingers of the left hand... let the left arm and hand act as a guide, and whack the hell out of the ball with the right hand.

On your long shots, hit the ball with the right hand just as hard as you can while keeping the body steady, and on the shorter iron shots, hit with the right hand briskly, and then, too, keep the body steady.

The reason for keeping the body steady is plain, if you'll stop and think. You can reason it out in the following logical steps:

- You know you must have clubhead speed to make the ball move far.
- Your hands are holding the club; therefore, your hands are the main elements in making the clubhead move. Your body and arms could remain in fixed positions, yet your hands alone could hit the ball a crisp blow.
- The faster your hands move, the faster the clubhead is going to move.

But, if your body is moving ahead, too, the relative speed of your hands will be diminished.

Therefore, to get the greatest speed of the clubhead, you must get the greatest speed in your hands, and that can't be secured unless your body is on a steadily fixed, upright axis.

Your right hand, being the human element closest to the clubhead, is the instrument located to produce the clubhead speed you want.

It all adds up to the swift-moving right hand being the source of the dynamic power.

The false idea that golf is a left-handed game for right-handed players shares with the keep-your-eye-on-the-ball idea, the guilt of wrecking the development of many potentially fairly good golfers.

The left-handed game notion grew out of failure to diagnose an error correctly. The error was in blaming the right hand for overpowering the left, when what really happened was that the left hand was too weak. That error accounted for many mistakes in golf instruction and learning, since it made weakness, rather than strength, the governing factor.

No right-handed player ever has naturally hit a golf ball with the left hand, from the very beginning of the game when some ingenious shepherd took a right-handed whack with his crook at a pebble.

There is offered as proof of the argument that golf is a left-handed game the statement that Hogan and Snead were originally left-handed players. Leaving aside the accident that they fell heirs to discarded left-handed clubs as their beginning implements, consider the logic that their left-handed starts gave them strong left hands which, when they switched to right-handed golf, provided them with firm control of the club. Naturally, then, they'd give the clubhead all the right hand they could get into the shot because they had no worries about the left hand being too weak.

And with Hogan, Snead, and every other star, it is the right-handed smash that accounts for masterly execution of the shots. Don't let anyone tell you otherwise.

Your Through-Swing Will Be a Reflex Action

1972 • John Jacobs with Ken Bowden

Englishman John Jacobs was an international star player in the 1950s, a Ryder Cup captain in the 1970s and 1980s, and the driving force behind the formation of the European Tour. A Hall of Fame instructor who probably has helped more golfers than anyone, Jacobs still teaches, writes, and breaks down the swing for his clients. Despite his complex life, Jacobs' approach to golf can be refreshingly simple and direct. His signature philosophy revolves around the physics of the game and how to apply clear principles of cause and effect to hitting the ball. In this excerpt from *Practical Golf*, he assures golfers that if the backswing has been completed correctly the downswing will be almost *reflexive*, in effect telling them to trust their swings. However, true to his calling, Jacobs then offers a detailed analysis of how the downswing unfolds, and urges golfers to apply that knowledge during practice.

There's a simple way of knowing whether you are coiling properly during your backswing. Try to hold your top-of-the-swing position for 10 seconds. If you've really coiled the spring, you'll find this, if not impossible, certainly a considerable muscular strain.

You will also find that the need to "unwind" is a *reflex* action. As your shoulders reach the limit of their turn, the opposing force in your resisting legs and hips will already be winning the battle. Almost before your shoulders have reached the limit of their turn in one direction, the lower half of your body will have started to pull in the opposite direction. This is what is meant by "starting the downswing with the legs and hips," a recommendation made by nearly every golf book author and modern teacher of the game.

This natural reflex action, the result of opposing forces acting upon each other irresistibly, is the start of the downswing.

Dustin Johnson, noted for his highly athletic and powerful swing, hits a shot during a practice round prior to the start of the 2011 PGA Championship. Johnson's coiled position at the top supports John Jacobs' assertion that if the backswing is completed correctly the downswing will be almost reflexive. (Stuart Franklin/Getty Images)

JOHN JACOBS' STROKESAVERS:

- Complete the backswing correctly, and the through-swing is reflexive.
- Allow the body's lower half to turn back toward the target, while the top half resists and the arms swing down.
- Keep the head behind the ball, and the wrists will uncock automatically just before impact.
- Save the mechanics for practice sessions.

It is an observable fact that in a good golf swing, the downswing begins before the backswing finishes. This change of direction, this victory of one force over an opposing force, is, for most golfers, a crossroads equal in magnitude to starting the club away from the ball. The clash of opposing forces *must* take place if the golfer is to get his maximum power into the shot. But it can only take place if he has wound up properly in the backswing. In the backswing, the top half of the body has been turning, the lower half resisting, as the arms swing up. In the downswing *the lower half turns while the top half resists and the arms swing down.*

As the lower half of the body wins the battle, the bulk of the player's weight shifts to his left foot while his head stays behind the ball. The legs move laterally to the left, and the hips begin to turn to face the hole, thereby clearing the way for the arms to swing the club *down and through* the ball. The right knee—which has been flexed throughout—"kicks in" as the left hip pulls the weight back to the left side. The right leg, now "released," adds thrust to the pull of the left side.

As I've stressed, all of this—subject to a proper wind-up—is largely a reflex action. You can hardly prevent it from happening if you've coiled properly. But the real trick is not in the lower-body action. It lies in the action of the top half, the torso and the head.

Throughout the downswing, the head must remain *back*; pretty much where it was at address and during the backswing, behind the ball. And the upper torso, notably the shoulders, must *resist* the pull of the lower half of the body until the arms have swung down. This is the key to power, the *natural cause* of the "late hit," which so many club golfers have sought so long in vain.

If your top half effectively reverses its backswing role (after resisting the pull and turn of the lower half), the arms and hands, instead of flinging the club from top—altering the swing's arc and plane, and dissipating power—will be pulled down *inside* the target line. The set or cock of the wrists established by the weight of the club at the top of the swing will be retained until—as the big muscles of the legs, hips, and back pull the hands down—the wrists automatically uncock, whipping the clubhead into the ball as the hands flash past it.

These are all the "mechanics" of the through-swing you ever need to know—and ideally you should not even think consciously of them, except in practice sessions.

From *Practical Golf*, by John Jacobs with Ken Bowden. Stanley Paul & Co., Ltd., an imprint of the Hutchinson Group. Copyright © 1972 John Jacobs and Ken Bowden. Used by permission of John Jacobs.

Step Five: Move Down to the Ball

1994 • Jim McLean

Although he played in two U.S. Opens and a Masters, Jim McLean soon found that he was more adept at helping others harness their swings than trying to tame his own, which he admits sometimes wilted under pressure. Studying under such diverse instructors as Carl Welty, Ken Venturi (a Hogan protégé), Johnny Revolta, and the master of "connection" Jimmy Ballard, McLean emerged with a unique and very successful teaching approach—one credited most recently by 2011 PGA champion Keegan Bradley. McLean focuses on eight checkpoints in the golfer's swing motion. But he isn't fanatical about exact positions for each stage in the way Hogan often could be, preferring that the golfer simply stay within acceptable ranges of motion—or what he calls "corridors of success." *The Eight-Step Swing*, a best-selling book and DVD, encapsulates the approach, and "Step Five" takes the golfer from the top of the backswing to just before the moment of truth at impact.

If there is a secret to employing a good golf swing, it occurs here.

In all of the great swings I have studied, there is no evidence of a "stop" and "start" that together reverse the direction of the club from backswing to downswing. Instead, I see a smooth, flowing transition. The arms, hands, and club respond to the actions of the lower body or lower center of body. In fine golf swings, the last thing to change direction at the top is the clubhead. This, of course, makes perfect sense, because all the centrifugal and centripetal force we apply in the swing is designed to do nothing else but load the clubhead with energy and deliver it down the proper path.

In the transition, your arms and hands are passive. The first move is backward and down. The clubhead sinks lower as your hips start to unwind. Your hands and wrists respond immediately to the reversal of direction. Your right elbow automatically drops into the proper slot by your right side. The Step Five checkpoint position in many ways resembles the Step Three position [the Three-Quarter Backswing Position] on the backswing. From a head-on view, it looks as if the hands and clubshaft were passing back through the same positions they were in at Step Three (*only considerably narrower*). There is a sense that the hands free-fall down to the delivery position.

The right shoulder helps determine the path of the downswing. If, in its first motion, your right shoulder rocks down, all systems are go. Thanks to the shoulder, your right elbow can now drop into its proper slot and align with your right hip. This lowering of the right shoulder is a response to the legs initiating the forward motion. But if the first motion is initiated by your right shoulder out toward the ball, you've got no chance to attain the correct positions at Step Five. The down tuck of the right shoulder can be overworked, so proceed with caution. You don't want to cause your left shoulder to "over-climb" through impact.

Note: to clear up any possible misconception, I have not said that the first move in the downswing is made by the right shoulder. The downswing starts with the hips or lower body center moving toward the target. The shoulder motion, good or bad, is a responsive motion that ties in with the hips or lower body.

In a model swing, the hands and arms are passive during this step and respond to rather than initiate any action. The right elbow gives the appearance of attaching to, then being glued to, the right side just above the right hip area. The left arm is fully extended from the body—straight. It is here that good players feel pull, but that is only a sensation, not a result of any conscious pull with the hands or arms. With your right elbow glued to your right side and your left arm straight, it is easy to see that Step Five is a very powerful position. Your hands and arms have not "run off" but are simply responding accurately and appropriately to the body motions. The clubshaft is very close to the same position it was in at Step Three—exceptions include 90 degrees of angle or more with the left arm and clubshaft. The downswing is inside (narrower than) the backswing. (This is one of my fundamentals.) Your wrists are in a fully cocked position. The club should not be outside your hands unless you intend to hit a cut. If it is outside the hands, this is a perfect illustration of "casting" (starting the release motion too soon) or exaggerating the initial rotation of the shoulders. The "*delivery position*," as I call it, will always show you the golfer's impact position. It is a critical spot in the swing that determines all ball flight. It is always a position I carefully analyze in my teaching.

At Step Five, body weight has shifted back noticeably to the left. It has re-centered the body and weight is shifting forward and *diagonally left*.

Your belt buckle as viewed from the front has slid seven to 12 inches toward the target, from Step Four to Step Six [Impact]. This slide is a natural response to the lower body—the feet and legs—initiating the downswing. It happens *automatically* in a sequenced swing. If you monitor the belt buckle on any top player, you'll immediately see this powerful lateral movement.

At Step Five, the shaft should have traveled down along a path that, when viewed down the target line, is between the tip of your shoulder and your right elbow. If the shaft stays in this Corridor of Success with the butt end of the club pointing to an extension of the ball-to-target line, this indicates an on-plane swing and promising solid contact and good trajectory.

In viewing the swings of the amateurs I teach, I sometimes see the shaft improperly low—dropped beneath the elbow. In this case, the dotted line from

JIM MCLEAN'S STROKESAVERS:

- Unwind the hips and let the hands free-fall at the start of the downswing.
- Allow the right shoulder to respond to the movement of the hips and lower body—it helps determine the club's path.
- If the right shoulder "rocks down," all systems are go.
- Shift the body weight back toward the left, recentering the body.

the shaft butt hits the ground at a point well beyond the target line. From this position you will push or hook the ball—if you make solid contact. Often, you will hit behind the ball from this inside, shallow swing arc.

A far more common problem I witness is indicated when the shaft moves downward on a path that takes it above the tip of the shoulder. In this instance, a line drawn from the butt of the club would point to the player's feet. We call this "shaft tip over." From this position at Step Five, you will usually contact the ball with the toe of the clubface and hit a weak slice—Death Position! If you manage to square the clubface, you'll pull the ball. Finally, this move is also characteristic of the shank.

STEP FIVE: FINAL CHECKPOINTS

- The right knee has kicked forward (toward the ball or target line), and there is a substantial space between your knees.
- The hips have shifted a few inches, in response to your weight-shifting action, and reached the square position. The shoulders trail the hips.
- The head is stabilized at, or slightly behind, its address position.
- The right heel is grounded or, at most, slightly off the ground. At this point in the swing, it should never be extra high.
- The flexed left knee is forward of your left hip. The left knee is more or less in a straight line with the middle of your left foot. The left leg is still flexed but is in the process of straightening.
- The body has entered the classic "sit-down" position many players and teachers have long observed.
- The clubshaft is on plane.
- The shoulders are unwinding at a rapid pace, yet still lag your hips in rotation. The golf swing depends heavily on "connection," but in the downswing we also see two instances of *separation*—first, the lower body "leaves" the shoulders, then the hands and arms "separate" from the shoulders. The distance between your hands and right shoulder increases as the club reaches our "delivery position."
- The right arm should be slightly visible under your left starting down.
- Your eyes are fixed on the ball.
- The clubhead is behind your body.
- Many golfers will benefit by *slowing down* the turn back to the target.

Sometimes it is useful to slow the upper torso—other times the lower—and sometimes both.

- A big secret to good shotmaking is the clubshaft position at Step Five and the square orientation of the clubface. I call this "the delivery position."
- Supinate the left wrist on the downward move. This happens during Step Five. Sometimes we actually teach this move. That is making the left wrist flat or slightly bowed. If the wrists, hands, and clubhead truly respond to the lower body this flattening should happen with no conscious thought. When it does not happen, we teach it. When you stop the club at Step Five, check your left wrist position. It must not be cupped.

Impact

2000 • Johnny Miller

In 1974 and 1975, Johnny Miller won 12 PGA tournaments, including one by 14 strokes and another by nine. Overall, he won 25 titles, including two majors, before burning out in the late 1970s and becoming a golf commentator. On the air, Miller is famous for his blunt, often controversial remarks, so it's not surprising that his ideas about his own golf swing are provocative. In more than a century of golf instruction, few have ventured where Miller does, focusing on that split second when the clubhead meets the ball. His knowledge of impact, he contends, is what elevated him to the top of his profession. In this excerpt from *Breaking 90*, he makes the intriguing claim that he developed muscle memory for the perfect impact position. He describes how to achieve this ideal by what professionals call "covering" the ball—a term related to Ben Hogan's "supination"—which involves maintaining a subtle, downward angle of the right palm.

I got my bachelor's degree in physical education from Brigham Young University in 1969. But I got my PhD in impact from 25 years of study, trial, and error on the PGA Tour.

From the time I started playing professionally in 1970, I made it my mission to develop a complete sense of swing feedback. I wanted to know exactly what the clubhead was doing at impact and how that affected my shots. To accomplish this, I didn't rely just on feel. I was one of the first pros to invest in stop-action and movie cameras to make pictures and videos of my swing. Just like Tony Gwynn, who has a video record of every baseball swing he's made during his career, I built a huge library of video and sequence pictures of my golf swing. After hours of studying those images and by hitting thousands of balls, I could pinpoint exactly what positions I needed to be in at impact to send the ball where I wanted it to go, with very few miss-hits. I actually developed muscle memory of the perfect impact position.

The result was that I played some stretches of golf that I can hardly believe myself. Everyone remembers the 63 I shot at Oakmont to win the 1973 U.S. Open, but that was only one dream round. For me, 1974 and 1975 were dream years. I won eight tournaments in '74, then three of the first four I played in '75.... I can say without bragging that for 16 months, anyway, I could play golf as well as anybody, ever.... For that...period...I was furious if I hit a mid- or short-iron more than five feet off line. I looked at that kind of miss—and we're talking birdie-range if my yardage was right—as a failure....

I'm not saying you're going to develop that level of confidence with your irons. But, if you become a student of impact, not only will you be able to understand why your shots do what they do, but you'll be able to take control and make the ball do what you want it to do. If you deliver the clubhead solidly and precisely to the ball, it doesn't make any difference what the rest of the swing looks like. That's why I am surprised that no instructors talk about impact. They tell you everything you want to know about the full swing, but leave out the most important part—the moment the clubhead connects with the ball. All the ball knows is impact.

Impact—which can be defined as the split second your club comes into contact with the ball to about an inch past when the ball leaves the clubhead—is everything in golf. Depending on where your clubhead is at that moment, you will hit a hook or a slice, a draw or a fade, a low runner or a high soft shot. If you can master impact, you can control and shape your shots. However, if you make a tiny mistake and your clubhead is left open as it hits the ball, even just a hair, you could slice the ball 20 yards wide of your target. That's how important impact is. In fact, a small but crucial difference in clubface position at impact is exactly what separates total hackers from the best players in the world. I've heard people say that golf is a game of inches, but when it comes to impact, it is a game of fractions of fractions of inches.

"The distance the ball travels is governed solely by the amount of power you unleash at impact."

—Julius Boros

If you're an average amateur player, your sense of feel isn't going to be fine enough to do more than make a rough estimate about what happens at impact. But even at that level, you can learn enough to make some really positive changes in your swing. At the absolute minimum, you need to know that every good professional golfer, from an aggressive swinger like Sergio Garcia to a controlled technician like Annika Sorenstam, reduces the loft on his or her mid- and short-iron shots, just before impact. That's called "covering" the ball....

A good golfer's palm faces down at impact, creating that reduced loft angle. If you took the club out of my hands at impact, you'd see that my right palm faces the target and is angled slightly toward the ground. I'm swinging down and through the ball. The shaft of the club is staying vertical long after the clubhead passes my left toe, and my right hand won't turn over until it gets to my left pocket.

Every bad player does the opposite—usually because he or she isn't convinced that the loft on the club is enough to get the ball airborne. Once you try to scoop the shot into the air with the club by rotating that right palm under and up toward the sky, at best you're going to hit a high, weak shot. In fact, most of the worst swing problems beginners have, from reverse pivoting to coming over the top, create more loft. With that right palm upward, not only does the club have more loft, but the face is flared open, causing even more of a left-to-right curve. It is impossible to hit consistently good shots if you add loft. Your only chance would be to hang back and pull one 20 yards left, and that would happen strictly by luck. To take the next step, you need to learn to cover the ball.

Watch an aggressive swinger like Garcia hit his 7 or 8 iron. He'll take a divot the size of a folded dinner napkin, yet his shots are struck cleanly and crisply. You're probably saying to yourself, *when I take a divot that size I'm hitting it fat and about 20 feet*. If you check out your divot on a fat shot, you'll see that it started before the ball. Once you jam the club into the ground behind the ball, you slow any clubhead speed you generated on the downswing. If the club can plow through all that turf and get to the ball, it usually sends it rolling about 20 or 30 feet. The difference in Garcia's shot is that he's hitting the ball, *then* hitting the turf. In other words, he's hitting the ball just before he gets to the bottom of his swing. He's angling that clubhead toward the ball, with his palm facing down, and striking the ball crisply with a descending blow. That divot is coming from the ground directly in front of the ball, after the ball is gone. He's pinching the ball between the ground and the club, causing the backspin that makes his irons hit the green, then stick like a scared cat.

If you spend enough time on the practice range hitting balls, you'll be able to get impact feedback through your hands and your ears. Just like a home run struck right on the sweet spot, when you hit a pure golf shot, you don't feel a thing—no vibrations. The sound is very distinctive, too. Go out and watch a PGA Tour player hit an iron from the fairway, and you'll know the sound of that pure strike—not the clattering of metal on balata, but a crisp click with a swooshing noise attached.

It's true that those last moves happen very quickly. I can remember playing a practice round with Jack Nicklaus early in 1975, when I was in the middle

JOHNNY MILLER'S STROKESAVERS:

- Most instructors talk about everything *but* impact; the ball knows only impact.
- Develop muscle memory for the perfect impact position.
- Try to make the right palm face the target and angle slightly down at impact—that results in an ideal swing down and through the ball.
- Get feedback from the hands and ears—a pure shot feels effortless, and produces a crisp click with a swooshing sound.

of that incredible run. We had played a few holes and I hit it to kick-in range on each one. As we got ready to tee off on the next hole, Jack asked me what I worked on in my practice sessions, and I told him about my ongoing quest to know impact. He looked at me like I was crazy. "It happens too fast—how can anybody know what happens at impact?" he said. Maybe that's why so many instructors spend so much time on swing mechanics and basically ignore impact. The swing takes time, so it can be shaped and fiddled with. Once they set you up in the proper position, most teachers think it's just a mater of firing away and letting the ball get in the way of the swing. I say that's leaving too much to chance. Jack hit some of the most solid iron shots I ever saw, so he knew something about impact. Don't sell your brain short. That impact move is very trainable. I've had great results working both with my kids and with average amateurs in just an hour or two on the range. You can easily work on it by yourself in front of a mirror.

"You must not begin the downward swing as if you were anxious to get it over."

—Alexander "Sandy" Herd,
early Scottish champion
(1902 British Open) and instructor

In a lot of ways, impact is the most important thing I can teach, because no matter how many other swing fundamentals or positions I talk about, your personal body shape and flexibility level are going to determine to what extent you can imitate what I suggest. Study the swings of the players who have had the most success over the years by watching videos of their swings or looking at swing-sequence photographs. It's easy to see what kinds of backswings and downswings promote that kind of solid impact. But that study also shows that there's more than one way to do it. Even when two swings are as different as, say, mine and Lee Trevino's, if you took a picture of the two clubheads at impact, you wouldn't be able to tell us apart.

If you want to get better at this game, you need to understand impact and what position you'll need to be in to achieve it just right. Then you can craft a swing with the body you've been given that will help you get where you need to be during those crucial split seconds of impact. Even if you understand the general mechanics of the swing, if you don't know impact, you're golfing in the dark.

Tiger Woods sinks the winning putt at the 1997 Masters and celebrates his arrival on the world stage. Barely 21 years old at the time, Woods annihilated the field with his prodigious length, but backed that up with a sparkling short game—especially his clutch putting—to take the tournament by a record 12 strokes and win his first major. (Augusta National/ Getty Images)

PART THREE

X

THE SHORT GAME

THE BEAUTY OF GOLF IS that players who aren't blessed with great power can best their more crowd-pleasing, long-hitting adversaries. They can do it with pinpoint pitches and chips, skilled bunker play, and accurate putting. That's as true today as it was in the late 1800s, although approach shots evolved from being primarily a ground game to more of an aerial assault. As equipment improved and golf moved from the seaside to inland forests and parks, instruction shifted from the low-flying chip—once the staple of links-type play and still a potent tool—to high-flying pitches for clearing bunkers and other hazards. Notions about bunker play also changed. Until Gene Sarazen debuted the sand wedge at the 1932 British Open, some regarded landing "on the beach" as a near calamity. But with this new weapon, instructors preached that escaping with "explosion" and "splash" shots was an easier challenge. Today, the consensus is that landing in a bunker is *preferable* to many other greenside lies. In the early twentieth century, outstanding putters Walter Travis and Jerome Travers developed the now standard reverse-overlap grip and pendulum motion. Later golfers, playing on well-manicured greens, would refine ideas about gauging speed and line, yet recommended combining sophisticated, modern technique with the artistry of early pioneers. Dave Pelz would introduce statistical analysis into putting. Confidence and consistency remain vital to steadying nerves, because as Bobby Jones said, "There is nothing so demoralizing as missing a short putt."

CHAPTER 8

CHIPPING AND PITCHING

Ground and Air Assault

Approaching

1896 • Willie Park, Jr

Willie Park, Jr.'s bewhiskered father was the first British Open champion in 1860 and fellow Scot Old Tom Morris' archrival for more than a decade. Uncle Mungo also won the Open, and Junior became champion himself in 1887 and 1889. When he played, *The New York Times* said, "He appeared to be encased in a triple armor of philosophical composure." A student of the game, who designed clubs and courses in Europe and North America, Park devoted an entire volume to putting in 1920, but is best remembered for *The Game of Golf*, the first complete instructional book by a professional. In this excerpt, he used terms that modern readers probably won't recognize—such as "wrist strokes" and "hitting off the left and right legs"—but they should realize he's describing how to chip, pitch, and execute tricky cut shots in ways not that different from current methods.

The approach is the most difficult, and sometimes the most delicate, stroke in the whole game.... In approaching, not only must the ball be hit truly, but the distance to the hole must be calculated and the force employed proportioned thereto, and consideration must be given to the nature of the ground to determine whether the ball is to be lofted or run up. These considerations make the stroke more complex. But in no part of the game is there afforded a greater opportunity for the display of skill, as opposed to force, than in this, and nowhere is skill better repaid....

Three-quarter and half strokes are to my mind much more difficult to play than full shots, especially the former. There is always a disposition to jerk the swing, as if to compensate for its being shortened, and this generally results in topping the ball.... Therefore, in playing these strokes, there should not, under any circumstances, be pressing: swing easily....

The position of the ball and the stance for playing half-shots is somewhat, though not materially, different from that [for a full shot].... The ball is [played] nearer the [golfer's] body, and nearer also to the line of the right foot. The right foot is also further advanced…[opening the stance]. It need hardly be pointed out that, as the club is not swung far round, the shoulders and body do not move so much as in playing a full stroke. The shoulders must move round, and the body must be eased…to a certain extent, it is true, but the less they do so the better, consistent with letting the club go sufficiently round.…

Of wrist strokes there is an infinite variety of gradation—anything less than a half-stroke falls under this definition. No further remarks on this subject require to be made, save that the ball should be nearer the player, and the feet closer together.… Both legs are slightly more bent at the knees than is the case in playing a full shot, and the body moves very little; in fact, wrist strokes are almost entirely played with the wrists, assisted to a small extent by the arms. I would only add: stand firmly, and do not move the feet at all; keep the right elbow well in to the side, and play from the wrists, giving the ball a quick, sharp hit.… It will be found of material assistance if the club be grasped farther down the shaft; and the shorter the distance of the stroke to be played, the shorter a grip of the club may be taken.

While the weight of the body is supported on both legs, the right really gives the greatest amount of support. This can be easily tested by trying to lift either foot off the ground. For the above reason, this mode of playing approaches has been termed "off the right leg," and it is the method most usually adopted. Hereafter an alternative method, termed "off the left leg," will be explained.

With the view of making iron approaches fall dead, more especially those played from shorter distances, it has been advocated that they should be played with slice, or cut, as it is more frequently termed in this case. This is done… by drawing the arms in toward the body in the act of hitting the ball, and omitting the follow-through. This probably may have the desired effect—and theoretically it is all very well—but practically it is exceedingly difficult to do

WILLIE PARK, JR.'S PITCHING STROKESAVERS:

- Choke down on the club for better feel.
- Narrow the stance.
- Keep the lower body quiet.
- Slide the leading edge of the clubhead under the ball.

successfully; and placing the risk of failure against the advantage to be gained, I do not think…it is worth attempting.

I therefore recommend that all approaches be played without slice. If, however, the player has sufficient confidence in his ability to put on cut, and is desirous of trying it, he will have to keep in view that the effect is to make the ball run to the right-hand side, and he must make allowance for this by playing, not straight on the flag, but to the left of it.…

It is not difficult to put on cut when a ball is teed or dropped on a fine piece of turf, simply for the purpose of illustrating the stroke; but it is quite a different matter to play approaches in this manner from the multifarious lies—good, bad, and indifferent—that occur in actual play.…

With wrist shots there is more run on the ball in proportion than with any others, and it may be absolutely necessary to make a wrist shot fall dead, as, for instance, where the hole lies between two bunkers, one in front over which the ball must be pitched, and one behind into which it will certainly roll if there is much run on it. There are other expedients resorted to for this purpose besides putting on cut. One is to lay back the face of the iron. To do this, the player must stand in such a position that the ball will be more in a line with his left foot. But this method is no better than using a club with a very great deal of pitch.…

There is another method, known as "cutting the feet from it," and this is the most effectual of all, and undoubtedly the proper way of playing the stroke. It is, however, somewhat difficult to play this stroke, and it is still more difficult to describe it. The stance and position are the same as for an ordinary iron approach, and so is the grip. The swing must, however, be much more of an up and down nature than in the ordinary approach, and played sharply. The head of the iron is slipped in between the ball and the turf (not swept over the ground), with the result that a large amount of backspin is imparted to the ball, and in the follow-through the arms are not thrown out in the line of play, but are lifted up straighter, with the object of "whipping up" the ball. The essence of the stroke lies in hitting the ball smartly and quickly; and the more quickly the ball is hit, the more backspin is put upon it, therefore the higher will it be lofted, and the shorter distance it will travel.… The stroke will be an utter failure unless the clubhead gets well under the ball. On a soft green such a stroke can invariably be played with success; but on a hard green, and out of a bad lie, it is difficult, but not impossible.…

The alternative mode of playing approaches is "off the left leg." The best exponent of this style is Mr. Laidlay, [who sets up with] the weight of [his] body thrown upon the left leg, and the club...held toward [his] left side. He also prefers to play approaches with an iron that has not a great deal of loft on it, thus getting a comparatively low shot, and allowing the ball to finish with a run after the pitch; but for lofted approaches he invariably uses a mashie....

Regard must always be had to the nature of the ground between the place where the ball lies and the hole, and upon that will depend the club to be used. If a putter be used, the ball will not, of course, rise at all, but will roll along the ground; if a cleek be used, the ball will rise but a few feet, depending upon the length and consequent strength of the stroke, and will roll a good bit after the pitch is exhausted; while using the iron, the stroke will be pitched up to the green and roll a comparatively short distance.

On a hard green, running up will be found most successful, because it is difficult to pitch a ball dead off an iron, and should it happen to alight on any irregularity it may shoot forward or may bound off in any direction; hence the superiority of running up, because there is much more forward motion on the ball, and it will not, if it hit some irregularity, be deflected to such an extent as if pitched. There is also this advantage, that, the straighter the face of the club, the less is a ball affected when not quite accurately struck, and it is easier to judge the distance—that is to say, an error in calculating the strength tells less against the stroke.

The more [loft] there is on a club the less striking surface is presented to the ball, and the more is any mistake magnified....

From *The Game of Golf*, by Willie Park, Jr., Longmans, Green & Co., London, England.

Approaching

circa 1928 • P.A. Vaile

Pembroke Arnold Vaile's long out-of-print books and old clubs, such as the "P.A. Vaile Stroke Saver," are items at auctions. Only collectors and historians seem to know the Chicago writer who learned golf late in life and then explained it in numerous books. Vaile wrote about international economic relations in *Cosmocracy, the Science of Peace*, and some of his golf books—and tennis books—were, if less high-minded, equally esoteric, bearing such titles as *The Soul of Golf*. Others, such as *Putting Made Easy* and 1936's *The Short Game* (originally a booklet in the late 1920s) could still be understood by readers who had never held a club. In this excerpt, Vaile told beginners to use a putting grip to chip and keep the body out of the shot, advice that still is golden. He reinforced his once disparaged theories by quoting similar views expressed by Johnny Farrell and Bobby Jones.

T he grip for the short approach strokes is almost the same as that for the putt....

The stance should be open...the left heel...in the open stance being a trifle farther from the line of flight than the right heel.

Be careful to keep the face of the club at right angles to the intended line of flight. Up to about 50 yards from the pin there is comparatively little knee and body movement, the hands and arms doing most of the work.

The grip must be firm with both hands, and the stroke should be crisp. Keep the left arm straight and the right elbow close to the side. The knees, hips, and shoulders start the downswing, which, even in the short strokes, is not entirely independent hand and arm movement. Keep the head still, and guard especially against ducking or lowering it during the stroke....

There must be *absolutely no lateral movement of the hips away from the hole*, or as it is termed, swaying. This unsettles the center, or base, of one's swing in a class of strokes wherein one should confidently strive for as much accuracy as in putting....

Luke Donald finished 2011 as the world's No. 1 player, and the first golfer to lead the money list on both the U.S. and European PGA Tours. The stylish Englishman, shown here executing a chip shot—a key to his success—exemplifies the form P.A. Vaile described over 80 years before: open the stance and swing the arms and hands close to the body in a pendulum-like motion, as if hitting a long putt. (Stuart Franklin/Getty Images)

THE CHIP SHOT—A LONG PUTT

An article by ex-Open champion of the United States, Johnny Farrell, in *The Amateur Golfer*, is practically a complete lesson in approaching itself…I shall quote only [from] the first two paragraphs here, as follows:

> The one point that I would like to impress upon golfers playing the chip shot is the fact *that it is nothing more than a long putt*. If the player will bring himself to realize this really important fact it will simplify the play greatly and create a mental condition that will reduce the tension that seems to be a handicap of the amateur golfer.…
>
> The most common fault that I have observed is that the player stands too far away from the ball, and the feet are usually too far apart. This fault makes the result of the stroke very uncertain as control of the wrist is lost. The proper method is for the player to stand as close to the ball as he can with comfort and freedom—without feeling cramped. Both arms should be tucked close to the side; the forearms and wrists only are used in swinging the club. The swing should simulate that of the putt. With the idea of a putt in mind, and by following the principles of the putt, the irritating and annoying habit of stubbing the ground is not likely to occur.

THE RUN-UP SHOT

Bobby Jones has recently published an interesting article on the run-up shot, from which I shall give a few extracts:

> Although lack of familiarity with the run-up has caused the majority of players to regard it as a very difficult shot, it is actually far simpler and far less risky than the pitch. That is the greatest virtue of the run-up—it will never finish very far away.
>
> The shot ought rarely to be played with any club of more loft than a No. 4 iron. I carry in my bag a cleek *shafted to a little more than putter length* which I use for run-up shots of 30 of 40 yards. It is very useful, for it makes of the stroke very little more than a long approach putt.

P.A. VAILE'S CHIPPING STROKESAVERS:

- Use a putting grip for better feel and control.
- Imagine the shot is just a long putt.
- Accelerate through the ball.

Note this carefully, for it is of great importance to golfers. We here have Bobby Jones' statement that the run-up shot up to 40 yards is "very little more than a long approach putt." We are now arriving at simplified golf within 40 yards of the pin—and it need not stop at 40 yards.

"Carry your putt back into your game as far as you can" has been persistently urged by me for years, and to have this instruction now supported by many of the country's most capable players and instructors is valuable corroboration which, combined with the use of proper clubs, must tend to improve the game where most it needs it.

The old slogan used by me more than 20 years ago, "A short putter for short putts," bids fair to be indefinitely extended to "Short clubs and short strokes for the short game."

Johnny Farrell, in one of his articles, recently said: "The chip is primarily a stroke-saver"—to which I replied, "Johnny is *nearly* right. It isn't *a* stroke saver. It is *the* stroke saver"—or as Bobby Jones puts it: "The great economist of golf strokes."

The Approach

1960 · Marlene Bauer Hagge

In 1950, child prodigies Marlene Bauer, almost 16, and sister Alice, 22, turned pro and were among the 13 charter members of the LPGA. In 1952, the Hall of Fame–bound Marlene became the youngest winner of an LPGA event, her first of 26 titles. Her father Dave Bauer boasted that his dainty daughters hit 200-yard drives in his 1951 book *Golf Techniques of the Bauer Sisters*, but Marlene, like Paul Runyan, viewed the short game as the great equalizer. Like her chips and pitches, her writing on the subject is well-reasoned and has teeth. Modernists may quibble with her advice on ball position for pitch shots, but few will disagree with her admonition not to "scoop" the ball or her chipping techniques. Modern wedges and "target golf"–necessitated by hazards near greens, particularly in America–have made the run-up shot she described almost obsolete, but high-handicappers may think it worth considering.

MASTERING THESE SHOTS WILL LOWER YOUR HANDICAP

With the approach shot—and this term includes the pitch, chip, and run-up—the golfer comes to the heart of the short game. These shots are important to every player, but it is imperative that they be played well by women. And here again, achievement is based first on learning the proper fundamentals and then on practicing these until they have truly become second nature.

For the pitch shot, the stance should be a little wide, the left foot drawn slightly back from the intended line of flight and the ball placed approximately off the heel of the right foot. This gives the player a fairly upright position, which she will need to make the downward swing that will connect with the ball first and the turf afterward.

This last point—that the ball be hit a descending blow—is perhaps the most important element in any of the approach shots, for only this motion will give it the backspin that means control, which is an absolute necessity at short distances from the green.

The hands should be placed slightly ahead of the clubhead at address, the weight distributed equally or over to the left. As with every other shot in golf, the approach needs a strong left side to hit into.

On this shot, I use either a 9 or an 11 iron. When the shot is a short one, anywhere from 30 yards in, I prefer the 11, but there are some definite don'ts in connection with this club. I've noticed that when a club with a definite loft is involved, most women tend to scoop the ball. This is dangerous anywhere; it can be fatal on the approach shot. Scooping will *not* get the ball into the air, let alone get it into the air for any distance. And another warning: those women who do not try to scoop the ball very often hood, or close, their clubface. Obviously, this error is just as severe as scooping, since it dissipates the loft intended for that particular club and necessary to the pitch shot. *I usually address the ball with a slightly open clubface*, which helps give the club its proper loft, and I keep it slightly open coming through the shot, with a very firm hand action, which means both hands working as a unit.

The golfer must always remember that the approach shot—and here we're specifically talking about the pitch—is one that is hit to the pin with a lot of backspin, so that the ball will bite. Too many golfers take a fairly long backswing and then baby the shot coming through. *The correct way, the only way, is to take a short backswing and remain firm throughout the swing....*

I usually take the clubhead back a bit on the outside and then hit across the intended line of flight. This gives me a slight cut shot and consequently a little extra bite on the ball.

Now for the run-up shot. Most players like it. I do and I know, too, that it can be an easy shot; just give it the proper attention. It's particularly handy if the distance between the edge of the green and the pin is short and the green doesn't hold well. In a case like this, it obviously would be impractical to use a lofted approach. Instead, the player should try hitting the ball into the green so that it will check or stop by the pin, which is what a successful run-up will do.

This approach can be made in either of two ways. The first involves a less-lofted club like the 5, 6, or 7 iron, and the ball is hit in much the same way as a putt. The ball is approximately centered in the stance, the line of the shoulders to clubhead is straight, and the swing is pendulum-like. Here, the center of the pendulum would be the shoulders, with very little wrist action involved, so that the ball is almost parallel to the ground when in flight. The second method of dealing with the run-up requires a club with a little more loft and, in this instance, it is permissible and even desirable to hood the face slightly. This is the run-up I prefer, since it affords more control. Here I usually use either the 7 or 8 iron.

I place the ball off the heel of my right foot, with my hands slightly ahead of the club at address. I start the club back with the left shoulder and arm and keep the clubhead low and close to the ground. The ball is hit with a descending blow—sharply enough so that I take a small divot. All these elements—the more lofted club, a slight hood to the face, and the descending blow—give a little more spin to the ball. Consequently, the player can pitch the ball farther, with less run on it. I feel that the more I can keep the ball in the air, the less chance I have of being defeated by the natural defects of the course: an unexpected bump, a small patch of rough, or another player's divot. In any case, the air *is* much smoother than the ground, so that the farther the ball travels through the air, and the more spin the player can get on her ball, the more successful the run-up shot.

"The chip is the greatest economist in golf."

—Bobby Jones

I will say this, however. The golfer's choice of run-up shot must be the one with which she feels more comfortable, the one in which she has more confidence. Confidence is probably 90 percent of a woman's golf game (really, of anyone's golf game), and since this means that golf is mental, it follows that if the player uses the shot she's happiest with, that shot is the one that will come off for her.

MARLENE BAUER HAGGE'S PITCHING AND CHIPPING STROKESAVERS:

- Open the clubface, play the ball back, and fully commit to the shot for pitches.
- Take the club back on the outside and cut across the ball for extra bite.
- Place the hands ahead of the clubhead for chips.
- Visualize the ball staying low and running early. Keep weight on the left side throughout the swing.

The chip—perhaps the most important of the approaches—is used for any shot from one to five feet off the green. It is important to keep the ball low to the ground, and you need to get some run on it. A 7, 8, or 9 iron is used, depending on the length the player has to carry over the edge of the green. Normally, I use an 8 for a chip. The stance here is slightly open, with the left foot drawn a little back from the intended line of flight, the ball placed off the heel of the right foot. The player's weight should be on the left side, and it remains there throughout the shot. As in the pitch and run-up, all movement—the downswing as well as the backswing—is initiated by that left shoulder and arm.

With the 8 iron, the clubface is hooded slightly at address, while the hands are ahead of the clubhead. The right elbow is kept close to the right side. For the chip shot, I grip the club down quite a bit farther than I do with the other approaches, and I bend more at the waist. The grip itself, while firm, particularly at impact, should be an easy one. That is, you're not gripping the club to death. Here again, the ball is hit a descending blow by the hooded face to give it backspin. This extra control makes it easier to judge the distance, and that is possibly the most important factor in chipping....

This short game is the part of golf that women should and must concentrate on, because it is the part of golf in which they can excel. A woman who can keep the ball in play on the other shots, while chipping and putting well, will be up there with the best of them. I should know because I'm a small girl. If it weren't for these areas of my game, I wouldn't have a chance.

From *Golf for Women*, edited by Louise Suggs. Chapter by Marlene Bauer Hagge. Copyright © 1960 by Rutledge Books. Used by permission of Doubleday & Co., a division of Random House, Inc.

The Basic Pitching Stroke

1983 · Tom Watson with Nick Seitz

Getting Up and Down was Tom Watson's first instructional book and one of golf's best sellers for more than a decade. The average hacker should find comfort in what he writes on the pitch shot. Most star players tell their readers how they easily can apply spin to the ball, but forget that for handicap golfers this is a highly advanced technique. Watson reassures the nonprofessional that even he does not complicate things by trying to add much, if any, extra spin. But he does emphasize avoiding the cardinal sin of the short game: decelerating the clubhead through impact. A student himself with a cautionary eye for pitfalls, Watson borrows ideas from golfers he admires: citing Byron Nelson, he invokes his mentor's famous "rocking chair" image for good weight transfer, and then offers a swing key from Tom Kite, who focuses on equalizing the length of his backswing and through-swing.

In my opinion, learning how to pitch the ball is the most difficult lesson for a golfer. Why? Because you must learn how to hit the ball with an abbreviated or less-than-full swing. You must feel how far to hit the ball, and feel is the most elusive part of golf.

Almost all golfers practice nothing but a full swing. Very few practice the short, 40-yard pitch shot. A full swing is easier to master, since the golfer is usually repeating the same swing for each club to make the ball go the maximum distance with that particular club. But to hit the ball less than maximum distance with a particular club, you must shorten the swing *yet still hit the ball firmly*. This shot causes many golfers to shake with fear and has resulted in the club as well as the ball being launched in disgust.

The two main requisites to good pitching are setting up well and making a firm swing that accelerates through the ball. When you face a less-than-full shot, you have to think in terms of a less-than-full backswing. The common error is taking the club back too far and decelerating through impact, which is like a boxer pulling his punches. It causes all sorts of miss-hit and misdirected pitch shots....

My philosophy is to play pitches [and chips] with as little spin as possible, because spin is hard to control and predict. Learning to pitch the ball with control and finesse, over hazards and near the pin, is a joyful part of the game and an art form in itself.

THE PROPER ADDRESS POSITION PREVIEWS THE IMPACT POSITION

My setup position [for a pitch], as in all my shots, is very similar to my impact position—a sneak preview. It's basically the same as my chipping setup. My stance is slightly open, 10 to 20 degrees, since I want my left side to be out of the way or slightly open at impact. The body weight favors the left foot and is centered on the balls of the feet. My knees are slightly flexed, my rear end stuck out so that I can hang my upper body and arms out over the ball. I call my rear end my "ballast." When stuck out properly, it serves as a counterweight to my upper body, which must hang out over the ball so that the arms can swing freely without running into the body on the downswing. I sole the club very lightly.

Two common faulty setup positions are:

- Standing too tall, which means the upper body doesn't hang over enough. The upper body then must either dip on the backswing or turn too horizontally, forcing the arms and club to swing too flatly around the body. Both of these swings result in poor balance and poor timing, causing inconsistency.

- The knees are too straight and the body slumps over the ball, forcing too much weight onto the toes. In this position you must rely on perfect hand-eye coordination for consistent shotmaking. With straight, unflexed knees you cannot transfer the weight properly during the swing.

I ADVOCATE BYRON NELSON'S "ROCKING CHAIR" WEIGHT TRANSFER

The pitch shot is made easier and more consistent when the lower body moves in timing with the arms and hands. Lack of movement in the lower body causes an inconsistent path of the club through impact. I jokingly refer to this bad habit as having "cement legs."

Do not stand still and just use your hands and arms. Use your hips and knees in the swing.

Tom Watson hits a short pitch during a practice round before the 2006 U.S. Senior Open. Watson's approach to the shot is straightforward—he emphasizes a synchronized movement of the arms and body and warns against decelerating the clubhead through impact. (AP Images)

How? I picture Byron Nelson, whose short, firm pitching swing was a smooth blend of both upper and lower body movement. Byron teaches a rocking-chair motion that coordinates the upper and lower body action, making possible a consistent hit time after time.

"There is no need to tell one who has played a great deal of championship golf that it's the short game that decides contests."

—Tommy Armour

The weight, which starts mostly on the left foot, transfers to the right foot and back to the left foot during the swing. The hit of the ball occurs during the transfer of weight from the right foot to the left foot. Byron couldn't help but hit the ball solidly and straight. His clubface stayed square just prior to and through impact the longest of any player I've ever watched—for nearly a foot; not only pitching but on his full swing as well.

A simple thought that Byron taught me is to return my hips and elbows to their original address position as I'm hitting through the ball. This forces me to synchronize the motion of my arms and lower body.

ACCELERATE THE CLUBHEAD AND DON'T OVER-SWING

Tom Kite, who is an excellent pitcher from 30 to 40 yards with a wedge, makes sure to avoid the common pitfall of decelerating the club through the impact zone. Tom's key thought is to swing the club back only as far as he swings it through.

Many high-handicap players swing with little or no weight transfer. Therefore they have to take the club back too far in the effort to produce the same clubhead

TOM WATSON'S PITCHING STROKESAVERS:

- Synchronize the movement of the arms and body.
- Swing the club back and through the same distance.
- Think of the pitch as an underarm toss of the ball.

speed they could produce with a proper weight transfer and shorter swing. If you have a problem over-swinging, first check your weight transfer. Then try swinging the club back shorter and accelerating it more firmly through the ball.

MAKE AN UNDERHANDED MOTION

Golf is an underhanded game. Since we are swinging down at the ball, we have to use an underhanded motion with the right hand and arm through the impact area. You can get the feeling by throwing a ball, because the underhanded motion we're talking about is similar to a throwing action.

The Pitching Supermodel: Tiger Woods

2000 • Jim McLean

Through a series of books and DVDs, frequent appearances on the Golf Channel, countless essays and lessons in *Golf* magazine and now *Golf Digest* (for which he serves as an "Instruction Editor"), and his school in Miami, the inexhaustible Jim McLean has established himself as one of the era's most familiar and influential golf theorists. This former PGA Teacher of the Year, who once played on a University of Houston team that featured future Tour stars Bruce Lietzke, Fuzzy Zoeller, and Bill Rodgers, is one of the best at analyzing the techniques, from setup to follow-through, of great golfers past and present. In this essay, he scrupulously breaks down Tiger Woods' 40- to 60-yard pitch shot, as developed under the auspices of his then-coach Butch Harmon. Beginners in particular should note the differences he points out between Tiger's approach to driving and his setup and backswing action for the pitch.

I love to see juniors copying a tour player's swing to learn a new shot. I think you do yourself a disservice by not taking a serious look at the pitching action used by Tiger Woods to hit high, soft-landing pitch shots from around 40 to 60 yards out from the green. This shot is magical, because the ball seems to stop the moment it hits the green. It doesn't spin back or take several hops forward. To quote a former golf commentator whose name escapes me, "it sits down like a hound dog in front of a fireplace."

Tiger is a short-game wizard, although most fans know him for his power-driving skills that allow him to drive par 4 holes and reach par 5 holes in 2 shots, instead of the regulation three. It's no wonder that Tiger won the 1999 PGA, his second major championship, and finished the year off at the top of the PGA Tour's money standing list.

I give Tiger and Butch Harmon, his [former] coach, a heck of a lot of credit for their hard practice and perseverance. There was a time when Tiger was criticized for not being able to control his wedge shots, with Butch taking much of the heat. They both had a plan a couple of years ago, and nobody can doubt it's been executed. Tiger has evolved into such a great wedge player that I consider him a supermodel.

SUPER SETUP

When watching Tiger set up to play a 40- to 60-yard wedge shot under normal conditions of lie and weather I have noticed that he's very careful not to position the ball well back in the stance. This is because he knows that such a position promotes a steep backswing action, sharp descending hit, and a shot that spins back. Tiger's priority is to hit the ball all the way to the hole and have it come down so softly you would think it was attached to a miniature parachute. Therefore, he plays the ball closer to his left heel than to the midpoint of his stance. He sets his hands even with the ball or slightly behind it. Ultimately, Tiger wants to come into impact with the clubface going nicely under the ball, not digging into the turf, so he is careful not to set his hands well ahead of the ball, which takes bounce off the wedge. I have noticed too that quite recently Tiger has widened his pitching stance some to prevent an overly steep swing and those *shooters* he was criticized for hitting early in his career. Don't get me wrong. Tiger's stance is still narrow, with the distance between his feet measuring about 10 inches.

Tiger's stance is slightly open, too, with the left foot a few inches farther from the target line than the right foot. His hips are also slightly open, pointing slightly left of target. This setup provides Tiger with a heightened sense of freedom. Because the hips are in a cleared, or open, position, he prevents an inside takeaway and too much action on the backswing. The added bonus of setting up this way is that he feels more confident about making square and solid contact with the ball. So will you.

Although Tiger opens his feet and hips, he's very careful to set his shoulders fairly square or just the slightest bit open to the target line.

JIM MCLEAN'S PITCHING STROKESAVERS:

- Open the feet and hips, but square the shoulders.
- Hinge the wrists freely on the backswing.
- Keep the left wrist stable, and hold the clubface open through impact on the downswing.
- Control the pace of the swing with a brisk body turn.

This pitching setup is much different from the one Tiger uses to launch the long ball on the golf course. When driving, he closes his feet as Ben Hogan did and opens his shoulders as Jack Nicklaus still does. This combination of closed feet and open shoulders was used by another great player, Sam Snead, also a super powerful driver of the ball.

When hitting the soft pitch, Tiger is not interested in generating power. He is looking to finesse the ball to the hole. This is why he sets up the way he does and tracks a line from the ball to the target with his eyes. This tracking work helps him sense or feel the distance in his hands. Incidentally, like Jack Nicklaus, Tiger uses an interlock grip rather than the overlap grip used by most PGA Tour players. The interlock grip should be considered simply because it provides you with a sense of unity to the hands. Further, and more important, when hitting this particular shot the way Tiger does, you must keep the clubface open through impact. Gripping like Tiger may help you avoid slippage in the hitting area. It certainly doesn't hurt.

When you feel you are comfortably correct at address, be sure to follow Tiger's other fundamentals to success: taking a nice fluid practice swing that matches the action he intends to employ when actually hitting the shot and visualizing the perfect shot in his mind's eyes before swinging.

SUPER BACKSWING

The wonderful thing about Tiger's backswing action is that it's relaxed, with the wrists hinging freely. It's very different from his full-power swing in which he has a late wrist set. There is no effort on his part to make a one-piece takeaway—that is, with the club straight back along the target line, low to the ground, and directed by the triangle formed by the shoulders and arms. Many high handicappers make this mistake, thinking all shots require this type of one-piece action.

Going back, Tiger's arms swing on a much more upright plane than his turning shoulders, while the club moves slightly outside the target line. As for the weight-shifting action, it is more of a mini-shift. I say that because Tiger leaves much more of his weight on his left foot and leg when hitting this shot than any full shot.

Tiger usually swings the club back to the three-quarter point, for this length shot. This helps him stay relaxed and maintain a certain good personal feel for the clubhead.

SUPER DOWNSWING

Indeed, Tiger employs perfect shifting and rotating action of the lower body, but the action is far less powerful or forceful. Another reason the shifting and rotating action is not so brisk and full is that Tiger is controlling the pace of his swing with the pace of his rotation.

A lot of speed Tiger generates on the downswing comes from the turn of his body. While he nudges the majority of his weight over to his left side, his upper body stays well behind the ball. As the shifting action continues, Tiger's arms accelerate faster. His arms bring the club through the ball, rather than down into it on a sharp angle, while his wrists unhinge.

Butch Harmon…worked with Tiger to maintain a firm pressure in his left hand to keep his left wrist stable in the hitting area. If the left wrist breaks down, the right hand and forearm tend to rotate rapidly in a counterclockwise direction, causing the clubface to close. The result is a low shot that runs upon landing. You want to keep the clubface of the sand wedge or lob wedge open when playing this shot so that you loft the ball nicely into the air and land it super softly onto the green, next to the hole.

CHAPTER 9

SAND PLAY

Toiling Through the
Bunkers of Repentance

How to Recover from Bunkers

1924 • Cyril J.H. Tolley

Cyril Tolley, a pipe-smoking, ascot-wearing former P.O.W., was one of Great Britain's top amateurs after WWI, but is best remembered for almost snuffing out Bobby Jones' 1930 Grand Slam bid—extending the Yank to 19 holes in the British Amateur. Tolley had already won that championship in 1920, the Welsh Championship in 1921 and 1923, and the French Open in 1924. Then he wrote an instructional book boldly called *The Modern Golfer*. Indeed, at times this piece about playing various bunker shots sounds as modern as later ones by Raymond Floyd and Ernie Els, especially concerning "explosion" shots—but with one important difference. Tolley and his compatriots—lacking a sand wedge—employed a "niblick," a club like today's 9 iron, and used a firm grip and little wrist break. The club almost stopped when it struck the sand, curtailing the follow-through—quite a contrast to the high finish today's teachers often recommend.

The common form of trouble all grades of players encounter is bunker trouble. There are many ways of trying to recover, but they all vary in execution, according to the situation of the particular bunker on the course. The bunkers around the green will be the first I shall deal with. I should have said that the texture of the sand will help you in deciding what kind of recovery you should attempt, and another factor will be what kind of lie you are fortunate enough to find in the bunker.

If you are lying badly, you have no option in the matter; the ball must be dug out, and the method employed is called the explosion shot. If the ball is lying well, you can either play an "explosion" or take the ball cleanly. It will be found from experience that the former is the one most generally used, for it is less dangerous and is also easier.

The theory of an explosive shot is that the ball is not hit by the club at all. The stroke is played by aiming at a mark some distance, anything up to three inches, behind the ball. As the club enters the sand, it displaces a certain amount, which has the effect of heaving out the ball. This displaced sand forms a wall between the clubhead and the ball, and it is this wall which causes the ball to move. As a general principle…the shorter the shot required the steeper should be the angle of descent of the club, and the less sand you aim at behind the ball. The longer the shot, the flatter must be the swing of the club, and the club has to enter the sand also but not quite as near the ball. If the sand is very light and loose, you can afford to take plenty of it, and you also can hit your hardest. If it is heavy and wet, there is no need to hit so hard or to take so much sand. To play any of these shots you must remember above all things that the head and body must be kept absolutely motionless; in other words, the body may pivot but must not move laterally.

You stand fairly open with the ball about opposite the left heel, and you play the stroke as a slice. That is to say, you aim to the left of the hole, and in taking the club back you take it away from the body. Your forward swing is across your body, and you will finish your stroke with the club well to the left of the line. The divot mark must also point to the left. You address the ball with the face of the club turned out, and the stroke must be played and finished with the face in relatively the same position…. On account of taking the sand well behind the ball, you will find that it is impossible to take a long follow-through. Try as hard as you like, and the clubhead will be found to have only just emerged from the sand. The hands must be kept low after the ball has been struck.

Very often you will find that the utmost you can hope for is to get the ball on the green, and having accomplished this you have to be satisfied. When the shot does not look so fearsome or difficult, you should try to get the ball out on that side of the hole which will give you the easiest putt. So many players do not consider the necessity of doing this, and rush headlong into the hazard, and have a terrific lash at the ball. Sometimes it will come out—generally it won't. Don't forget that golf is a thinking game, and must be treated as such….

If you are unfortunate enough to be caught in a bunker midway between the tee and the green, the type of shot you employ to recover depends firstly on the

CYRIL J.H. TOLLEY'S STROKESAVERS:

- Use an open stance, with the ball about opposite the left heel.
- Swing out-to-in, as if hitting a slice.
- Open the clubface, and try to keep it open through impact.

position of the ball in the bunker. If you are lying well back you have, provided the lie is not a bad one, a reasonable chance of completely recovering the resultant loss of distance caused by your faulty tee shot. Sometimes you can take as strong a club as a light iron, and to play the shot successfully you should play slightly across the back of the ball, but you must allow for the ball to swing to the right near the end of its flight.

"If your opponent is playing several shots in vain attempts to extricate himself from a bunker, do not stand near him and audibly count his strokes. It would be justifiable homicide if he wound up his pitiable exhibition by applying his niblick to your head."

—HARRY VARDON

Take a long, flat swing with the face of the club turned out, and endeavor to strike the sand not more than half an inch behind the ball. If you follow-through close to the sand, the loft of the club will get the ball up quickly enough. Take great care not to move your head or body, and concentrate on looking at the sand under the ball. Play the stroke in a similar way to an iron shot, only with this difference: that you hit the sand before the ball, instead of the ball before the sand.

If, on the other hand, you are lying badly, or are too close to the face of the bunker to get any distance, you must first see in what direction you should hit the ball to give you the easiest possible next stroke to put you on the green. Sometimes you can only just get out of the bunker, and then you must try to get out with the least possible chance of failure. Never try to do too much out of a hazard, for you must not forget you are considerably handicapped in not being allowed to sole your club in the sand. The great thing to remember in bunker play, and in all golf for that matter, is always to play the easy shot; do not try to play the difficult and spectacular shot; you will only look ridiculous and your remorse will be 10 times greater if you fail to get the ball in play.

From *The Modern Golfer*, by Cyril J.H. Tolley. W. Collins Sons & Co., Ltd., Glasgow, Scotland. Copyright © 1924 by Alfred A. Knopf, Inc.

Getting Out of Traps Easily

1949 • Johnny Revolta and Charles B. Cleveland

In his prime, Johnny Revolta won the 1935 PGA and competed in the Ryder Cup that year and again in 1937. His teammates on the American "Dream Team" that captured the 1935 Cup were Walter Hagen, Gene Sarazen, Horton Smith, Paul Runyan, and Henry Picard, all short-game wizards. Years later, as teachers and writers for *Golf Digest*, Runyan and Revolta became perhaps America's leading short-game authorities. If Runyan wrote for students of the game, Revolta wrote for the masses, pitching a system that would have sold well on late-night infomercials. He made everything sound easy, including bunker shots. In his 1949 book, which ThinkandReachPar.com reissued and turned into a three-part video, Revolta said one needs merely to trust the sand wedge and use the "modern" variation of the explosion shot, assuring readers they have a wide margin for error.

The sand trap shot is—and should be—the easiest shot in the bag. There is more room for error in this shot than in any other. You can hit a half inch, an inch, or even two inches behind the ball and still be all right. With other shots, that margin of error would result in a bad shot.

An explosion shot out of a sand trap is easy with a 9 iron. With a sand iron this shot is a lead-pipe cinch.

Ordinarily sand traps are located in two places—bordering the fairways between the tee and green or right around the putting green. Golfers just taking up the game often don't get into these bunkers because their shots are generally short enough to miss them. As your game gets better you'll find yourself in these traps fairly often. The fellows who lay out golf courses specifically locate these traps so as to catch the better golfer either when his shots go a little off line or when his fairway shots get enough distance to carry to the edge of the green. So don't overlook this phase of your game.

Beginners have a great fear of sand traps. I presume this is due to some mental quirk which ties up traps with the difficulties of the game. They try to roll the ball out with a putter, scoop it out with an iron—anything, in fact, just to get the ball out. And generally they wind up taking several strokes to do it.

There are, of course, all kinds of sand traps. Some are so shallow they are little more than dents in the fairways filled with sand. Others are so deep that you need a ladder to climb in and out of them. And there are those in between.

In some the sand is loose, and in other traps it is packed tight. Especially after a rain the sand is most likely to be packed hard in any trap.

In very loose sand, the ball occasionally will fall in with such force as to become partially buried. Sometimes in demonstrations I take a golf ball and stamp on it so that it is completely buried and then blast it out onto the green. You are not likely to encounter that tough a problem. But I have found it an effective means of showing what can be done with an explosion shot.

Occasionally—but very rarely—a chip shot or an approach shot [similar to those taken off grass]…are feasible out of a sand trap. These few possibilities exist when you have a shallow bunker. Sometimes a professional, gambling, may even use a No. 4 wood out of a shallow bunker for a long shot.

But I can't advise gambling for the average player. The odds are too much against him. In at least 90 percent of the cases, the explosion shot is the surest, safest, and best way out of sand.

And—with the sand iron—the easiest.

A very open stance is needed for an explosion shot. The left foot will be drawn back even farther from the line of flight than it [is] in the chip and approach shots.…

Take your approach stance; then shift the clubface slightly back and readjust your grip. Rearrange your stance so that the clubface is square to the hole. Then follow with your natural swing. Seemingly you will be aiming to the left of

JOHNNY REVOLTA'S STROKESAVERS:

- Open the clubface first, then take the grip.
- Wiggle the feet into the sand, establishing a firm stance.
- Trust the loft of the club, freeing the mind to focus on the proper swing moves.
- Aim for a spot in the sand one half to two inches behind the ball— not at the ball.
- Don't be afraid to hit hard.

the cup as you swing, but don't worry about it. The maneuver will send the ball straight for the hole. Just follow your normal swing.

Let me encourage you to work on this explosion stance until you have it well in mind....

Sand, as you know, shifts. So it is especially important that you get your feet well anchored. As you take your proper stance, wiggle your feet until you get a good footing.

As in most other shots, you play the explosion off your left instep.

But—and this is an important difference—you aim for a spot just behind the ball instead of aiming to hit the ball itself.

The reason is that you want to hit the sand before the ball. Your clubface hits first the sand and then the ball. The sand acts as a cushion. Actually the force of the blow drives the sand against the ball, and the pressure pops it out onto the green.

For this reason don't be afraid to hit it too hard. The sand will deaden most of the force and leave just enough to toss the ball out onto the green.

In getting ready for this shot, take your proper stance for an explosion. Then pick the spot you want to hit in the sand—about a half inch to an inch behind the ball—and aim for it. It is against the rules to ground your club in the sand and mark your spot, so it will take a little practice to adjust your sights.

But remember, you don't have to worry. You have plenty of room to hit and still make a good explosion shot.

Using my system for getting out of traps, you will find it easy whether the sand is fluffy or packed hard—whether your ball is lying on top or buried in the sand. If the ball is buried deeply, just aim a little farther behind and put a little more speed in your swing.

Where does Danny the Duffer go wrong? He makes his error in failing to have confidence in his club. The sand iron is designed to get the ball out of the sand. It has the heavy flange to keep from being buried. It has a big clubface to give you plenty of hitting surface. It has a lot of loft to get the ball into the air. Everything is built into the club.

Danny the Duffer, however, doesn't trust his club. He wants to help get the ball into the air. He scoops at the ball. As a result the club either digs into the sand or he tops the ball. And it is still in the sand trap.

Trust your club to do the job. For yourself, simply concentrate on swinging it properly.

WHAT GOES UP

While riding shotgun for "aviator" Howard Hughes, Gene Sarazen was inspired to create the sand wedge that revolutionized bunker play. After observing that lowering the flaps makes an airplane go up, he added gobs of lead to an old niblick, creating a flange that tilted the leading edge of the face upward. Thus, when struck downward, it would slide, or "bounce" through sand, rather than dig in. After using his "secret weapon" to win the 1932 British Open, he likened wielding it to how "you would swing an axe when chopping a tree."

This shot to be effective has to travel through the sand and emerge in the normal fashion, just like any other swing. It can't hit into the sand and stay there. You can't hit down at the ball and have the club stop as it reaches the ball. It has to cut through, spraying sand, and follow on through.

Combined with chip shots, the average player will cut 6 to 8 strokes off his score with good explosion shots. And there isn't anyone who wouldn't give plenty to knock his score down that much.

From *Johnny Revolta's Short Cuts to Better Golf*, by Johnny Revolta and Charles B. Cleveland. Thomas Y. Crowell Company, New York, N.Y. Copyright © 1949 by Johnny Revolta and Charles B. Cleveland. Used by permission of Richard Myers and New South Media, LLC, as publisher of and agent for the re-issued copyrighted book. (www.thinkandreachpar.com 864-675-0038)

The Blaster

1962 · Gary Player

Gary Player, golf's eternal optimist and greatest ambassador, never saw a course he didn't like best. And he never saw a bunker he didn't enjoy hitting out of. Johnny Revolta insisted sand was an easy challenge, but Player went further by claiming it was often the preferable lie around the green, and saying bunker shots, while sometimes problematic, were part of the short game, distinguishable from *trouble shots* that can be executed only by advanced players. By 1962, the young, fit, 155-pound, practice-obsessed South African had won three of an eventual nine majors and joined Arnold Palmer and Jack Nicklaus in the era's "Big Three." He also began writing instructional books, including the nearly forgotten *Play Golf with Player* in which he endorsed the explosion shot, or "blaster." We pay strict attention because, as Jack Nicklaus stated, "The best sand player I have ever seen is, without doubt, Gary Player."

I am not going to start off by telling you that the bunker shot is the easiest to play. It is not, but I do think it is not half as difficult to play as some golfers imagine. With only a little know-how you should always succeed in getting the ball out. It takes a lot of practice to get it close.

Preparation for a bunker shot starts immediately after you walk into the trap, for you must quickly decide whether the sand is hard, wet, or soft, because a slightly different technique is required in each case.

Start by taking a firm stance. You are allowed by the rules to imbed your feet into the sand. If you think it necessary don't hesitate to dig deep—but please, please smooth the sand again when you have completed your shot. A man who leaves his marks in a bunker is one of the worst pests in golf, and if I had my way I would penalize him two shots. There is enough chance in golf without an innocent party having to play out of your footmarks.

For the normal bunker shot, i.e. soft sand, the feet are comfortably close together and the stance is opened fairly wide, the left foot drawn about eight inches back of the right. With the clubface slightly open at address, the club is taken back *outside* the line of flight to the hole. This is one of the few occasions this happens in the swing and will result in you hitting from outside to in, across the ball.

This action would normally cause a slice, but in this case it helps the clubhead cut through the sand. Some left-to-right spin is imparted to the ball however, and this should be allowed for by *aiming left* of the hole, depending of course on slope.

For bunkers close into the green, the club must enter the sand *two inches behind the ball*, so the club is held in that position at address. Do not watch the ball. Watch the spot of impact, which in this case is the sand. In bunkers 20 yards or so from the green, hit one inch behind the ball. Farther out than that you can hit the ball cleanly.

No matter where your ball lies in a bunker, position it opposite the left heel, otherwise the club is inclined to bury itself in the ground. The bunker shot does not require strength, and before describing the swing you should appreciate that it is not a case of punching down into the sand, but of cutting through the sand.

The most important aspect of the swing is that it must be firm throughout. If you hold back, or quit on the shot as the Americans say, you have little chance of making a good stroke.

The stroke is played mostly with the hands and arms and the natural movement of the knees. The backswing is curtailed, with the wrists cocking naturally, but the follow-through is full. In a bunker you can never follow-through too far.

"The more I practice, the luckier I get."

—GARY PLAYER

The method just described is for a normal, good lie in a bunker. If the ball should be plugged, or in a foot mark, or if you are prevented from swinging back, play short of the hole, because the ball is going to run farther than it normally would.

Many Americans play this shot with a square face at address, but I still prefer to open the face and concentrate more on hitting deep than following through.

I think the *most difficult lie* in a bunker is when the ball rests in the bunker face. Here the tendency is to sky the ball by hitting too far behind it. In this

Gary Player executes a tricky bunker shot during the 1961 British Open. Jack Nicklaus once called the South African "the best sand player I have ever seen." (Bob Thomas/Getty Images)

position hit only one inch behind the ball and apply more force to counteract the height which is bound to result. It is difficult to follow through fully on an up-slope, but try and swing normally.

When the reverse position applies and your ball lies on the down-slope, hit two inches behind and again concentrate on hitting down. This is one time you really must trust the loft of the club to pop the ball out.

Playing from a side-slope, or hanging lie, when the ball is higher than the feet, you will be inclined to hook the ball, so grip the club short to enable you to swing more upright and aim right. When the ball lies below your feet, grip the club fully, play normally, and aim left.

For a normal bunker shot I grip the club an inch or so short of the top because I get better feel this way.

If sand in a bunker is wet or hard, the clubhead will skid in the first instance and bounce in the second. Play this shot more softly than the others, for the tendency here is to be too strong. It will help if you imagine the pin three yards closer than it really is. Still hit two inches behind the ball.

The only time you hit with all your might in a bunker is when a clod or stone or some similar obstruction lodges between the ball and club. Then you hit hard behind the obstruction—and hope.

Normally in a bunker I am very confident of getting close to the hole. I try my best to hole out every bunker shot. This is not arrogance on my part, only my way of training myself not to funk the shot. It paid off handsomely in the 1959 British Open when I was in 12 traps near the green and only once failed to get down in two.

If I had to back any particular phase of my game against the best in the world I think it would be out of a bunker....

One last word to handicap players. Make sure you get out of the sand at your first attempt, even if you do knock the ball over the back of the green to start with. When you are out, at least you might have a chance to chip close to the hole, or even putt. If you stay in the sand, the chances are you will be rattled and will still hit a bad shot at your second attempt anyway.

From *Play Golf with Player*, by Gary Player. Collins, London, England and Glasgow, Scotland. Copyright © 1962 by Gary Player. Reprinted with the permission of Gary Player Group, Inc.

GARY PLAYER'S STROKESAVERS:

- Check the sand first: is it hard, wet, or soft? Then size up the lie.
- Vary the stance, depth of hit, and swing speed accordingly.
- Grip down on the club for better feel.
- Bunker play isn't easy, but know-how and practice lead to success.
- Advanced players should try to hole every bunker shot.
- High handicappers should just focus on getting it out.

Relax, Here's How to Master the Sand

1989 • Ray Floyd with Larry Dennis

Raymond Floyd, who joined the Tour in 1963, and Sam Snead are the only individuals to win PGA titles in four decades. Unlike Snead, Floyd won the U.S. Open, as well as a Masters and two PGAs, as his confident short game contributed to his clutch play. Mark O'Meara said Floyd was "the most intimidating player I've ever played against. He plays every shot like it's the last shot of his life. He's like a black leopard, stalking the jungle." Despite this description, Floyd, in this essay from his popular book, instructed readers to *relax* when hitting the relatively easy sand shot. Floyd, whose swing was less steep than Gary Player's, described the splashier *modern* explosion shot, saying the follow-through should match the length of the backswing. He also offered a "flight-plan," detailing how far the ball will carry, and then roll—plus instructions on how to apply spin.

I've been named Sand Player of the Year on three occasions by *Golf* magazine, an honor determined by vote of the Tour players, so I guess I know something about getting out of bunkers. Maybe it's because I get in so many of them. But anybody who plays much golf is going to get in a lot of them, too, so he had better find a way to consistently play the ball out and onto the green, hopefully with a chance for a one-putt....

You need a method to get the ball from sand repetitively and well, and it must be one that incorporates some kind of blast or explosion shot. Picking and putting out of sand usually doesn't work unless the bunker is flat with no lip, and you don't see many of those around.

Let me quickly mention a few different techniques. One technique I call the skimming method, which calls for more of a wide, shallow swing, taking a very shallow cut of sand very close to the back of the ball. Ken Venturi, among other good players, is an advocate of this style. He almost (but not quite) picks the ball off the sand. Kenny has described it as "clipping the ball off a carpet." It's an excellent method from good lies and when the sand is shallow and firm. Properly executed, the shot puts a lot of spin on the ball. But I feel it's rather dangerous for most players, mainly because you must strike the sand so close to the ball.

The opposite method is one in which a steep, V-shaped swing is used, striking down farther behind the ball and making a steep entry into the sand. The club cuts deeply under the ball and throws out a lot of sand. Gary Player, Lee Trevino, and Billy Casper, among others, use this method, which is very good from poor lies and deep, softer sand. Because it lets you strike farther behind the ball, it allows a great margin for error, but because of the steep angle you have to be careful not to leave the club in the sand. I think you have to work too hard with this method, because you are digging out a lot of sand, and I don't use it myself. But the three guys I just mentioned are among the best sand players in history, so who am I to say it's wrong?

I use what I call the explosion method, as do many good players, and I recommend it for you. It is more or less a compromise between the two styles I've just described. I think it's the easiest method with the least chance for error.

You will encounter many different kinds of shots in a bunker. The explosion method, with variations, will handle all of them. I can play any kind of bunker shot I desire. I can play a low, running shot, a low shot that spins, a high lob, [and] a high shot that spins. I can hit 10 inches behind the ball in a footprint and pop it out nicely. I literally can take a 4 wood into the sand and play a pretty decent shot onto the green.…

THE NORMAL SAND SHOT

First, let's get rid of your fear. Most amateur players are afraid of the sand for two related reasons: the shot is an unknown, one they don't know how to handle because they don't know the proper technique to use; and they seldom, if ever, practice it, probably because they don't know how to do it in the first place. Let me explain how to do it, which will take care of both problems.

The normal sand shot, one in which the ball is sitting reasonably well on top of the sand and on a reasonably level surface, is really a pretty easy shot. I know you've heard that before, and you probably don't believe it, but it's true. It's one that does not require precise club-to-ball contact, and so allows a considerable margin for error.…

All sand shots require that you create an explosion of sand that carries the ball out. Think of having a handful of sand with the ball perched on top, then just making an underhand toss out of the bunker. That same motion removes the ball from the sand with a club, only now the clubface sliding through the sand creates the handful of sand with the ball sitting on top....

Open the clubface about 30 or 35 degrees to allow the flange or bounce—remember, that's the bottom portion of the club that on a sand wedge hangs below the leading edge—to work properly. The clubface should be open to your *stance line*, which is pointing to the left of your target, but the face should be pointing at your target, which is the flag or wherever you want the ball to start. Then swing the club back along your stance line, a little to the outside of your target line and on an upright plane. It will come back down across and to the inside of your target line on the follow-through, but because the clubface is aimed at the target, the ball will start there. It's not something you have to worry about. During the swing, keep your eyes focused on [a] point two or three inches behind the ball. Be a little wristy, letting the hands hinge and unhinge freely, and use your right hand to send the clubhead down and underneath the ball and up again in a slicing action. The impact will force the sand up, carrying the ball with it....

RAYMOND FLOYD'S STROKESAVERS:

- Be fearless—this shot has a high margin for error.
- Visualize the ball perched on a handful of sand.
- Imagine making an underhand toss that carries both out of the bunker.
- Expect the shot to carry about three-quarters of the distance to the hole, and roll the rest of the way.

The finish is critically important. Do not let the club stop in the sand, because if you do the ball will stop there too. A good rule of thumb is to make your follow-through as long as your backswing.

The consistency of the sand—how course or fine it is, how soft or firm—has a great effect on the shot. With practice, you will learn how to handle it. In coarser, more firmly packed sand, the ball will come out hotter and travel farther, so you swing easier; soft, fluffy sand tends to deaden the impact, so you must create more speed with a longer swing.

Practice also will help you determine how much swing speed—thus, how long a swing—you need to carry the ball certain distances from sand of certain consistencies.

"For a right-handed player, the sand shot is executed almost entirely by the right hand slapping or thumping the sand behind the ball."

—CLAUDE HARMON

The arc of your swing—how steep or shallow it is—also determines the height and length of your shot. The ball will come out of the sand at about the same angle that the club enters the sand. To get a higher, shorter shot, make a steeper, more sharply descending entry into the sand. For a lower, longer shot, make a shallower, more sweeping entry.

In general, shots from the sand should carry about three-quarters of the way to the hole and roll the rest of the way. Thus, on a 60-foot shot you should try to carry the ball 45 feet and let it roll 15 feet. That will vary, of course, depending on the slope from which you are playing and the lie of the ball…. On certain shots, when you have a good lie on firm sand, you also can make a shallower cut closer to the ball that will apply more spin and stop the ball more quickly.

The Downhill Bunker Shot *and* The Long Bunker Shot

1989 • Nick Faldo with Vivien Saunders

Nick Faldo was inspired to become a golfer watching Jack Nicklaus and Tom Watson on TV. Playing his initial Ryder Cup in 1977, the 20-year-old Brit and Peter Oosterhuis beat Nicklaus and Raymond Floyd in fourball, and he defeated Watson in singles. In time he'd be a Ryder Cup star and win three British Opens and Masters. During most of his time as the world's best player, he surprised traditionalists by having a female caddie, Fanny Sunesson. A year before hiring her, he broke a literary tradition by writing an instructional book with a woman: the former champion player and highly celebrated golf teacher Vivien Saunders. In this essay about two of the toughest bunker shots, Faldo and Saunders describe how to hit from the devilish downhill lie, and tackle the equally vexing problem of fairway bunkers. On the latter, they offer advice that goes back to Vardon and Tolley, cautioning against being too greedy.

Perhaps the most difficult of all bunker shots is the one where the ball just runs into the back of the bunker and leaves you with a ball sitting on a down-slope, still with the face of the bunker in front of you to negotiate.... You are going to get less height to the shot and may be faced with one which is virtually unplayable. Don't expect to get the ball up quickly and even if you do get good height, it isn't going to stop easily on the green. The ball is probably going to run as far if not farther than it carries....

The difficulty with the downhill lie is that there is in effect no sand directly in front of the ball but lots of sand to negotiate behind it. You need to produce a fairly steep up-and-down action where the clubhead rises well in the backswing, then gets down into the sand behind the ball and very definitely is held down beyond impact as the ball starts on its way.

To play this shot you need to get the wrists cocking early and suddenly to get sufficient steepness in the backswing. I play the shot with a wide stance, the

Nick Faldo hits a downhill bunker shot during the 2000 European Masters. Faldo's approach to this tough shot emphasizes balance and a special technique. He counsels that golfers align their shoulders with the lie and hold the club down well beyond impact, following the slope. (AP Images)

NICK FALDO'S STROKESAVERS:

- Take several rehearsal swings for downhill bunker shots—balance is key.
- Play the downhill bunker shot with a wide stance, the ball back, and an early wrist cock.
- Hold the club down well beyond impact, following the slope.
- Don't be too greedy on long bunker shots. Take a short iron and just get it out if the ball is sitting down.
- Try a long iron—or even a fairway wood—and pick the ball cleanly off the sand if it's sitting up.

weight well on my left foot and with the right shoulder held high at address. This helps to get the swing moving up and down the slope, with the added feeling of picking the club up sharply.... It is well worth having a couple of rehearsals of the backswing....

I keep the clubface open, ensuring that the clubhead goes into the sand about an inch behind the ball. The last thing you want is to catch too much sand behind the ball. For this reason you should play the ball quite well back in the feet.... The swing is now one which goes very much up and down beyond the ball through impact, working hard at maintaining balance as you do this.

THE LONG BUNKER SHOT

The golden rule with long bunker shots is not to be too greedy.... Don't take risks unnecessarily and...choose a sensible route back to safety.... In some countries fairway bunkers give you a really good chance for getting length. They hardly have any lip, and you can even take a long iron or a wood if the lie permits. But on most championship courses in Britain, and indeed elsewhere, the fairway bunkers are relatively punishing, and you have to look carefully at the face of the bunker in front of you to see what loft you need.... Look at the bunker shot from the side, and really do gauge what height is needed.

Next look at the lie. If the ball sits down at all in the sand you need to produce a contact which is the equivalent of a ball-divot contact on grass. This kind of shot should be played exactly like a normal iron shot, making absolutely certain that there is no question of taking any sand before the ball. You want a clean but slightly downward attack, taking the ball with a little bit of sand beyond. This time the danger is in a slightly fluffed contact which won't get the length you require. With a lie like this I would always be hesitant about taking a medium iron and certainly a long iron, unless there really is no bank in front of you.

If on the other hand the whole of the ball sits above the sand, you can pick the ball off almost cleanly, but again paying particular attention to the height you need. If the bunker is one of those low traps with nothing to negotiate then you can in effect try to catch the ball slightly cleanly or almost thinly for maximum distance....

The danger here for the really good golfer is in catching a "flyer" which goes a little farther than you expect and may run a little more on landing.... Long shots from a bunker are always very slightly hit-or-miss even for the very good player, the slightest contact with the sand taking the sting and distance out of the shot.

FACE UP

Vijay Singh won nine times in 2004, including the PGA Championship, to vault to the No. 1 ranking in the world. Although famous for his booming drives and lengthy practice sessions, his short game skills are often overlooked. In *Golf Digest*, he offered a tip for putting more spin on sand shots—to freeze the ball on the green—by holding the club open through impact and well into the finish, leaving the face pointing upward.

Sand Play Made Simple

1998 • Ernie Els with Steve Newell

Ernie Els, who has won three majors and a record seven World Match Play titles, reached his position in the pantheon of today's golfers with a flawless all-around game and a laidback temperament—evident during stressful situations—that earned him the nickname "The Big Easy." He's so calm and creative on bunker shots that he recalls fellow South African Gary Player at his peak. In this essay, Els approaches bunker shots with the positive, keep-it-simple attitude of Player, but provides more specific advice in the characteristic way of modern instruction. And instead of advocating "blasting" the ball free, he concentrates more on the genial "bounce" and "splash" effects. His point is that the sand iron's weight and the momentum of a free swing will give golfers the necessary shallow angle of attack and a smooth, accelerating swing that slides through the sand—*if* they allow the club to do its work.

THE TOOLS OF THE SAND TRADE

The first thing I want you to understand is that your sand wedge is designed to help you a lot more than you probably realize. Gene Sarazen, a golfer known as "The Squire," and one of only [five] players to have won all four major championships, invented this club way back in the 1930s. And he did it for a good reason. The wide flange on the sole of the club encourages the clubhead to slide through the sand. And that is the essence of good bunker play. The clubhead slides through the sand, throwing the ball up and out on the green. This is known as the "bounce effect." In many ways, though, it is better to think of it as the "splash effect." The clubhead splashes the ball out on a cushion of sand.

If you have a sharp leading edge, which was the case with the pre-1930s sand wedge and every other iron club in your bag today, the clubhead tends to dig into the sand rather than slide through it. And from a decent lie that's definitely not what you want. That's why Gene Sarazen reinvented the sand wedge. If it weren't for his good thinking, you can be certain that bunker play would be a lot more difficult today. Not a nice thought, is it?

THE STANDARD GREENSIDE BUNKER SHOT

Bunker play becomes 10 times easier if you stick to a few basic principles at address and 100 times more difficult if you ignore them…. The bounce effect on your sand wedge works best when the clubface is open—there's absolutely no way that clubface can dig too deep into the sand if it stays open. So that's your first principle of good bunker play, you have to open the clubface at address so that it actually faces right of the flag. It's important that you open the clubface first and then form your grip, which should be a little weaker than normal. If you grip it first and then open the face, it'll return to square at impact and cause you problems with height and accuracy.

Open your stance, too. That means your shoulders, hips, and toes need to be aiming, say, 30 feet left of the target. Spread your weight pretty evenly on both feet and, as you look down at your grip, I want you to check that your hands are level and with the ball, maybe even a fraction behind it. Finally, ease the pressure on your grip approximately 20 percent to ensure a nice, sensitive hold on the club. Now you're in good shape.

SWING ALONG YOUR BODY-LINE

The key now is to swing along the line of your toes and body—that's why the angles you establish at address are so important. Using a harmonious blend of body rotation and arm swing, try to make sure the clubhead follows the line of your toes as you swing it smoothly away from the ball. Then hinge your wrists to "set" the club in position at the top. Keep your grip pressure light and, as you change direction into your downswing, you'll sense a little bit of "lag" in your hands and wrists. That's good.

Now focus on an exact spot a couple of inches behind the ball to help regulate your point of entry and swing the clubhead through the sand. Your open stance will ensure that the clubhead travels on the necessary out-to-in path, but it helps if you sense that your hands stay close to your body through impact. The design of your sand wedge will take care of the rest for you. Also…my knees stay nice and flexed, stabilizing my swing as the club swings back and forth. The ball sets off a little left of target and then spins to the right, with a little bit of run on landing.

Once you've sorted out your technique, controlling distance will come a lot sooner than you think…. Simply alter the distance you want the ball to fly by lengthening or shortening your swing. The actual tempo of your swing and the pace at which you accelerate the clubhead through the sand should feel pretty much the same every time. That's a far more reliable method than trying to hit harder or softer from identical length swings.

HOW TO MAKE THE BALL FLY HIGH AND SIT DOWN

When there isn't much green to work with...I adapt my technique slightly to produce a higher, softer trajectory with virtually no run on the ball. I also use my 60-degree rather than my 56-degree sand wedge. Maximum loft for maximum height.

The changes you need to make couldn't be easier. Place the ball more central in your stance and feel that your weight favors your left side just a fraction. Then in your swing consciously hinge your wrists a little earlier in the takeaway, basically pointing the shaft of the club more at the sky. That establishes the steeper swing plane that you need for this shot.

In the downswing there are two things to bear in mind. Firstly, take a little less sand at impact—aim to hit behind the ball, say, one inch instead of two. Secondly, make a slightly longer swing than you would for a regular bunker shot from the same distance and really "zip" the clubhead through the sand under the ball to help generate the extra carry necessary to get it to the hole.

Take these thoughts into the bunker with you and commit yourself to being 100 percent positive. Remember, with this shot, the ball will have virtually no run on landing so you can afford to pitch it right up to the flag. Get this one right, and it's a very satisfying, spectacular-looking shot.

ERNIE ELS' STROKESAVERS:

- Spread the weight evenly and place the hands level, or a fraction behind the ball.
- Keep grip pressure light throughout, and maintain knee flex.
- Hit every sand shot with consistent tempo and pace of acceleration.
- Lengthen or shorten the swing to alter the distance the ball will fly.
- Use a 60-degree wedge when there isn't much green with which to work.
- Move the weight forward, swing more steeply, and really *zip* the clubhead through the sand.

DRILL: RIGHT-HANDED SWINGS KEEP THE CLUBHEAD MOVING

There are two features of good bunker play that are worth mentioning again. First is the necessity to keep the clubhead moving through the sand. This sounds obvious, but I mean keep it moving in a smooth, flowing motion. Sadly, I don't see that too often when amateurs play this shot. Second is the angle of attack. The clubhead needs to swing on a shallow path into the sand, not a steeply descending one. The following exercise gives you the right feeling for both.

> *"Rotate the face open with your right hand before taking your grip, making sure that the grooves on the face continue to point skyward."*
>
> —ANNIKA SORENSTAM

Assume good bunker play posture, and take your left hand off the grip. Let your left hand hang free or put it in your pocket or behind your back, whatever feels most comfortable. Also, open the clubface. Now using your right hand only, make slow, rhythmical, almost lazy practice swings down and through the sand. Grip mega-lightly and keep the movement very free, almost as though you are letting go of the club.

Notice how the clubhead just slides through the sand? You don't even have to force it. And the clubhead doesn't bury itself, either. Simply the weight of the club and the momentum of a free swing give you the two key ingredients I was talking about—a shallow angle of attack and a smoothly accelerating swing. Introduce the sensations from this practice drill into your proper swing, and you've cracked it. You'll have a better technique in no time at all.

From *The Complete Short Game,* by Ernie Els with Steve Newell. CollinsWillow, London, England. Copyright ©1998 by Tee-2-Green Enterprises. Reprinted by permission of HarperCollins Publishers, Ltd.

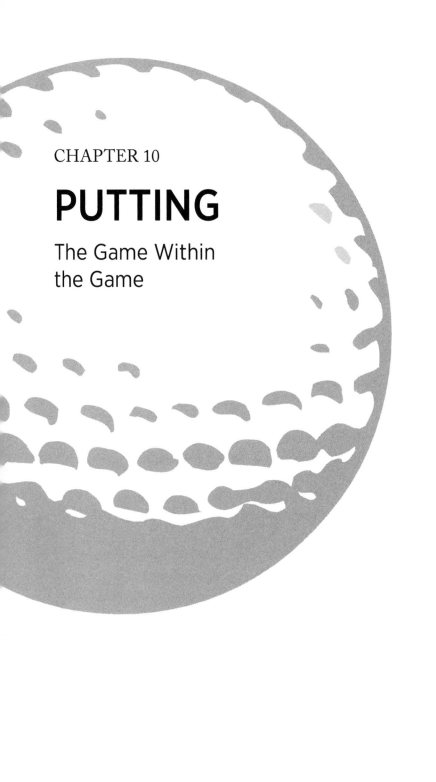

CHAPTER 10

PUTTING

The Game Within
the Game

Holing the Ball

1901 • Walter J. Travis

Walter Travis, who came from Australia to America as a child, was called "The Old Man" because he first played golf at age 34. Four years later he won his first championship, the U.S. Amateur, and defended the title in 1901 using the revolutionary rubber-cored ball patented in 1899 by Coburn Haskell. Playing with a dangling black cigar, he'd win another U.S. championship and shock the British by taking their title in 1904. Called "a deep thinker," Travis founded and edited *The American Golfer*, and wrote books to popularize the sport, emphasizing putting, at which he replaced Willie Park, Jr. as the world's best. In his historic *Practical Golf*, he was among the first to promote the now standard reverse-overlap putting grip—which he taught Bobby Jones—and discourage overuse of the wrists. He also furthered the concepts of "straight-line putting"—taking the putter straight back and through—and picking an intermediate target.

O nce the golfer has managed, more or less successfully, to get on the green, the serious business of getting the ball into the hole in one or two strokes presents itself. And mighty serious business it is, too. Putting, that is consistently good putting, is perhaps the most difficult part of the game…[and] calls for the highest degree of skill and the nicest kind of judgment both as regards accuracy and strength. By accuracy is meant the passage of the ball over an imaginary line between it and the hole. You may possibly be able to keep your ball along this line, but if it is hit too hard it will probably jump the cup, while if the necessary strength is lacking it certainly cannot go in. It all seems easy enough, especially to the man who has never tried it, and who is not saddled with recollections of innumerable misses in the past, sins of commission and omission.…

ACCURACY IN PUTTING

Let us examine…the character of the stroke in reference to accuracy, more particularly dismissing for the time being the question of strength. If one can succeed in getting the ball to run true, more than half of the terrors of putting are gotten rid of at the outset, and the mind may then be concentrated on the important matter of strength.

In respect to accuracy, it is imperative that you should act upon some well-defined principles. Proceed first by taking a glance back of the ball toward the hole, and trace the line over which it must pass, noting for subsequent guidance a particular blade of grass on this imaginary line. Take your stance and square the face of the putter at perfect right angles to the blade of grass you have picked out by resting it immediately in front of the ball. By resting the club in this way…it is easier to get the correct baseline, and, furthermore, it assists in going through the ball properly when the stroke is made.

Now withdraw the club and let it rest gently on the turf close behind the ball, taking care to preserve the correct angle. Let the eye run quickly over the imaginary line to the hole, so as to determine the requisite force to be applied, and then make the stroke.

If the club presents a perfect right angle in reference to the line of play during the period of contact with the ball, and no irregularities of surface or obstructions interfere, the ball will almost certainly run straight, and assuming that the right amount of strength has been employed it will stand a much better chance of finding the hole than if the player simply trusted to luck, and with each new putt changed his method according to the whim of the moment.…

REGARDING THE GRIP

The…grip affected by [this] writer [is different from the conventional one]. It is not contended that [my grip] is in any way better than the orthodox grip for the general run of players, but exhaustive tests—and under fire—have demonstrated conclusively that it serves its purpose somewhat better than does the prevailing style. It will be observed that both thumbs are laid down the shaft, and that the index-finger of the right hand touches it also at the tip, toward the back of the shaft. Grasping the club in this way, with the fingers, one seems to feel it better and to be able more accurately to determine the proper degree of strength to be applied to the stroke. Then too it lessens one's innate tendency to pull the ball, a tendency which the orthodox grip rather encourages.… Throwing the burden of the work on the right forefinger seems to counteract any such fault, and not only is the club guided better, but greater delicacy of touch is apparent, and consequently the matter of strength is better controlled and regulated.

It will be found, generally speaking, that the better results follow by gripping the club pretty firmly with the fingers—firmly but not tightly. A very light grip is usually at the sacrifice of delicacy. A firm grip insures the ball keeping its line more accurately and not being deflected by irregularities of any land. The rougher the green the more is this essential.

PUTT THE BALL; DON'T HIT IT

The club should be taken away from and brought back to and follow-through the ball with a smooth, even movement, free from any jerk. Endeavor to take the club back and let it follow after the ball on the correct line of the putt. Aim to strike the ball exactly in the center, and don't be in any hurry to look up after the stroke.

In addressing the ball do not allow the club to weigh heavily on the turf; rather let the touch be very delicate. Whatever the distance may be, always go for the hole; in other words, be up. In this way a certain proportion of long putts will be brought off. Aim to be just a shade *over* the hole, but not so far beyond as to make at all uncertain the holing out of the next, in case of missing....

KEEP THE BODY IMMOVABLE

In putting, it is of prime importance that the body should be kept immovable, the hands, wrists, arms, and to a certain extent, the shoulders only entering into the stroke. Neither should the wrists alone play any undue part. The less they are employed the better, for uniformity. They should act in perfect harmony with the other factors, the whole so blending and merging into each other as to produce a rhythmical unison, and leave the player wholly unconscious of any particular element being present. There should be more or less of an air of stiffness about the stroke, free, however, from any rigidity born of tautened muscles.

WALTER J. TRAVIS' STROKESAVERS:

- Develop a consistent pre-shot routine.
- Pick an intermediate target, and square the putter blade to it.
- Take the putter straight back, and then straight through the ball.
- Don't look up until the ball is well on its way to the hole.

KEEP THE EYE FIXED ON THE BALL

The head, of course, must be kept absolutely still. At the moment of striking, the eyes—particularly the left—should be intently fastened, not only on the ball, but on the dead center of the ball toward the back, where you intend hitting it. It has been suggested that the left eye more especially should be directed at the ball. As a further aid, it is advisable to get both elbows in line, parallel with the line of the putt. This will necessitate the turning of the left elbow away from the body, the right being somewhat tucked in toward the thigh, but not being allowed to rest on it. By letting the club swing in the manner described it will be noticed that it meets and goes through the ball with the face at a perfect right angle with reference to the line to the hole, and that is the whole essence of good putting. There is no mystery at all about it. The laws of motion are unchangeable, and given that the ball be hit truly on scientific principles, such as I have endeavored to outline, it will assuredly run straight on a smooth and true green, and be far more liable to keep a straight line on an indifferent one than if hit "in any old way."

From *Practical Golf*, by Walter J. Travis. Harper & Brothers Publishers, New York, N.Y.

PENDULUM PUTTING MOTION

Around the turn of the last century, Walter Travis, the "Old Man" of golf, dominated the amateur game with his deadly accurate putting. But in 1905, youth was served as Jerome Travers, 17, upset Travis in the first of their many head-to-head competitions over the next decade. An icy, enigmatic player, Travers often copied his older rival's technique on the green—and even used the same "Schenectady" putter—though Travers was the first to coin the phrase that best described the new putting stroke they both adopted, likening it to a "pendulum-like" motion. "Remember that the wrists and arms should work in unison," Travers wrote in his 1913 *Travers' Golf Book*. "The true putting stroke is best described a pendulum movement in which neither the wrists nor arms predominate." Travers' method is the preferred putting stroke to this day.

Four Main Factors in Putting

1943 • Mildred Didrikson Zaharias

The daughter of Norwegian immigrants, gregarious Texan "Babe" Didrikson Zaharias may have been the greatest athlete ever. After winning two golds at the 1932 Olympics, she competed in almost every sport, from bowling, boxing, baseball, and basketball to diving, tennis, and shooting. Then she became serious about golf. Evolving from a long hitter to a fabulous all-around player, she dominated both the amateur game—winning 17 of 18 tournaments in 1946–47—and later the professional ranks until her early death in 1956. An LPGA cofounder, she is credited with 41 professional wins and 10 majors. In this deceptively simple excerpt from her book, *Championship Golf*, Zaharias wrote about the twists and turns that golfers encounter on the greens of championship courses, giving a quick brief on how to study those breaks for the proper line and read the grain to gauge speed. Like Walter Hagen had before her, she also advised golfers to *hit* with topspin.

You read a golf green like you read a book. When you learn to do this, you are on the way toward getting those all-important last shots in the cup.

There are four important factors in putting, aside from grip and stance, [and] if these are followed closely you *will* get results:

- Contour of the green
- Texture or grain
- Lining up the putt
- Swinging the clubhead to get over-spin on the ball

In studying the surface of the green you look for rises and depressions to determine the borrow to compensate for rolls to the right or left. Obviously, if the green slopes from right to left, you would not attempt to putt on a true line, which would cause the ball to roll past the cup on the left side.

You will learn to adjust your putts to the contour with experience, which is the only way this factor can be learned.

The same goes for learning to govern the speed of your putt by the grain of the green, whether you are putting with, against, or across the grain, which is the equivalent of the surface on a rug.

In lining up the putt, you take into consideration the contour and the grain and with a couple of easy practice swings determine how hard you should strike the ball to get a true putt into the cup. Remember to be up to the cup on putts.

BABE DIDRIKSON ZAHARIAS' STROKESAVERS:

- Read the green like a roadmap to the hole.
- Determine how hard to hit the ball during a couple of practice strokes.
- Turn your head—not lift it—after the ball is struck.

It is advisable to look the putt over at least from behind and from one side before hitting it. And take your time. An old saying on the greens is "miss 'em quick." It is better to take a little more time and sink them, but don't delay needlessly to the point where you are tied in knots. Some people may be born putters, but serious thoughtful practice will go a long way toward improving any golfer's play on the greens.

Remember to determine the speed of the green and the other factors before you stroke the ball and concentrate solely on the stroke finally.

My putting grip is the conventional reverse overlapping grip with both thumbs on the very center of the top of the club handle.

By reverse overlapping grip is meant that the forefinger of the left hand overlaps the little finger of the right hand, which is the opposite of the grip used on the other clubs.

My hands work together on a putt, but I have the feeling that the forefinger and the thumb of my right hand are doing most of the work. They serve as the guide to the stroke. This is a matter of individuality.

My feet are fairly close together—about eight inches apart. Weight should be fairly evenly distributed between the two feet, with just slightly more of the weight on the left foot. You lean forward so as to be looking down on the ball. Whether you putt with a slight bend in your knees or with your legs straight

An LPGA cofounder, Babe Didrikson Zaharias is credited with 41 professional wins and 10 majors. She emphasized reading the green "like a book," taking special note of both the contour and grain when sizing up a putt. (Hulton Archive/Getty Images)

is a matter of choice. I putt with a slight knee-bend. I hit the ball from a point exactly opposite the left toe.

My right elbow rests against my lower side, and my left elbow points toward the cup.

I hit short putts and stroke the long ones.

Whatever you decide upon as your putting style, always remember:

- Check on the contour, or break of the green.
- Determine the speed of the green by the grain.
- Check your grip and your stance.

Line up the clubhead behind the ball so that it is square to the hole. Take the clubhead back slowly and bring it into the ball close to the ground in a free, smooth motion which catches the ball on a slight upswing to impart over-spin. This helps to keep the ball on a true line.

After the putting blade has made contact with the ball, follow-through and gradually turn your head with the stroke *without* lifting your head.

Don't try to putt with a jerky, indecisive stroke.

Make you putts with confidence.

A trick I employ in lining up a putt may be helpful to you. Pick a blade of grass or some other similar mark a foot or so in front of the ball and in line with the hole and use it as a guide. This will help you to avoid pushing or pulling your putts offline.

From *Championship Golf*, by Mildred Didrikson Zaharias. A.S. Barnes and Company, New York, N.Y. Reprinted with the permission of the Babe Didrikson Zaharias Foundation.

BETWEEN THE EYES

In *Amy Alcott's Guide to Women's Golf*, the former LPGA star and Hall of Famer recommended positioning the body so the eyes are right over the ball or just inside the target line when putting. If the eyes are outside the target line, the golfer will pull putts to the left. To check, she counseled, put a ball down, take a putting stance, and then drop another ball from the bridge of the nose—or from right between the eyes—onto the ball below. The golfer also can use a putter to do this, putting the tip of the grip handle between the eyes and then sighting down the shaft.

Borrow and Break

1961 • Horton Smith and Dawson Taylor

Horton Smith broke onto the professional tour with a start that anticipated Tiger Woods. At age 21, he won eight titles in 1929, beginning a career that would include 32 victories. The lanky Missourian had an all-around game—he even preceded Gene Sarazan by using a specially designed club for sand play (a concave-faced model that would be banned)—but he's still known for his brilliant putting. His most famous victory, by one stroke in the inaugural Masters in 1934, was the result of an 18-foot birdie putt on the 71st hole. He won a second single-stroke Masters title in 1936. Twenty-five years later, the retired PGA president covered every aspect of putting in *The Secret of Holing Putts!*, reissued as *The Secret of Perfect Putting!* Especially helpful is this thorough piece on how to master breaking putts and on why playing for the "pro side of the cup" is so important.

"How much should I borrow?" "How far do you think this putt will break?" You will hear these expressions time and again as golfers seek advice from their partners or their caddies. So let's explain them with a few illustrations.

Think of steel balls in a pinball machine rolling up one slope and then down one side or the other. Or think of the banked corners around the Indianapolis Speedway, where the racers go high up into the corners and then come down into the straightaway. Or think of the way a boomerang sails out on a cushion of air and curves back so gracefully to the arms of the thrower: these are three illustrations of the same principle that makes a golf ball "borrow" and "break."

As you know already or will soon discover as you play golf and learn putting, many golf course greens are "banked." Consequently, you will have to allow for the curving roll of the golf ball as it travels over their slopes. How much should you allow? Obviously, the more the "bank" or "tilt" of the green, the more the allowance for the alteration in the roll of the ball from a true, normal, straight path. As you play, experience will be your teacher. You will also find that for a long while you will tend to underestimate the amount of effect a banked slope will have on your ball.

Suppose you are contemplating a 20-foot putt on a green that is banked higher on the right than on the left. Obviously, you would have to hit this putt off to the right of a straight line between the ball and the cup. The degree to which you hit the ball to the right is the "borrow" from the right. The tendency of the ball to curve to the left is called its "break."

You "borrow" so many inches from the slope, but your putt "breaks" so many inches from the slope toward the cup. A green banked from left to right would naturally work in exactly the opposite fashion. That is, you would be "borrowing" from the slope on the left and your putt would be "breaking" to the right. I hope you are not confused, but that is the language of golf.

TOLERANCE FOR ERROR

It is my firm conviction, based on years of my own experience, and on watching thousands of golfers attempt putts on a "borrowed" line, that 90 percent are missed on the "low" side of the cup....

Perhaps you have never seen a greens keeper cut a fresh cup on your course. Well, he uses a tool that might be likened to a huge cookie cutter to slice a circular cut into the ground, in order to remove a cylinder of turf about 10 inches long. He must necessarily pull this section out of the ground from directly above

IF THE GRASS IS GREENER

Billy Casper won two U.S. Opens, a Masters, and ranks seventh on the PGA's all-time victory list. And he compiled that record while playing with a serene air of confidence and a deadly accurate—if unconventionally wristy—putting stroke. In *Billy Casper's Golf Tips*, he revealed a putting secret that separates pros from amateurs: how to judge speed and break by reading the grain. If the grass is shiny behind the ball, he said, the grain is with the golfer and the ball will run fairly true. But if the grass is dull, the grain is against and the ball must be hit harder to hold its line. If the grain runs across the line, uphill putts will break less than normally, but downhill putts will break more dramatically.

so as to have a perfectly level cup. Very rarely does the greens keeper, much as he might try or wish to do so, actually remove the cut turf straight up. The result is, even on a supposedly level area, a cup with one side higher than the other.

HORTON SMITH'S STROKESAVERS:

- Never leave a putt short—hit to the high, or "pro side," of the hole.
- Most golfers underestimate the break—add 25 percent.
- Hone the skill of reading borrow and break on the practice green.

When the cup has been cut from an area with slight or even great slope in it, you will nearly always find the "high" side of that cup on the side toward the slope. This is very important for you to know, understand, and act upon. For when the ball is slowing down and is near the "high" side of the cup, it acts as though a magnet is there to draw it into the cup. I have seen this happen many times when it might appear that the ball is at least half an inch away from the line of the cup and cannot possibly be expected to fall.

Now, let us go back to my first statement that 90 percent of "borrowed" putts are missed on the low side of the cup. Suppose you are surveying a 10-foot putt with a right-to-left break or "borrow" of six inches.... The normal track of this putt necessary to hole the ball [is] in the exact center of the cup. But knowing two things about this situation changes your strategy for sinking this putt. First, your eye has informed you that the right side of the cup is the high side (this is also called "the pro side of the cup," for the obvious reason that the pros play for it all the time), and therefore this is the side you will aim for. Second, since you and probably most golfers are inclined to underestimate the amount of roll on a "borrowed" putt, I suggest that you add an arbitrary 25 percent to your original estimate of the required degree of "borrow." This gives you what I call "tolerance for error," or margin for error. By allowing this margin, you can take advantage of the chance to enter the cup from the "high" side.

Remember too that the "dying ball" is much more affected by the contour of the green than a ball that is still moving from the power supplied by the putter. So why not make sure that the "dying ball" curves into the cup? Don't take my suggestion of a 25 percent compensation too literally. It may be that your eye consistently overestimates the necessary roll or break. Only you can be the judge of that. In general, however, golfers tend to underestimate, so 25 percent is generally sound.

When you are putting on the practice green you should experiment with various amounts of roll in the following fashion: put down a ball 10 feet from the cup and arbitrarily try to figure the break. You might, for example, figure the putt to break four inches right to left. Then place a tee four inches to the right of the cup and putt for the tee. Watch most carefully to be sure you are putting on the line four inches right of the cup. By experimenting with this system you will have a graphic illustration of the points I have been trying to make. After a while you can discard the tee and simply imagine the point toward which you are putting.

"You drive for show, but putt for dough."

—Bobby Locke

Another way to approach this problem is to decide that on right-to-left putts of lengths from six feet and up, you will arbitrarily open the blade a little bit more than your eye tells you to, and, in the opposite fashion, on left-to-right putts of the same distance, close your blade slightly more than your eye tells you.

Whichever method works best you should adopt as a general rule and work at strenuously on the practice green until you have established your exact formula or percentage of over-allowance. It is entirely possible that you will even wish to try this system on shorter putts.

You should also experiment with the ball position on borrowed putts. I find it more effective to have the ball slightly back toward the center of my stance on left-to-right putts and slightly in front of normal position on right-to-left putts. I feel that these variations in ball position are merely individual "margins for error" which help me to hit the ball on the line more often. Perhaps this method will help you too.

Putting Overview

2000 • Dave Pelz

When Phil Mickelson hired Dave Pelz to help him win his first major, it underlined the status of the Texas instructor and *Golf* magazine's Technical and Short Game Consultant as today's leading putting guru. Pelz's 1991 book *Putt Like the Pros* was straightforward nuts and bolts mixed with scientific analysis of his putting experiments. It is primitive compared to the best-selling *Dave Pelz's Putting Bible* (a companion to *Dave Pelz's Short Game Bible*), which the former NASA research scientist filled with graphs and statistics to support his recommendations for approaching every kind of putt. Much of his data-backed theory is perhaps too remote for beginners, but this excerpt, culled from three chapters, can be useful to all golfers. There is no instruction and no charts, but readers can better understand the odds of making putts of various lengths, and learn how to use that knowledge both to focus their practices and make better judgments when they play.

G olfers are always looking for a cause-and-effect relationship. It's human nature to want an explanation or reasons why things happen, especially when you are trying to enjoy yourself, but you keep seeing putts miss the hole. In golf, as in other areas of life, the phrase "the easy way out" comes into play. Many golfers chose to hope or spend money in an attempt to buy improvement rather than have to read, practice, or learn how to improve. But putting does not succumb to such desires or offers of cash. Rather, just to make things interesting, the game throws in a number of unknown and unknowable factors that make success a statistical uncertainty.

The statistical nature of putting is one of its charms.... The world's best putters (the golfers on the PGA Tour) make only about half of all their putts from six feet away; however, if they were on perfect and known surfaces, their strokes are so good that they would hole approximately 90 percent of these same putts.

Short game coach Dave Pelz works with Phil Mickelson before the 2006 British Open. Pelz emphasizes simplicity when it comes to putting. "The simpler and easier the stroke is to execute," he wrote, "the more precisely and repetitively you'll be able to learn to execute it, especially under pressure." (Ross Kinnaird/ Getty Images)

HOW WELL CAN YOU PUTT?

Something…you need to think about before actually beginning to work on your stroke are the answers to a few questions. They are important questions, but only if you want to know just how good your putting can get: 1) How good are the world's best putters? 2) How well do you putt now? 3) How good can one get at putting? 4) How good will your putting be in the future?

Let me answer these as best I can:

I believe the best putters in the world are playing on the PGA Tour. My proof is the results of the first two World Putting Championships, where the Tour pros were seriously challenged by some Senior Tour players, several LPGA Tour players, and a number of amateurs, both young and old. However, the PGA Tour players placed higher as a group than any other.

Also, my data on the percentage of putts holed from different distances show that the PGA Tour players lead all other groups. Don't think that you can look at the statistics quoted in the newspapers and find this information, because the number that the papers publish (provided by the Tour) simply shows how many putts the players average on greens hit in regulation, which is affected by the quality of their iron shots (the better the iron play, the shorter the putts). And these are the new putting stats. Years ago, the Tour's statistics measured putts taken per green, which was influenced by how many greens players missed and how consistently they chipped close to the hole (again, leaving them shorter putts). Neither of these statistics measures the quality of a player's putting, because both are strongly influenced by the quality of different shots (approaches and chips).

The true measure of the Tour pros' putting is indicated by the percentage of putts they make ("convert") based solely on the length of putts.…

If you want an answer to Question 2—"How well do you putt?"—you must measure your percentage of putts holed from each distance. You can do this, but it will take some effort. You have to record the distance of each putt on your scorecard as you move around the course, and indicate those you hole. After 10 to 15 rounds (and at least 5 to 10 putts from each distance), you'll begin to be able to plot your own conversion chart and compare it to those of the pros.

As for Question 3—"How good can one get at putting?"—the answer depends on a number of things: the quality of the greens, how well a player reads those greens, and the quality of the player's stroke and touch. Although none of these questions can be answered definitively in this book, I assure you that all of the above are getting better all the time. As greens improve, putting strokes improve, and golfers learn to read greens better, a higher percentage of putts from every distance will be made in the future.

Finally, "How good will your putting be in the future?" That depends on your ability to learn the mechanics of a better putting stroke, your ability to learn better putting feel and touch, your ability to learn to read greens better, and your ability to produce the right stroke at the right time. Depending on your lifestyle, your determination and intensity, your focus, your self-discipline and practice habits, and your ability to learn, only you can provide this answer.

STOP THREE-PUTTING

For most golfers to improve their scores, it is often easier to reduce their number of three-putts than it is to increase their number of one-putts. This is generally true for golfers with handicaps greater than 20, although it is even true for some very fine, lower-handicap players.... The length of the most frequent first putt on greens hit from outside 60 yards is 38 feet. (This distance varies a little with the handicap of the players measured, but obviously there are many more long first putts than short ones.) The most frequent first putt to follow shots hit from inside 60 yards is an 18-footer....

This means that you shouldn't practice only short putts; the long ones are also important. And you must stop three-putting those long ones if you want to be a good putter....

DAVE PELZ'S STROKESAVERS:

- Simpler is better in putting technique.
- Be realistic: PGA pros make only half of *their* six footers.
- Practice long putts as well as short ones—that's the key to reducing three putts.

SIMPLER IS BETTER

There are many different ways for golfers to putt. Having said that, it does not mean that I'm advocating all or any of these methods. But it's important that you are aware of the choices a golfer has, and even a few he doesn't, unless he doesn't care about *The Rules of Golf* (which I think you must if you're going to be serious about this game).

The old adage "different strokes for different folks" is very meaningful, because some putting strokes work better than others for certain players, while no one stroke works perfectly for everyone. While no strokes, even perfect ones, make all their putts, some really awful strokes do make some putts. And sometimes the differences between good and bad strokes are very difficult to measure or see. But believe me, the differences are there.

Let me pass on to you the one thought, the one axiom that governs all my theories on putting. It is this: simpler is better. You'll find research test results in many different disciplines that validate this conclusion. It is certainly true in almost all of sports. Why? Because regardless of your level of talent, the less you give yourself to do (and still get the job done), the more consistently you can learn to do it. Whereas the more compensations that must be made in your putting stroke, the more difficult it will be to repeat in such a way that it actually makes your putts. The more complex a putting stroke (that is, the more compensations that must be made to make it effective), the more uncertain (or inconsistent) its results by any golfer regardless of skill level.

All this may sound routine, and you may have heard it many times before, but that doesn't mean it isn't true. And more important, that doesn't mean it shouldn't be taken seriously. So there's no question about it: in putting, simpler is better. The simpler and easier the stroke is to execute, the more precisely and repetitively you'll be able to learn to execute it, especially under pressure. And that's why all my teaching begins with that principle.

How to Square Your Putterface and Hole More Putts

2003 • Tiger Woods with Pete McDaniel

During Tiger Woods' long reign as golf's top-ranked player, he was the most consistent clutch putter on the PGA Tour. Woods attributes his success to his pre-putt routine, a ritual that provides a few moments of needed serenity. What precisely goes through his mind before he pulls the trigger is his secret, but when it comes to the mechanics, Tiger is a pure traditionalist. He commits to line and speed—which he says is the most important element in putting—aims at where the putt will break, and keeps his head down to avoid yanking putts off line. In this brief piece for *Golf Digest,* Woods wrote about another essential to good putting—keeping the clubface square to the target line. When he writes to practice putting along a string to make squaring the clubface automatic, it carries weight because he claims he has used this classic drill himself.

Good, consistent putting involves several factors, not the least of which is the ability to visualize the line and get the ball started on that line. You can get the ball rolling properly if you can square the putterface to the target line at impact without having to manipulate the putterhead.

I recommend using a string or chalk line to help you practice squaring the putter. You can buy a ready-made string drill training aid or make your own by tying a piece of string to two small stakes—a couple of pencils will do. Stretch the string taut on level ground, high enough so your putter can travel under it.

I used the string drill during my rehab from knee surgery, before I could make full swings. The extra work on my short game paid off my first tournament back, the Buick Invitational. I struggled with the pace of the greens early because of rainy conditions, but my alignment was sharp, which contributed to a lot of par-saving putts. To win right out of the blocks felt pretty good, too.

GETTING A LINE ON SQUARE CONTACT

The string drill gives you great feedback on the path of your stroke, the angle of the putterface, and the target line. Here's what I do:

TIGER WOODS' STROKESAVERS:

- Use a string—tied off between two small stakes or pencils—to practice squaring the putterhead to the intended line of a putt at impact.

- Focus on swinging straight back and through on short putts, using the string for feedback.

- Make sure the putterhead is square to the swing path when hitting longer putts.

On putts of five feet or less, I swing the putter straight back and through. I use the string to practice keeping the putterface square, or perpendicular, to the string throughout the stroke.

On longer putts…where you make more of a shoulder turn to take the putter farther back, the putterhead tends to move to the inside a little. It also moves a little inside on the through stroke. The key is that the putterface stays square *to the swing path* throughout the stroke. This should happen naturally.

Free-swinging lefty Bubba Watson tees off during the 2008 Arnold Palmer Invitational. Never content to simply bomb the ball down the fairway, Watson is a master of hitting highly sophisticated shots that produce either a cut or— as above—a draw. (Chris Condon/ US PGA TOUR/Getty Images)

PART FOUR

SHOTMAKING

WALTER HAGEN FAMOUSLY MAINTAINED THAT golf was a game of managed imperfection, and modern golfers would do well to accept that to err is human and only the divine can hope to consistently split the fairway. Since Harry Vardon's time, golf books have included chapters on "faults and cures," but it was Vardon's great rival, J.H. Taylor, who earlier set the tone for future discussions on such problems as slicing, hooking, topping, and shanking. Dismissing those who would rely on "natural" methodology, Taylor advised the golfer to learn precise technique from the ground up. Decades later, John Jacobs would reverse that concept—while still embracing the core lesson—when he suggested first watching the flight of the ball, and then working back to cure the fundamentals. Alongside such advice inevitably comes an examination of how to deal with "trouble" when the anticipated error does occur. Since the 1880s, instructors have advised how to cope with a multitude of bad lies as well as the vagaries of the weather. Early instructors were often folksy and less thorough, while modern instructors, such as Chi Chi Rodriguez, offer ideas that mix flair, cold-blooded analysis, and recuperative drills. In complement to such teachings, golf writers consistently evolved theories on that most exquisite phase of the game: employing advanced techniques. From early twentieth century champions to Tiger Woods came methods for mastering intentional slices and hooks that can steer players *over*, *under*, and *around* obstacles, and manufacturing shots that laugh at the wind and nullify slick greens.

CHAPTER 11

FAULTS AND CURES

Prescriptions for the Ailing Swing

Mashie Play

1904 • G.W. Beldam and J.H. Taylor

When Horace Hutchinson came home from Oxford on holiday, one of his parents'
servants caddied for him at the famous Westward Ho! links nearby. The caddy,
also a greens keeper, was John Henry Taylor, and within a few years, Hutchinson
was writing about the former houseboy beating the Scots at their own game. The
first of the Triumvirate to win a British Open title—he'd win five overall between
1894–1913—Taylor was the superior putter and was renowned for his approach shots
with his favorite club, the versatile, mid-iron mashie. In this excerpt from their book of
articles that appeared in *C.B. Fry's Magazine*, Taylor and pioneer golf-and-cricket-
action photographer George Beldam set the precedent for instruction on faults and
cures. Refuting those who contended golf is a "natural" sport, Taylor offered "stern and
unsympathetic detail" about correct technique and how to stop hitting fat shots and
shanking the ball.

I have heard it said many times—and even by golfers whose experience
should have taught them better—that the easiest way—viz., the way
which comes naturally to each player—is the only right way for him to
adopt. In my experience I can count many golfing failures entirely due
to the too ready acceptance of this fallacious theory. I go so far as to state that
this so-called natural way is generally the wrong way, and often violates the
fundamental principles of the game. I quite sympathize with anyone who is
lured on to play the game in this "natural" way; but to yield to the temptation is
not to his best interests, as he may discover in after years when it is too late. A
little perseverance, application, and determination to master the difficulties at
the outset will bring a full and certain reward.

To come to stern and unsympathetic detail, which in such practice is met
with by all, strong and flexible wrists are undoubtedly necessary, but these will
be of no avail if other requisites are neglected. The head *must* be kept perfectly
steady during the upward stroke, and until after the ball has fairly started on its

way; this to obviate the prevalent fault of looking up too soon. The eyes, during the upward stroke, *must* be riveted *on the ground*, at a point immediately behind and almost underneath the ball, but still on the ground. If this is really done, there will be fewer half-topped balls.

"It's a strange thing that we know just how to do a thing at golf, and yet cannot do it."

—Bernard Darwin

[Hitting fat or behind the ball is] one of the most general of faults indulged in not only by novices but also by golfers of more mature experience.... The fault consists in the over-anxiety of the player to "get down" to the ball. To do this he bends the right knee too soon, and this causes the right shoulder to drop, with the probable result that the ground in front of the ball is struck first. The knuckling in of the right knee tends to throw the hands forward just before the moment of impact, and this is one of the most frequent causes of socketing [or shanking] that I know. If, however, the ball be struck with the face of the club, and not off the socket, it will most probably be pushed out, and fly, sooner or later, to the right of the intended flight. The left arm has left the side, and therefore power also has been lost. It then follows that the right forearm must be in the ascendant, over-powering the left. Indeed, in most pushed out shots the right hand obtains the mastery....

[Many golfers try to help the ball into the air by drawing the club] across the ball...[then] pulling the arms in close to the side directly the ball has been struck. Some players do this to put "cut" on the ball, and that they accomplish this I readily admit, but I consider it must be at the expense of accuracy and command of the ball. With this system too much cut, at the expense of propelling power, is obtained. This finish would be alright if distance were no object, and the ball were required to leave the club in a perpendicular manner to clear some steep obstacle. If I were to finish my pitching strokes of, say, about 60 yards in [such a] manner, I should be "cutting the legs from under the ball," and be short. As the ball ought to go well up into the air, it has to travel considerably more than 60 yards in its flight. It will therefore be seen that, to get this distance with cut, it is essential neither to pull the arms nor the club across the ball....

[In] the correct finish of a pitching stroke with cut...the arms are carried through much more than [in the above example.] The position of the clubhead [would have]

Keegan Bradley hits his second shot on the first playoff hole during the final round of the 2011 PGA Championship—which the PGA Tour rookie won while playing in his first-ever major. Bradley keeps a steady head and spine angle through the shot, which as J.H. Taylor stressed more than a century earlier, helps prevent all sorts of swing errors. (Stuart Franklin/Getty Images)

J.H. TAYLOR'S STROKESAVERS:

- Master the fundamentals – golf is not a "natural game."
- Keep a steady head and eye position to avoid topping the ball.
- Avoid anxiously trying to get down to the ball – it causes fat shots and shanking.
- Don't try to *help* the ball up – doing so is one of golf's cardinal sins.

the face looking upward [with] the left forearm controlling the club.... Combined with [an open] stance, [this] produces natural cut; and...distance is more accurately gauged when the stroke is played in this straightforward manner.

From *Golf Faults Illustrated* (1904), by G.W. Beldam and J.H. Taylor. George Newnes, Ltd., Southampton Street, London, England.

Common Faults and How to Cure Them

1927 • Abe Mitchell

Abe Mitchell, who hit balls almost 300 yards with a hickory-shafted driver, was Britain's best golfer between the Triumvirate and Henry Cotton. Cotton wrote, "No golf balls have ever been struck harder and truer than those struck by Abe Mitchell... from about 1910 to 1933." Cotton also believed Mitchell was too nice to close out big tournaments, the reason he'd be known as the best golfer not to win the British Open. He was a superb match player, however, and the star of three Ryder Cup teams. Hired by multimillionaire seed merchant Samuel Ryder for private tutoring, Mitchell became the model for the golfer atop the Ryder Cup trophy. In this essay from Mitchell's 1927 book, he offered still-relevant instruction on how to cure slicing, pulling, and topping the ball. Notable are his remedies for a reverse pivot and his advice on how to check for grip and posture problems.

The faults dealt with in this chapter are the commonest in golf. Everyone may be said to pull and slice occasionally in every round; some commit one or other of these faults at almost every hole. If they are only slight deviations from the straight line, there is little wrong and the errors will right themselves. Once the player starts altering his stance or grip or swing, the change produced is almost certain to do more than correct the error; a slice will probably give place to a wicked hook, a hook to a depressing slice, and so on, the remedy proving much worse than the disease.

But many players have spells of one particular form or other of these golfing maladies, and obviously some remedy is necessary in their case. It is for these unfortunate people that this chapter has been written....

SLICING

Cause: Wrong grip

This may be contributory to the slicing habit but is unlikely to be the root cause. See that the grip is normal for the shot. For an ordinary drive two knuckles of the left hand should be visible and if the back of that hand is too much in front of the shaft, it should be slightly altered, but very slightly.

The right hand grip should...not be allowed to creep farther over the shaft.

Cause: A stiff upright stance

This is a common fault among lady players. There is scarcely any pivot, and both sections of the swing are largely arm movements. The first movement in the swing is usually a backward sway of both the trunk and the head accompanied by a lift of the hands.

The hips appear to be locked in the address and to remain so, thus preventing either a hip swing or a shoulder movement. This is really the root of the trouble.

Similarly in the downswing, the absence of body twist prevents the hands from going through and thus the clubhead is brought inward across the ball.

Cause: Stance too open

The remedy in every case is the same, viz. get more width in the backswing. Decide in the address that the backswing is to be a dragging back as far as possible of the clubhead along the line of flight, until the right hip has gone back to its braced position. If this movement has been consciously prepared for, or been actively in the mind, the faults of stance and grip [already] mentioned will remedy themselves....

If there is difficultly in getting extra width, the player should, for a time, stand more square, for this will facilitate a wider backswing. Also, at impact, he should be thinking keenly of his clubhead and should have the courage to roll his right forearm in the follow-through. He may pull horribly for a time, but the slice will disappear and a much longer ball will result. Firm up the grip, keep the head down, and have courage.

PULLING

Cause: A wrong grip

The grip is frequently contributory to the pulling habit, more so than to the slice. It is more natural for the right hand to get under the shaft than over the top and, usually, the players who grip habitually with the right in this way are right-handed players; that is, the blow is delivered largely by the right. With the hand in this position, the knuckling over at impact or just before is apt to be exaggerated, especially if the grip with that hand throughout the swing be very tight, as it is apt to be. The puller's grip, then, must be altered to the normal grip....

Cause: The right side is braced in the address

This throws undue weight on the right foot. The first movement is a draw away of the whole body along the line of flight, the right hand lifting but keeping the clubhead shut.

The right hand is in control, but unlike the slicing positions, the right elbow is away from the body.... From this position it is difficult to get the elbow down to...the proper position for a normal swing. Instead, it describes a circular outward arc, and the clubhead comes onto the ball with a shut face and the result is a pull from the very commencement of the flight.

Remedy

See that the grip is normal and that the left hand has control. Let the grip with the right be slack in the address. Get width in the backswing, and keep the right elbow well in to the side. It ought to be noted in connection with pulling and slicing that the method of grounding the club in the address may have a distinct influence on the backswing. Thus, if the clubface be open in the address there is a tendency to swing at once round the feet; thus width is lost, the left elbow bends,

ABE MITCHELL'S STROKESAVERS:

- Strengthen the grip slightly to cure a slice.
- Keep the right elbow in to avoid a pull.
- Honing a better backswing will cure any number of swing errors.

and a slice results. On the other hand, if the face be too shut, a pull may ensue.

It is best, in the long run, to address the ball with the clubface fairly shut, that is, with the toe well forward. This mode of address invariably tends to a wider backswing and fuller pivot.

TOPPING, BALLOONING, DIPPING THE RIGHT SHOULDER, ETC.
Cause

These are all symptoms of the same faulty backswing already dealt with…. The right hip has not moved laterally, the right hand has had control and the club has been lifted rather than slung.

At the top, the player feels mewed up. Both elbows are spread-eagled, and as there has been little pivoting the player is conscious that the body is now cut out and that the downswing is largely dependent on the arms and wrists. Consequently, the downswing becomes a snatchy movement, as the arms are not actuated from a braced trunk.

Anything may happen. The clubhead may hit the ground behind, and the caddie or partner on being appealed to will probably tell the player that he is dropping his right shoulder in the downswing, as it is the most obvious thing to say. The real fault, of course, occurred in the backswing and escaped notice.

From *Essentials of Golf*, by Abe Mitchell. Edited and arranged by J. Martin (Verulum Golf Club of St. Albans). Hodder and Stoughton Ltd., London, England, and George H. Doran Company, New York, N.Y. Reproduced by permission of Hodder and Stoughton, Ltd.

Curing Golf Ailments

1951 • Johnny Farrell

Stylish Johnny Farrell—who twice was selected America's best-dressed golfer—is arguably the best player not in the World Golf Hall of Fame. He won 22 tournaments—including seven straight in 1927—and played on the first three Ryder Cup teams. Because of family obligations, he retired and became the head pro at Baltusrol for 38 years. And this son of poor Irish immigrants gave lessons to presidents, British royalty, the social set, and celebrities. Perhaps his biggest admirer was Bobby Jones, whom Farrell upset by sinking an eight-footer in a 36-hole playoff in the 1928 Open. In his introduction to Farrell's book, Jones called him a "great golfer and a fine teacher." In this excerpt, Farrell took a different approach than Abe Mitchell to "prescribe medicine" to cure slicing, hooking, shanking, topping, and skying the ball. His process was to scrutinize the stance, timing, and swing path.

Nobody needs a professional to tell him what's *good* with his game. The weekend golfer probably likes to hear that he has got good hand action in his swing or that he is all in one piece coming back; but as soon as you comment on it, he invariably eyes you sourly and says, "A devil of a lot of good that did me today, I was slicing the ball all over the place!"

So I'm going to tell you about slicing—as well as some of the other common ailments that creep into any man's game on occasion—and try to prescribe some medicine....

THE SLICE

There are many reasons for a slice but there's only one way *how* it's done, and that's by bringing the clubhead across the ball—outside in—and giving it a right-way spin.

Of the ways *to* slice, the No. 1 enemy is getting the right side into the shot too quickly. You generally do this because you *sway* on the backswing, rather than *pivoting* around on your hip.

An inside arc going back that becomes an outside downswing is another fatal slice producer and usually is caused by losing control of the shaft at the top of the backswing.

A slice can also come from a left arm that isn't firm, and because it isn't firm, the *right* elbow strays. Tuck that right arm in, and when you unwind your left hip it will follow the inside arc naturally.

But both the loss of hand control and the straying elbow are generally the result of (a) rushing the backswing and (b) not waiting for the downswing. Hand in glove with a rushed swing is a tendency to lunge at the ball—to drive it 15 miles. This causes you to leave your hips out of the shot entirely, so that it is the arms, and not the clubhead, that are swinging at the ball. My advice, then, is to practice coming back extra-slow—all in one piece…then unwind, keeping the right shoulder behind the shot, and let the clubhead come through the ball.

Many golfers slice, too, because they *die on the shot*, as the expression goes. They come back in one piece, wait, come back down again, and then quit completely as the clubhead strikes the ball.…

Finally, a slice may be traced to your grip. Be certain that your left hand is around the shaft and not slipping to the left so that the palm is facing up. Check, always, that the V of the forefinger and thumb points [to the right] shoulder. Don't waste the power of that all-important left arm, hand, and wrist. The right hand—thanks to the overlapping grip—is meant to be nothing more than a guide for the swing. And be sure that you are holding the clubshaft in the fingers of your right hand and not palming it. You must, at all times, have *live hands* that can feel the whip in the shaft and control the swing.

THE HOOK

It has been my observation that the beginners do most of the slicing—it takes an experienced golfer to develop a bad hook. It's true. During the first five years that a man plays golf he tries so many things to rid himself of a slice that he suddenly finds he is faced with the problem of losing a disastrous hook. But "Hookitis" is not confined to any one group of golfers, for the simple reason that a hook is most often the result of timing that has gone bad. And when the expert golfer hooks a drive or a long iron it is generally spectacular because he *trusts* his swing. He bends back and lets go—and if his timing is off, however slightly—the hook that follows is sometimes unbelievable.…

First of all, keep your left foot in contact with the ground throughout the

Johnny Farrell's process to avoid swing faults was to scrutinize the grip, stance, timing, and swing path.
(AP Images)

swing. In practice, do it consciously and make yourself aware that you are pivoting all at one time and all in one piece....

Your timing may also be off at the top of the backswing. You may be failing to *wait* for the shift of power to the left side and allowing your hands to come down far ahead of the hip. This gets the clubhead out *ahead* of the hands, and the ball takes an impact that curves it to the left after it has left the tee. Failure to wait also causes the ball to be *pulled*—which is a straight flying ball that veers sharply to the left when hit.

A *smothered hook* results from a swing that is too flat, and this can be corrected at the stance. "Stand tall and swing tall" should be your reminder, with knees relaxed and slightly bent. If your back is straight, without being stiff, the arc of your backswing will be bigger. Don't crouch over the ball or you will find that you're getting too much of your caboose into the shot.

Check, too, that your left hand is not over too far on the shaft. Beware the creeping left hand! Don't let it swing to the right—as opposed to palming it for the slice—and be sure that you can see no more than the first three knuckles after you've taken your grip. If you have been hooking then you had the recent company of Ben Hogan who told me that he corrected his by allowing only *two* knuckles of the left hand to show on the grip.... A hook may also be caused by a clubface that is closed at point of impact, or toed in as the backswing starts. Hold the face of the club upright and square with the ball....

JOHNNY FARRELL'S STROKESAVERS:

- Throwing the right shoulder at the ball produces a slice.
- Take the club back extra slowly—all in one piece—and then let the hips unwind.
- Weaken the grip slightly to prevent a hook.
- Hit *down* into the ball to avoid topping it.

SKYING THE BALL

A common complaint, especially from the tees or with the woods, is that the ball is popped high in the air. It comes from hitting too hard from the top of the swing, which causes the right shoulder to drop and the ball to be scooped skyward by the downward force of the clubhead. You correct this by slowing down on your downswing and not *pressing* the shot. If you really want to hit the ball a long way, let the *clubhead* do the work. Never rush a shot.

TOPPING THE BALL

On the fairway, many golfers have a tendency to try and *lift* the ball into the air, and in doing so, they lift their body on the downswing as though their arms were going to pick the ball up and send it away. But the only way to get a ball in the air is to *hit down into it.* The loft of the club, plus the down-and-through motion of the downswing, gets the ball in the air and makes it impossible to top it.

SHANKING

To correct a shank, come back straight from the ball and stay in that same inside arc on the downswing. Have the feeling that the ball must get over a high tree and you will stay back on your heels and not lunge forward on the shot and hit it from the outside.

Shanking usually develops from hooking the ball. To avoid going to the left, you come too much from the inside of the line and push your hands through to avoid hooking. This causes the locking of the wrists at impact. Take the club straight back and have more action with your wrists at impact of the ball.

From *If I Were in Your Golf Shoes*, by Johnny Farrell. Henry Holt and Co., New York, N.Y. Copyright © 1951 by Johnny Farrell. Reprinted with the permission of the family of Johnny Farrell.

THE SECRET IS IN THE PREPARATION

Sweden's Annika Sorenstam was admired for her remarkable consistency. Her secret was in preparation and strategic thinking. In an article in *LPGA's Guide to Every Shot* (2000), she wrote: "During the game you must…come up with a strategy for playing each hole. The first step is recognizing your own strengths and limitations when it comes to executing certain shots. The second step involves carefully scoping out the hole and noting any potential trouble areas, like sand or water, high rough, etc. From this you can designate certain areas as 'safe' places to land the ball. By comparing your strengths and weaknesses to the layout of the hole, you can decide the best path to the green and the club you should use to get there."

The Major Faults

1972 • John Jacobs with Ken Bowden

A half century after J. H. Taylor first offered cures for awkward mashie play, fellow Englishman John Jacobs revolutionized the study of faulty swings simply by looking up. Jacobs concluded that it was more *practical* to diagnose a problem by watching ball flight than working to correct fundamentals. In effect, where the ball went told Jacobs what the golfer was doing at impact, a revelation that led to his theory of cause and effect. Jack Nicklaus endorsed the idea, a flock of studies examining the physics of hitting a golf ball confirmed it, and eventually the concept was expanded by Dr. Gary Wiren and enshrined in *The PGA Teaching Manual* under the banner "Ball Flight Laws." In this excerpt from *Practical Golf*, Jacobs wrote about specific faults, such as slices, hooks, tops, and fat shots, from his unique perspective, and offered detailed solutions every golfer can take immediately to the range.

YOU CAN STOP SLICING FOREVER IN FIVE MINUTES

I'm writing this chapter hot—and hot under the collar—from some marathon teaching sessions at my Golf Centers. Never before have I realized quite so emphatically how major a problem the slice in golf is. It really is the golfer's curse! I'm sure that at least 80 percent of the people I've seen in these sessions have sliced ever since they started trying to play the game. But the really devastating thing is their ignorance of why they slice. Not one in 50 really knows what causes his ball time and again to start left and dribble away weakly to the right.

"Why do you slice?" I ask, and usually I get the same answer: "Because I hit across the ball." This is a *contributory* factor in a slice, but it is not the basic cause. Hitting across the ball may produce a pull, or, if the clubface is shut, a quick hook. The *basic* cause of a slice—the common factor in every shot started left that bends right toward the end of its flight—*is a clubface that is open to the swing line at impact*.

You slice because the clubface is open—pointing right of the direction in which your club is traveling—as you hit the ball. Please, *please* get that fact implanted in your golfing consciousness if you really want to eradicate this disastrous shot.

The slice, like so many other faults, stems basically from the grip. Golf is such a difficult and frustrating game for so many people because they can never be bothered to develop an effective grip. Indeed, the very last thing the average golfer wants to be told by a pro is to change his grip. It's too much bother, it's too uncomfortable, it couldn't possibly make that much difference, and anyway, he's sure his faults are in his backswing or his downswing or his follow-through. Because he has never thought out the simple ballistics of the game, he doesn't appreciate the fundamental and very simple fact that *everything* in golf stems from the way the clubface meets the ball.

The habitual slicers are the worst in this way. They go on playing with a hold on the club that brings the clubface to the ball in an open position. Then, because with this grip if they stand square to the target line their shots go straight out to the right, subconsciously they angle themselves around until they are facing miles left of the target. The effect of this shoulder alignment is actually to increase the slice potential of their grip. Then, of course, they swing out-to-in across the ball—the only way they can swing with such a setup. With the clubface now very open to this line of swing, nothing but a sliced shot can *possibly* result.

I will repeat once again what I must have said 10,000 times: you must find a grip that returns the clubface square to your line of swing at impact. If you will not or cannot do this, your golf will always be inconsistent and, in most cases, downright lousy.

In teaching I am often able to stop a lot of golfers slicing inside five minutes. I do it simply by persuading—sometimes forcing!—them to aim the clubface at the target, with the right shoulder pulled well around—probably six or eight inches back from the position it has been in. This in itself immediately improves their grip, because it pulls the hands at address away from the left side and brings them more toward the center of the body. From this address position, I then ask the pupil to have the feeling in the takeaway that he is closing the clubface. This is essential in the early cure of a slicer, because in his previous action, with his very open body setup and hands well forward, he is almost certain to have been rolling the clubface open with his hands and wrists in the takeaway—the only way he can get the club away from the ball on what seems to be the right path when his body is aligned miles to the left of his intended target.

The first essential, then, for the consistent slicer is to square his shoulders to the target line at address. Often this will give him the feeling that he is closed—aiming right of target. But it is *imperative* that he gets his shoulders square, and he will usually only do this if at first he feels closed in his upper-body alignment.

The golfer now has made room for his arms to swing up—and consequently down—on the inside. He no longer feels the need to make the pronounced rotary movement of his body to get the club back on the inside that was necessary from his open-shouldered address position—a movement that produced a reciprocal rotary body swivel on the downswing that threw the club outside the target line. It is easy for him now to develop the feeling of swinging his arms *up on the inside* in the backswing. From here they will surely swing down on the inside, causing his right shoulder to trail his arms instead of leading them.

I guarantee that anyone who can master this setup and arm-swing will stop slicing in five minutes. I also guarantee that he or she will be staggered and delighted by the feeling of solid striking that results. Indeed, many golfers realize after a few dozen shots like this that, for the first time in their lives, they are playing golf in a way that enables them to apply the clubhead fast and solidly into *the back* of the ball. It is a whole new experience for most.

The next stage, of course, is to modify the action according to the flight of the ball by experimenting with the grip and shoulder alignment. If the ball hooks, the shoulders may be a little too closed at address. If it is pushed straight out to the right, the grip may be a little weak and the hands can be moved slightly more to the right. Trial and error is necessary to consistently produce straight shots—but it must, for the congenital slicer, be within the framework of a square or slightly closed shoulder position at address and no independent action of the hands and wrists in the takeaway of the club, instead of a swivel of the body and roll of the wrists.

Another vital factor for the inveterate slicer is head position at address. Most slicers set their heads too far to the left—over or even in front of the ball—which forces them into the open-shouldered, open-bladed setup that guarantees a slice. They should observe how the very good golfer *always* sets his head behind the ball, and looks into the back of it—the bit he wants to hit.

If you stand so that you must look at the front (or even the top) of the ball, not only are you set up for an across-the-ball swing, but your whole left side is almost certainly going to collapse as you start down. Looking at the back of the ball from behind it establishes a strong left side. Remember, when your game goes bad, the set of the head affects the shoulder alignment and that the alignment of the shoulders has a big effect on the type of shots you will hit.

We cannot get away from the fact that golf is basically a matter of grip and setup. If you set yourself so that you must swing across the ball with an open clubface, you are doomed to slice—no other shot is possible. And the problem is that golfers who don't understand how important the setup is aggravate their faults by purely instinctive movements.

The slicer indeed is the supreme example. The ball goes to the right, and the more it does, the more he sets himself to the left—shoulders open, head in front of the ball, and, worst of all, a slicer's weak grip. Eventually, poor soul, he gets to the stage where the only thing he can possibly do is produce feeble banana shots from far left to far right.

Thus, the slicer's first task must *always* be to get himself into a square address position—shoulders, hips, knees, and feet parallel to the target line, or even slightly "inside" it. This will enable him to grip the club in a way that will let him swing the clubface through the ball looking at the target.

HELP FOR HOOKERS—AND PULLERS WHO THINK THEY'RE HOOKERS

The fact that there are fewer "natural" hookers in golf than slicers is very little consolation to the player whose every other shot darts sharply off to the left. True, he is likely to be a better golfer than his opposite number, but at times he will be in such a mess as to be virtually a non-starter. A genuine hook—a hard-hit ball swinging violently left—is a shot ranking in the disaster quotient with the shank.

The slicer, although a weak striker and short hitter, can usually at least remain in the park, because a "cut" ball flies, lands, and rolls more softly than a hooked ball. It is for this reason that so many professionals and first-class amateurs favor a slight fade, and why at the highest levels of the game one hears so much about "blocking" shots. To the good player, especially if he hits the ball a long way, a hook is a constant threat.

Even though a hooker usually has some knowledge of golf, like the slicer his problem stems from a lack of basic analysis of cause and effect. He may have thought hard and long about his swing, but he hasn't taken the problem to its root, which is the direction in which the clubhead approaches the ball and the alignment of its face at impact.

JOHN JACOBS' STROKESAVERS:

- Strengthen the grip, square the shoulders, and set the head behind the ball to fix a slice.
- Cure the tendency to slice—that also results in less topped balls.
- Weaken the grip slightly and again square the shoulders to straighten a hook.
- Prevent fat shots with better posture, balance, and timing.

I have proof of this daily. Good players come to me and say they are hooking. I ask them to do so. They hit a few shots, and, true enough, the ball goes to the left. But in many cases it does not "bend" to the left. It flies straight to the left, or starts left and then goes more left. These shots are not hooks. They are pulls and pulled hooks. And the important thing is that they do not stem from the sort of action that produces a genuine hook. They stem, indeed, from the very opposite, from a slicer's action, an out-to-in swing. All they lack is the slicer's open clubface at impact. If these self-described "hookers" were to hit the ball with an open clubface, they would in fact slice. If they were just to swing the club through the ball in the right direction, all would be well.

In golf, it really does help to know what you are actually doing before you try to alter it!

The genuinely hooked shot starts to the *right* of the target, then swings away to the left. If its turn is gentle, the shot is described as being "drawn"—perhaps the most useful "shape" for the average player, in that the kind of spin imparted to the ball increases both carry and run. If the turn is violent, the shot is disastrous at any level of the game. In both instances, and in every variation in between, the shot is made by the club coming to the ball from inside the target line with the face at impact closed to the line of swing.

(I might add here, for the benefit of people who hit the ball straight to the right and think they slice, that in fact they have a hooker's action, except that the clubface is square to their inside-out swing.)

It should be clear by now that the hooker hooks because something in his action brings his club to the ball on an "inside" path with the face closed to that path. What is that something, and how does he adjust to it?

We must go back, as always, to the clubface. If it comes into the ball closed, an in-to-out swing will naturally follow due to the golfer instinctively trying to swing the club to the right to counteract the "bend" in his shots. The hooker's first job, then, is simple: to square his clubface, which will make the ball fly straight along its starting path—in the same direction as he is swinging. This usually requires nothing more than some intelligent grip adjustment.

If you are a true hooker it is more than likely that you close the clubface at impact because your grip is too "strong"—your left hand is too much on top and your right too much underneath the shaft. Move both hands bit by bit to the left. It will feel uncomfortable for a while, but it will be worth the effort in the long run. A loose grip with the left hand very often closes the clubface, too, so make sure your hands work as a unit during the swing.

Persevering like this, you will eventually find that the ball, instead of starting right and turning left, starts right and continues that way. You have now swapped your hook for a push. Don't be disappointed. You have made the first of two adjustments, and are now ready to tackle the second.

If the ball now flies straight, your hands must be returning the clubface square to the line of your swing. It follows, therefore, that if the ball is not going where you think you are aiming, either your aim or your direction of swing is wrong. In this case you are pushing the ball straight to the right of your intended target. What does that mean? Simply that you are aiming to the right of the target when you set up to the shot in order to allow for your old hook, and thus are swinging the club along that line of aim—i.e., too much from inside to outside the proper ball-to-target line.

Your second task, therefore, is simple: aim and set yourself correctly. Arrange your feet, knees, hips, and shoulders—especially shoulders—parallel to the target line with your clubface looking squarely at the target. As a hooker, you may feel as though you are now aiming miles left. You can check your feet by lining up with a club on the ground. Get someone to check your shoulders by laying a club across them after you've taken your stance.

IF YOU TOP SHOTS, YOUR SWING IS TOO "STEEP"

Ask golfers what causes a topped shot and most will immediately say "head up." You hear it time and again on golf courses all over the world. One member of a fourball scuttles a shot along the ground. "Head up!" exclaim the other three. They haven't actually seen their chum lift his head—indeed, they may not even have been watching him swing. But that doesn't matter. It has to be "head up."

Usually they are wrong. Lifting the head can cause the body to lift also, and when this happens it is true that the ball may be topped. But only a small proportion of thinly-hit shots stem from such a movement. Even if you anchored their heads in cement, a great many poor players would still manage to top the ball quite effectively because the fault is not in their superstructure, it is built into their games by faulty swing patterns.

There are two basic causes of topping, they are closely allied to each other, and they emanate from a particular kind of swing geometry.

To achieve flush contact with the back of the ball, the clubhead must be square and also travel through the impact zone on a reasonably shallow arc, moving from inside the target line to straight along it to inside again.

The chronic slicer never achieves this shallow arc at impact or an inside-straight-through-inside clubhead path. For various reasons, usually arising from his setup, he brings the club to the ball from well outside the target line—across the ball. Even the most elementary knowledge of geometrical principles indicates that this must severely steepen, or narrow, the arc described by the clubhead as it approaches the ball.

It can easily be understood that, even if the shot is reasonably effective—and 70 percent of golfers play all their lives like this—the club has not hit the ball squarely in the back. To a greater or lesser degree, impact has been made on the top far-side corner of the ball as the golfer sees it at address. Now imagine what happens if the downswing becomes just a little more across the target line from out to in, and thus even steeper. The angle of attack becomes so acute that the clubhead cannot connect even with two-thirds of the ball, as happens in the normal slice. Its approach is so steep that it can contact, if anything, only the top half of the ball, or perhaps even only the top quarter of an inch. Result: a top—usually a top along the ground to the left.

From this, it should be clear that topping has little to do with your head, but is really the ultimate expression of a steep out-to-in, slicing-and-pulling swing pattern. That, in fact, is why the fault is so common among long and middle-handicap golfers, and so rare among good players.

The cure is equally obvious. To stop topping, you must stop slicing! You must in fact set yourself in such a position at address and use the club in such a way that you can swing into the back of the ball from behind and inside it, not over and down on it.

The second cause of topping is very much allied to the foregoing. Again, it is largely a poor player's fault, but it also sometimes afflicts the competent golfer, because it can happen even when the setup, swing arc, and plane are good.

At address on every golf shot, the radius of the swing—the measurement from player to ball—is established by the unit of the left arm and the club, held in a more-or-less straight line. In the early part of the backswing this radius is maintained by the "one-piece" (no independent movements) combination of arm swing and shoulder turn. But at some point in the action, where we cock our wrists, the radius obviously decreases. If, then, in hitting the ball, the wrists do not uncock sufficiently to reestablish the radius of the swing at impact—reestablishing the left arm and club as a straight-line unit—the ball is likely to be topped, or at least hit "thin." Among fairly competent players this is the commonest cause of topping.

In the simplest terms, what basically causes both these "tops"—and also most thin or "bladed" shots—is too little use of the arms, hands, and clubhead in the downswing. The inveterate slicer should understand that this problem is built into his game because of his steep downswing, which in turn emanates from his open clubface and out-to-in swing path. In the case of the better player, such lack of arm and wrist action arises usually from a deliberate attempt to "hit late." He would benefit from thinking of the downswing as a "re-measuring"— of getting his left arm and club back to the full radius of the address position before impact.

"FAT" SHOTS AT ADDRESS

Fluffing is hitting the ground behind the ball, or hitting shots "fat." There are two common causes of this depressing disease.

Among both good and indifferent golfers alike, it can often be caused by nothing more complicated than bad posture at address, leading to loss of balance during the swing. The golfer stands to the ball in such a way—usually crouching or reaching for it—that his weight is pulled forward onto his toes. Inevitably the momentum of the downswing throws him even farther forward, with the result that he either "falls into" the shot, or is forced to dip his head and shoulders to get the clubhead to meet the ball. To avoid such a destructive fault is just one more reason why we must always start the swing from the correct setup, remembering particularly in this case that the back must be reasonably straight.

The most common cause of fluffing among reasonably accomplished golfers is poor coordination of body and hand action in the downswing. It is the opposite of a topper's problem—a tendency to hit *too early* with the hands and wrists, before the hips have cleared a way for them to swing past the body and out toward the target.

As most slicers are prone to topping, so most hookers are liable to fluff occasional shots. What happens is that the fluffer lengthens his swing radius by letting the clubhead catch up with and pass his hands before they have arrived back at the ball. In other words, the arc the clubhead is describing as it approaches impact is too wide—the hit is too "early" with the hands and arms. It is, indeed, to avoid catching the ground that ladies—most of whom must hit "early" to get the clubhead moving at maximum speed by impact—instinctively rise on their toes during the downswing.

For men golfers, however, the cure for this fault is definitely not to be found in ballet dancing. The fluffer's basic problem is to better coordinate his downswing leg-hip movement with his arm and hand action—even to the point, for a time, of deliberately restricting his wrist action—deliberately hitting "later" with the hands and wrists.

From *Practical Golf,* by John Jacobs with Ken Bowden. Stanley Paul & Co., Ltd., an imprint of the Hutchinson Group. Copyright © 1972 John Jacobs and Ken Bowden. Used with the permission of John Jacobs.

What'd I Do Wrong, Coach?

2000 • Kellie Stenzel

"I assume that the reader knows nothing about the game," Kellie Stenzel wrote in her first book, *The Women's Guide to Golf: A Handbook for Beginners.* Since then, Stenzel, a popular instructor in Palm Beach, Florida, has been named a Top 100 Teacher by *Golf* magazine and broadened her target audience by writing more instructional volumes. Beginners still flock to her, but, significantly, even with more advanced readers and students, she caters to the insecure novice that lurks inside *all* golfers. In this excerpt from her first book, Stenzel plays coach to the proverbial duffer, providing a highly evolved, beautifully organized, and very welcome mode of instructional writing that details how to cure errors such as shanking, topping, and hitting fat. Senzel identifies several possible causes for each fault, and then offers advice for corrections that involve checking various fundamentals or performing specifically tailored drills.

By now in your golf career, you may have concluded that there are unlimited ways of hitting the ball badly, simply by combining your bad shots. So when your teaching professional asks you at your next lesson what your predominant shotmaking error is, you don't have to respond with a puzzled look. Your capability to describe your most prevalent shotmaking error guides your teaching professional to the most direct route to your error....

SHANK

A shank is definitely not a fun miss. In the resulting shot, not a pretty one, the ball often travels directly right and low.

Once the manager at Atlantic (the club in Bridgehampton, New York, where I teach) was out playing golf with the manager from another club on Long Island, and since they were playing quicker than my foursome we waved them to play through. The visiting manager had a brutal case of the shanks. He just kept shanking the golf ball in a circle right around the green. Eventually he just picked up his golf ball. It was painful to watch him circle around the green, shanking the golf ball, ending up farther away from the pin after each shot.

Cause: The clubhead getting outside the ball, so that the ball is contacted in the neck or hosel of the club.

Correction: Obtain a headcover or a towel from off your golf bag. Lay it down about three or four inches away from your golf ball, on the side of the ball farther away from you and on your intended line of flight. Then swing the club without contacting the headcover or towel. If your club crosses outside the ball, the ball will probably hit the heel. Practice with the headcover or towel until you stop hitting the box, and your shanks should disappear. In my opinion, you do not want to place anything solid on the outside of the ball; if you shank the ball, you *do* get your club outside the ball. Place something soft, so that when you do make this incorrect motion you will be aware of your mistake, but you will not run the risk of injuring yourself. I have seen people practicing this with wooden boards. It does not seem worth the risk to me. So if this is your problem, please use something soft.

Cause: Not properly squaring the clubface at impact, which will leave the face of the club open, exposing the hosel of the club to the ball.

Correction: Practice making half-swings. Hold your finish to check to see if the toe of your club is up or skyward, rather than having the face of the club skyward. If your clubface is pointing to the sky so that you could serve a drink on your clubface you have not allowed the club to naturally rotate through with your body.

Cause: Addressing the ball in the hosel at setup.

Correction: Address the ball in the center of the clubface. It may appear more out toward the toe of the club from the player's perspective.

Cause: Left hand grip rotated too far to the left.

Correction: Hold grip in fingers, so that the palm faces toward your body and you can see two to three knuckles.

Players who shank their shots will not like their irons. They will tend to prefer the woods, simply because the woods do not have a hosel and the irons do. You can spot shankers by their golf bags. They will have a lot of woods, and their irons will have dimple marks in the heels of the clubs. When they first start to understand the reason that they do not like their irons, because they are contacting the ball in the hosel, they are on the road to being able to correct the problem. You must first understand what you are doing incorrectly, and then you must understand what you need to change to make that correction.

TOPPED BALL

A topped ball, though very common, can be very frustrating to a new golfer. You will hit some tops. It is just part of your initiation process into the game of golf. Over time your percentage of tops should decrease, but expect some of this in the first couple of years. The suggestions here are to help you minimize your tops.

When I arrived at Furman University with approximately a 4-handicap, I would top my fairway woods once in a while. I was so embarrassed, I would wait to practice them when the range was nearly empty. If a 4-handicap can top the ball, it is okay for you. I forced myself to practice the fairway woods. Working on the weak points of your game is not as much fun as practicing what you are good at, but it will help you improve.

I was giving a playing lesson when one of my students, Carole, topped the golf ball off the tee of a par 3. I quickly picked up the golf ball and placed it back onto her tee to try again. She then proceeded to knock the golf ball into the hole. It was quite an impressive par!

Cause: If you have a great deal of tension in your arms, this will cause the muscles in your arms to contract, which in turn causes your arms to pull in toward you.
Correction: Relax adequately so that you can feel the clubhead swinging freely.

Cause: Terraphobi, fear of hitting the ground.
Correction: Place a tee in the ground in front of your golf ball, and allow the clubhead to stay very low to the ground in front of the ball, which will allow you to use the loft of the club properly. Many women fear hitting the ground for two reasons: it will hurt or it will make a mess. It should not hurt unless you are "death-gripping" the club, and it is okay to make a mess, also known as a divot.

Cause: A lack of understanding of how the ball gets into the air.
Correction: Understand that the lower side of the club must be allowed to swing

down to the ground to get the ball into the air. There is a phrase in golf "let the clubhead do the work." The true meaning is "permit the loft of the club to lift the ball into the air for you." Our tennis players must specifically watch this. In tennis you must swing up to get the ball into the air, because the tennis racket has no loft. In golf we must get the club down to the ground to get the ball into the air. So in other words, we are hitting the ball as the club travels on a descending path.

Cause: Standing too far away from the golf ball.
Correction: Check your setup to make sure that there is only one hand's distance between the end of the grip of the club and your body.

Cause: Your weight is too much back toward your heels.
Correction: Bend forward from your hip joint so that your chest is over your toes.

Cause: Loss of spine angle, also known as "standing up."
Correction: Maintain posture throughout the swing until contact with the ball.

"FAT" SHOT

A fat shot occurs when you hit the ground before the golf ball. The ball will travel significantly shorter than anticipated.

Cause: Standing too close to the ball.
Correction: Back away from the ball adequately so that you have approximately a hand's width, fingers outstretched, between the end of the golf club and your legs.

KELLIE STENZEL'S STROKESAVERS:

- Practice half-swings—rotating the clubhead through impact—to fix a shank.
- Check the setup to avoid topping—make sure the club is no more than a hand's width from the body.
- Turn the shoulders—don't tilt them—to prevent hitting fat.
- Stop skying by teeing the ball higher—not lower—and placing it inside the left foot.
- Keep a notebook detailing specific faults, then ask a pro for targeted instruction.

Cause: Tilting, rather than turning on your swing.

Correction: If your shoulders dip, rather than turn around your spine, when your right shoulder drops on the forward swing the ground will often be contacted before the ball. Cross your arms across your chest and practice turning around your spine so that your sternum turns away from the target rather than the shoulders' teeter-tottering.

Cause: Staying too flat-footed on your forward swing.

Correction: As you make a natural underhand throwing motion on your forward swing you should allow your body to turn to face the target so that your right foot comes up to the toe in reaction to the body turning to face the target. The turning of the body toward the target will pull the club to swing through toward the target.

TOED SHOT

This is a shot hit off the toe or tip of the club. It usually goes 90 degrees to the right and is potentially lethal. Do not allow anyone to stand directly to the right of you when you are practicing if you tend to toe your shots. Or place something like your golf bag to the right of the ball, to stop the ball from advancing too far to the right.

I was giving a lesson in New York right next to two other lessons. My student proceeded to toe the ball excessively off the end of the wood. The ball ever so softly lofted right over the instructor and the student directly to our right and landed like a marshmallow on the chest of the instructor two doors down. It landed so softly it was unbelievable. Nobody was hurt, but it was amazing to see the golf ball go so high, so right, and so short.

Cause: Standing too far away from the ball.

Correction: Determine if you have only one hand's distance (fingers extended) between the end of the club and your legs.

Cause: Arms pulling in on forward swing.

Correction: Work on swinging wide on the forward swing. Place a tee several inches ahead of your ball, along your flight line. Try to hit that tee as you swing through the ball. You will also want to check hand position in your grip. If your grip is too weak or, in other words, your hands rotated too far to the left, you will often try to pull across the ball to square the clubface, causing you to pull in and toe the ball.

Cause: Loss of spine angle.
Correction: Maintain posture throughout the swing, as opposed to standing up. Your weight should maintain its position on the balls of your feet and not throw back to your heels at any point in the swing.

SKIED SHOT

A skied shot or a pop-up with your teed woods is a ball that travels excessively high and not very far.

Cause: Incorrect ball position.
Correction: Make sure that your ball position for your teed woods is left in your stance, in line with the inside of your left foot.

Cause: Too steep an angle of attack. The angle at which the clubhead comes into the golf ball is the angle at which the ball will come off the clubhead.
Correction: Feel that your swing is more circular, rather than resembling the letter V. Take practice swings where your club sweeps an extended patch of grass, rather than digging into the ground. You should not take a divot with a teed wood.

Bad advice that is often given to the beginner who is popping the golf ball up is to tee the ball lower. What you actually want to do is tee the ball higher. When the ball is teed too low, the student feels the necessity to go down to get the golf ball and dives, producing too steep an angle of approach. So tee the ball higher and practice not hitting the ground by sweeping the golf ball off the high tee....

KEEP A NOTEBOOK FOR PROGRESS

We all tend to repeat our mistakes, so keep a small notebook of your problems with your golf and what you and your professional do to correct the particular problem. If that particular problem resurfaces, you can refer back to your notebook and correct your problems quicker. If we learn from our mistakes, they are worth making!

From *The Women's Guide to Golf*, by Kellie Stenzel. Copyright © 2000 by Kellie Stenzel. Reprinted by permission of St. Martin's Press, LLC.

CHAPTER 12

TROUBLE
SHOTS

How to Get Out of Jail

Recovering from the Rough and Playing from Difficulties

1924 • Cecil Leitch

Charlotte Cecilia (Cecil) Pitcairn Leitch grew up on the windy, hilly links of Silloth—a championship course in northern England—playing with the boys and imitating their swings. She emerged with an aggressive style that set a new tone for British women golfers prior to World War I and into the 1920s. She won 12 national titles—including the British Women's Amateur Championship a record four times—while engaging in a ferocious rivalry with Joyce Wethered. She beat Wethered in 1921 but lost to her in 1922 and 1925. In this excerpt from her book, *Golf Simplified*, Leitch offered timeless advice on coping with the difficulties free-wheeling players such as herself inevitably encountered. She included an engaging description of how despite wearing the restrictive long skirts of the period, she managed to scramble, straddle, and improvise shots from a variety of sloping lies, and creatively bend the ball in howling winds.

There are many lady players who are as good as the best so long as they keep down the middle and on the fairway, but when they are called upon to recover from the rough, or play from difficulties, their weaknesses are disclosed. Then, again, the majority of lady players are very poor performers in a wind. I shall try, therefore, to make these difficulties appear less terrifying by explaining the methods of play which I have found to be the most satisfactory under these varying conditions.

When the ball is lying in the rough, the player is inclined to overestimate the difficulty of the shot. Instead of trying to get as far as possible many players are quite content to find the fairway. This may be a wise precaution under certain circumstances, but playing for safety does not tend to improve one's form. It must be admitted, however, that it is almost impossible to get any length from the thick juicy grass, which is a difficulty to be feared by every player on an inland course during the summer. This type of grass has an unpleasant habit of

Alexis "Lexi" Thompson, 16, became the youngest woman ever to win an LPGA tournament, helping herself by executing this tough downhill lie shot on the 10ᵗʰ hole of the 2011 Navistar LPGA Classic. Thompson played the ball back, aligned her shoulders with the slope, and swung down and fully through the ball. (Darren Carroll/Getty Images)

winding itself round the shaft of the club and taking the sting out of the shot. To recover from a lie of this kind the niblick must be used and gripped very firmly, the player must stand well over the ball, and the swing must be of an upright nature. A point about an inch behind the ball should be aimed at, and the action should be more of a chop than a sweep.... From difficulties of this kind the player must apply all the force at her command, and in order to do so she will have to use a well-controlled full backward swing. No mere half or three-quarter swing will remove the ball....

The ordinary wiry grass of a seaside links or that to be found on an inland course during the winter is not really so trying.... The player must use her discretion as to which club is the right one, but here I should like to point out the value of a spoon for use in the rough.… Unless the ball is cupped in the rough, I invariably take my spoon, and standing well over the ball, use a swing similar to that employed in the push shot.

For a more cupped lie a mashie iron, [or a mashie-niblick], should be taken and the ball stabbed out. It is utterly useless to try to get a ball out of the rough with the ordinary sweep and hit of a full drive or brassy shot.

When playing a ball that is teed up in the rough, it is essential that the player address it with the club off the ground. She who puts the clubhead on the ground in such circumstances, instead of keeping it on a level with the ball, not only runs the risk of causing the ball to move, but will be almost certain to cut right under it.

Heather should be treated in the same way as grass, but here again I must refer to the versatile qualities of the spoon. Having been brought up on a links where heather abounds, there are few things I do not know about it. From thick heather the player must be content to regain the fairway by methods similar to those employed when in the thick grass of an inland course; but when the ball is lying even reasonably well the spoon is by far the best club to use. It is strange, but nevertheless true, that heather has far less effect upon a spoon or even a brassy than it has upon an iron club. In some strange way a spoon seems to glide over the heather and meet the ball truly, but the player must assist it to do so by putting a little bit of "push" into the stroke.

THE HANGING LIE

We have been in the rough long enough; we must now deal with difficult lies on the fairway, of which the "hanging lie" is the one most feared by lady players. When called upon to play in this position many players use a lofted iron club and play for safety, but there are many occasions that make a brassy or spoon the more effective club. Provided there is not a sharp rise immediately ahead, the player need not lose very much distance from a clean hanging lie. There are two methods which can be adopted, but the easier, to my mind, is as follows. Use the ordinary grip and take up a stance rather behind the ball, putting most of the weight on the right foot. Address the ball about an inch behind and use a full easy swing and follow-through, similar to an ordinary brassy shot allowing the clubhead to travel along the slope of the ground in the direction of the hole. Many players are inclined to dig at a ball lying in this position, but this is quite unnecessary and every player would be well advised to depend upon the loft of the club to raise the ball. It will do so naturally if this smooth sweeping action and hit are employed.

The other method of playing from a downward slope with a wooden club is to use an open stance; stand behind the ball, placing most of the weight on the right foot; and draw the face of the club across the ball by means of a swing which imparts a slice or cut. In this swing the clubhead is taken back in a line outside the ball and is brought down sharply by bending the right knee at the moment of impact. This is the more difficult method of playing the shot as the player has to allow for the slice, but I must admit there are times when it is the only one to play. Risks have to be taken sometimes, and when rising ground has to be avoided and the ball has to be played from a hanging lie onto a green which can only be reached with a brassy or spoon, this shot must be attempted, as it gets the ball up sharply.

THE UPHILL LIE

The "uphill" lie is a very simple one from which to play, and a brassy, spoon, or iron can be used according to the length of shot required. Throughout the playing of the stroke the right leg is used to support the body and in order to do so it must be stiff. The head must be kept still, as there is always a tendency to fall back from the ball. The right shoulder should be dropped slightly in the address in order to bring it and the left shoulder parallel to the slope of the ground. Provided these points are observed, the player can play the stroke in the same manner as she would if the ball were lying on level ground, in that the clubhead must be allowed to follow the slope of the ground.

It is as well to add that when playing to the green from an uphill lie the player should always use a club one higher in power.... The upward slope causes the ball to be thrown high in the air and so takes from the distance.

ABOVE AND BELOW THE BALL

The variety of lies and stances to be found, especially on a seaside links, compels me to mention those in which the player is standing above or below the ball.

For the former, the player must grip the club as near the end of the leather as possible. The player is obliged to adopt a rather stooping position, but if she keeps her head still the shot should not present any further difficulties and can be played as an ordinary brassy or spoon shot. Should an iron club be used, it will be played in the usual manner.

CECIL LEITCH'S STROKESAVERS:

- Use anything from a 3 wood to a wedge in the rough, depending on the lie.
- Don't ground the club when the ball is sitting up in the rough.
- Swing with the slope on a downhill lie.
- Take an extra club for uphill lies.
- Play for a slice when the ball is below the feet.
- Choke down on the club when the ball is above.
- Grip down and abbreviate the follow-through to keep the ball low in the wind.

When standing above the ball, there is a tendency to slice with a wooden club, but this is due to the player's failure to follow through. It is wise to allow for a slice by playing to the left of the direct line. The majority of players will probably agree that it is easier to play a shot when standing above the ball than when standing below it. The latter is an unpleasant position, as one feels unable to get any power into the stroke. When length is required I find my spoon a most accommodating implement. The rounded sole does not object to being dropped at the heel as would that of an iron or brassy. I have often played satisfactory shots with this club when the ball has been lying on a level with my waist. A still head, a shortened firm grip, and a stance slightly behind the ball are the chief essentials. This alteration in stance is the simplest way to overcome the inevitable pull from such a lie and stance....

PLAYING IN THE WIND

Lucky is the golfer who started to play the game on a windy seaside links. There is no finer nor fairer hazard than a stiff breeze or young gale, and she who can play well in a wind will find all other conditions simple. There is no doubt that any successes with which I have met are largely the result of the experience I gained as a child on the Silloth links, where the wind blows hard and often. Let me, therefore, try to help those who have not been so fortunate, by handing on certain points which I have discovered and found effective when playing in a wind.

When playing against the wind a low ball is essential and the well-hit ball will not be seriously affected. In order to hit a low ball I have found the following method the best and safest. With a driver, brassy, or spoon, I shorten my grip, hold the club very firmly and stand rather nearer the ball with my feet gripping the ground, the weight rather more on the left foot, and my knees stiff. My backward swing is flat, slow, and not as full as usual. The forward swing is well controlled and finishes with a low follow through.... The player must endeavor to make the clubhead follow along the line of play for a few inches after it has met the ball, in order to avoid the tendency to fall back onto the right leg at the moment of impact.

"I'd like to see the fairways more narrow. Then everybody would have to play from the rough, not just me."

—Seve Ballesteros

The "push" shot should be used with all iron clubs when playing against the wind. The ball that is hit in the more ordinary...manner is absolutely at the mercy of the wind, and can be blown hither and thither like a feather, but the ball that is hit with a punch will cut through the wind like a bullet....

Playing downwind is also a simple business, but I should warn the player against the tendency to stand too far behind the ball. After playing against the wind for a number of holes, the first drive downwind is invariably topped on account of the player's anxiety to get behind the ball and hit it up for the wind to assist it on its way.

I always consider the iron shot downwind onto the green with a bunker just short as one of the most difficult shots. This is one of the few occasions when the "floppy" iron shot is preferable to the "push" shot. The latter will race over the green, but the former will drop in a tired manner if hit high. [However,] when approaching with the wind behind [and no hazard in front of the green] it is advisable to keep the ball as low as possible. The pitch and run will generally give the best results....

The difficulties of playing against the wind or downwind are nothing compared to those to be encountered when a strong wind is sweeping across the course. Ladies are at a greater disadvantage than men under these conditions as skirts are a handicap, and there is nothing so tiring nor so trying as endeavoring to keep one's balance, when the wind is blowing on one's back or face. A firm

L ee Trevino offered classic advice for playing out of the rough, the only shot in golf where gripping the club tightly *is* a good idea. "The deeper the grass, the tighter the grip," Trevino said in the August 1985 edition of *Golf Digest*. Golfers as far back as Cecil Leitch offered the same counsel because a tight grip keeps the club from twisting and closing in the cabbage.

stance and a still head are terribly difficult to retain under these conditions, but they are essential.

Some players make use of the wind by playing for a slice when it is blowing from left to right, and for a pull when it is blowing from right to left. Personally I do not recommend such tactics, and I always try to hit the ball through the wind. It is surprising how little the flight of a well-hit ball is affected by a cross-wind. Once a player begins to tamper with her game by trying to use the wind she will find herself in all kinds of trouble.... When playing in a right-to-left wind I prefer slicing my wooden-club shots rather than pulling them. A sliced shot may not go so far, but it is invariably kept on the fairway with the help of the wind, and to be on the fairway is the main thing after all.

From *Golf Simplified*, by Cecil Leitch. Thornton Butterworth, Ltd., London, England.

Rainy Day Play

1960 • Doug Ford

If golf writers bother to discuss playing in rainy conditions, the advice is usually terse and basic, much like a mother might say: bundle up, keep your grips dry, and try to grin and bear it. But in this brief but original piece, Doug Ford, a star during the 1950s—he won a Masters and a PGA—and a much-respected instructional writer, presented strategies for how to actually *play* in the rain, and even related certain advantages that soggy conditions afford. Most noteworthy is that Ford insisted that club selection should be much different in the rain, and explained why golfers should adjust their short game techniques in order to handle different conditions on the greens.

So next time you play during or after a downpour, you'd be advised to take along Ford's recommendations, wrap them in clear plastic, and tape them to the underside of your umbrella.

Your pattern of play should change considerably in wet weather, yet so few average golfers seem to appreciate this fact that I feel a brief word on playing in the rain can help the club golfer considerably.

The choice of clubs, particularly on long shots, changes a great deal in rainy weather. It should be dictated by the lie, the ground to be covered ahead, and the condition of the turf underfoot. Bear in mind that a golf ball will fly, or float higher in the air, when hit off wet turf. This happens because the ball sits up more, and a wet face gives the ball more up-spin. Because of this it is bound to carry much farther in the air from soft ground. This is important to remember, because in such going, a club with more loft than would be used from a dry lie should be used. Bear in mind, too, this applies to the long clubs.

In rain or dampness, I think the 4 wood becomes the most essential club in your bag. Many of the circuit stars will leave their 2 or 3 irons in the clubhouse when the weather gets heavy. [Today, these clubs are usually replaced with various hybrids and fairway woods of 15 or 19 degrees.]

The important thing is to make sure to keep the ball airborne. With turf conditions aiding you, you can get as much distance with the more lofted 4 as with a 2 iron in dry weather. And a 6 iron will fly the ball as far as a 5 iron from unsoaked turf.

Also keep in mind, however, that the absolute reverse is true in the use of the deep-faced pitching clubs when the turf is wet. As an example, let's take a pitch with an 8 iron from just off the green. Normally, the division on such a shot should be to pitch about one-third of the distance to the pin, with a roll the remaining two-thirds.

When the rains come and the grass is saturated, you don't get the bounce and roll, so therefore you must be bolder and hit the ball more firmly. Now you should pitch two-thirds of the distance and expect the roll to be about one-third.

To me, playing in the rain offers a big bonus, particularly on the greens. I know the ball will roll much better and truer, though certainly slower. Wet greens call for firmness, and a firm putt is always the best.

Reprinted with the permission of Simon & Schuster Adult Publishing Group, from *How I Play Inside Golf*, by Doug Ford. Copyright © 1960 by Prentice-Hall, Inc.

DOUG FORD'S STROKESAVERS:

- Use less club in the rain—a shot off wet turf will fly longer and higher.
- Fire at the flag when the green is damp.
- Putt firmly; the ball will roll better and truer, but also slower.

Six Super Shots

1990 • Chi Chi Rodriguez with John Andrisani

Chi Chi Rodriguez's hardscrabble life started in the sugar cane fields of Puerto Rico, where he fashioned his first golf club from the branch of a guava tree. Whacking tin cans when he couldn't find balls, Rodriquez envisioned an escape route. His break came when he was caddying at a local resort and his game caught the eye of Laurence Rockefeller, who staked him to $12,000 for a fling at the pros. A half century later, Chi Chi is in the Hall of Fame after a solid career on the PGA Tour, and a stellar one on the Champions Tour, where he had 22 victories, including a record four straight. In this excerpt, golf's flamboyant master of adversity—whose foundation helps poor, at-risk kids—details how to overcome the toughest lies in golf from leaves, pine needles, hardpan, heather, and even "off the knees," and how to do it with "pizzazz."

THE OFF-THE-LEAF LIFT

The trickiest part of playing this shot takes place at the address. Avoid moving a ball that sits on a leaf, otherwise be prepared to accept a 1-stroke penalty for violating The Rules of Golf. Fearing this penalty, I never rest my club behind the ball in this situation; I let it hover slightly above the ground, just behind the ball.

Since good balance is key to playing this shot well, I flex my knees quite deeply and distribute my weight evenly between the ball and heel of each foot.

Because the ball must be *picked* off the leaf as cleanly as possible, good hand action is also critical. A light grip will greatly help you liven your hand action.

Pick the club up quickly in the backswing to set yourself up for a nice firm downswing hit. Keep the entire backswing action compact.

Drive both knees toward the target, and pull the club down and *through the ball*, making sure your hands lead the way.

THE SOFT TOUCH

Wiry Bermuda rough reminds me of steel wool. It's very hard to spin a ball that lodges itself in this dense grass that lines the fairways of many southern courses in the United States. Nevertheless, you can get the ball to sit down on the green pretty quickly if you switch from your normal technique to a highly unorthodox yet easily workable swing.

To hit this shot, I address the ball with my feet, knees, hips, and shoulders aligned precisely parallel to the target line. Then rather than balancing my weight evenly on each foot I put 65 percent of it on my left foot. This manner of distributing my weight helps me propel the club on an upright arc. That arc, in turn, promotes a down-and-through hit rather than an upward sweep with the clubface at impact. Trying to sweep the ball with the clubface at impact will not work for this type of lie. You must hit down and across the ball to get it to land softly on the green.

The key to setting up a reciprocal across-the-ball downward hit is swinging the club outside the target line on the backswing.

On the downswing, keep your head behind the ball, and pull the club down very hard with both hands. Again, because you swung the club outside the imaginary ball-target line, you'll automatically swing down and across when you're coming through.

Bill Haas won the 2011 Tour Championship and FedEx Cup in large part by perfectly executing this shot on the second playoff hole. The secret is partly luck—at least half the ball must lie above the water line—and lots of guts. Haas opened his stance and clubface, and played the shot as if the ball were in a bunker. (AP Images)

Due to the out-to-in shape of your swing path, enough cut-spin will be placed on the ball to make it land softly on the putting surface.

THE OFF-THE-KNEES HIT

The average golfer sometimes takes a penalty drop when he shouldn't. Most often he does this whenever his ball lies under a bush or small tree. Granted, dropping clear of trouble and taking a 1-stroke penalty is often the smartest solution. Nevertheless, don't be so quick to drop a ball until you have first carefully examined the situation and stretched your imagination, looking as hard for a shot as a lawyer does for a legal loophole.

CHI CHI RODRIGUEZ'S STROKESAVERS:

- Lighten the grip and pick the ball clean off loose leaves.
- Shift the weight forward and hit down and through to beat wiry Bermuda rough.
- Kneel down and swing with the arms for a shot from under a bush or small tree.
- Set up firmly and swing wide, using little wrist cock, to hit off slippery pine needles.
- Take a very upright backswing, and a crisp downward stroke to hit off hardpan.
- Keep the weight left, and lead the club down with the hands when the ball is in Scottish heather.

Actually, it upsets me to see a golfer take a drop from under a tree, if I know he could have hit the ball pretty solidly and accurately by playing off his knees. Kneeling down can give you ample room to swing the club so that you'll be able to at least hit the ball down the fairway. That's better than losing a shot and then still playing from the rough.

In setting up, spread your knees wide apart, as if to build a solid and balanced foundation for swinging the club back, down, and through mostly with your arms. Let both arms stretch out, since this extension keeps your hands and wrists quiet during the action and prevents the club from catching the ground well before contact is made with the ball. Quite a portion of the clubhead's sole will be off the ground as you jockey yourself into position. So to guarantee that you'll trap the ball at impact and make solid contact, close the face of the club a bit.

Lock your hips and swing the club back on a flat arc, being careful to let the arms control the action. Rotate your shoulders in a counterclockwise fashion while swinging your arms freely through to sweep the ball cleanly off the light rough grass.

THE PIZZAZZ PLAY OFF PINE NEEDLES

Whenever your ball lands on pine needles you must exercise extreme care. Not only is the ball sitting in a precarious position, but also your footing is usually unstable.

If you intend to move any loose impediments near the ball—twigs, leaves, etc.—proceed with caution. One false move could set off a chain reaction that will dislodge the ball, costing you a penalty stroke. For an identical reason, don't ever ground your clubhead when you address a ball resting on pine needles. Hold it just above the needles, and be certain to grip down on the club's handle to increase your control over the shot.

To play a solid shot off pine needles, *good footing* is very important; therefore, set up firmly and carefully in a square stance. Also, since pine needles are very slippery you must take a slightly wider stance than normal.

Make a wide flowing backswing with minimal wrist cock. This type of action will dissuade you from flicking the club through the ball and hitting a fat shot. What you want to do is pull the club down squarely into the back of the ball, with as little interference from the needles as is possible. So stay steady and wait for impact.

THE HARDPAN HANDLER

Patches of worn-down ground, or hardpan, are often found off the lush fairways of golf courses. The uneducated player who hits a shot haphazardly off hardpan gets a big surprise watching his ball shoot far to the right, often into bigger trouble.

After the club has swung from inside the target line on the backswing, hardpan prevents the clubface from squaring itself to the ball. At the moment of impact the clubface is open to the target—looking right of it. Consequently, you have two choices at the address: to set up open to the target to allow for the ball's inevitable left-to-right flight (more open if the club you're hitting with features a low degree of loft), or to set up square, with the clubface toed in a few degrees, so that it faces left of the target when it's set behind the ball…offsetting the blade's tendency to open at impact.

I n the July 1991 issue of *Today's Golfer*, two-time Masters champion José María Olazábal wrote that when the ball ends up against a tree, wall, or fence, right-handers should play the shot left-handed (or vice versa for left-handed players). Take a 7 or 8 iron, turn it upside down so the toe is pointing at the ground, aim a bit left, reverse the position of the hands on the club (left below right grip), and take a short, controlled swing. The objective is to get out of jail rather than hit it long and to save the penalty stroke for an unplayable lie. Harry Vardon used to carry one left-handed club in his bag just for such rescue shots, but modern golfers will want to carry an extra wedge, which they are more likely to need on today's courses.

In my youth, when I experimented even more than I do today with different swings and shots, I tried to discover a way to get a solid hit on a ball lying on hardpan. When I tried to pick it cleanly off the hardpan by exaggerating the sweeping motion of the clubhead through impact, I usually topped it. This happened because the clubhead actually bounced off the hardpan into the ball.

I got my best results, and so will you, from employing a very upright backswing, which makes for a very crisp downward hit. Don't misunderstand me. You'll never feel as if you're hitting the ball as solidly as you do from fairway grass. At least with this type of swing, however, you will avoid hitting the hardpan behind the ball.

The most critical thing you must do in setting up is to set your hands two inches in front of the ball. Make a very short upright swing, being sure not to sway off the ball. On the downswing, encourage a full, free, fast swing, and a *whip* of the club through the hitting area, by trying to straighten your right arm.

THE SURE OUT FROM HEATHER

Chances are you're a golf nut, which means that one day you'll probably play St. Andrews, in Scotland, the most historic course in the world, where the game is believed to have begun over 500 years ago. Whether you play that famous course, or any other links, be prepared to tackle heather, a wiry purple-flowered plant that will grab the neck of a golf club and close its face as surely as a Venus Flytrap catches flies.

A ball that lands in heather rarely perches high on the plant's upper branches; therefore, you'll usually face a tough lie that requires you to hit a pitching wedge shot back to the fairway. Don't mess with this stuff by gambling foolishly or you'll quickly chalk up strokes. Get the ball back to safety, and try to make a great par or a good bogey.

In setting up for this shot, assume an open alignment and put 65 percent of your weight on your left foot. Let the clubhead hover *above* the springy-textured heather with its face open, because the gentlest touch will move the ball out of position, costing you a penalty stroke.

In swinging back, pull the club almost straight up in the air.

Lead the clubhead down into the ball with your hands.

CHAPTER 13

ADVANCED TECHNIQUES

Master Class for the
Precocious Golfer

The Niblick, the Cut Shot, and How to Apply Backspin

circa 1928 • P.A. Vaile

Modern golfers may be surprised to learn this: a century before Phil Mickelson made galleries gasp with shots that land softly on greens and then roll back 10 feet—as if yanked by an invisible chain—the grand old men of golf could do the same. In this excerpt, the writer P.A. Vaile described how Johnny Farrell hit highly effective "cut" shots with a rudimentary niblick. Using a "lazy" swing and a "crisp" hit, Farrell could freeze the rubbery balls of the time—manufactured in Cleveland of all places—dead on the tracks of rock-hard greens throughout the country. The technique, which contemporary golfers might wish to try after reading this delightful piece of archaism, also pays homage to J.H. Taylor, the first genius of cut spin. Vaile insisted somewhat audaciously that if golfers can hit a slice—which most certainly can—they also can hit the delicate cut shot.

The niblick, in its ordinary construction—that is with the full-length shaft for full strokes—is admittedly a treacherous club. It requires considerable practice to master it, but for many shots it is indispensable.

With most players this club is used for pitching over and out of obstructions such as bunkers. It is seldom used for full strokes, and being used for shots just around the greens, 25 to 50 yards or nearer, should be played with the nearest possible approximation to the putting stroke....

The construction of [a] special short niblick [with a shorter shaft] allows the golfer to play an extraordinarily delicate shot with a very short swing back, which naturally tends to much greater accuracy in strokes where grounding of the club is prohibited.

Substantially endorsing my emphatic advice to golfers to carry the putt and its principles back into their game as far as they can, Johnny Farrell, Open

Champion of the United States in 1928, tells how to play a niblick shot over a mound or hazard and hold the green with backspin.

He says, "A great number of golfers have asked me what particular chip shot I use in pitching over mounds, hazards, and rough spots. I do not advise any particular club for these shots, because each condition calls for a different club to obtain the best results. Sometimes, for example, it is necessary to chip over a mound or hazard and hold the green. This requires a shot with sufficient backspin to cause the ball to remain near the hole. In such a case I use a niblick, standing close to the ball, and have the face of the club open—well laid back. A slow backswing is taken, and the ball should be hit through smoothly with the right hand. This is called the 'float' shot and must be played with a 'lazy,' slow swing with a rather sharp or crisp hit at the moment of impact. This shot is ideal for all short pitches over an object from five yards to 50 yards—an elevated putt, if you will…."

I understand Farrell's expression, "A lazy, slow swing with a rather sharp or crisp hit at the moment of impact," to mean putting the hand action, commonly called "the wrists," into the stroke only when very close to the ball….

Instead of being difficult to acquire, "cut" is so easy to get that it seems to come naturally to most people. Nobody ever heard anyone saying that it is difficult to slice. Well, a cut mashie or niblick shot is merely another variety of slice….

Place the ball on the turf at, say, 20 yards from the hole. Address it with an open stance. Swing your club—mashie or niblick—backward across the line to the hole and away from you.

SPIN DOCTOR

Applying backspin to the ball on delicate cut shots around the green is a highly skilled technique. But no matter how talented a golfer is, doing so will be impossible if the clubhead is dirty and the grooves can't grip the ball and give it that extra spin. Butch Harmon is known for instructing golfers to wipe clean their clubheads before hitting. But as long ago as the early 1900s, Harry Vardon was offering similar advice, saying "I like to see a golfer play with bright irons…that gives evidence of tender and affectionate care."

Come down on the ball with the clubhead swinging inwardly across the line toward you.

At first bring the club in toward you at about a right angle to the line of run or flight so that it merely "brushes" the ball and scarcely moves it from its base. It is, of course, obvious that this can be done.

P.A. VAILE'S STROKESAVERS:

- Open the clubface and take a slow backswing for a flop shot—what P.A. Vaile called the "float" shot.

- Hit crisply through impact, with the right hand overtaking the left.

- Open the stance and swing across the target line for a lob—a shot that is also sometimes called a "cut."

- Slip the clubhead under the ball to generate backspin.

When you have satisfied yourself of this it will be clear to anyone of much less acute mentality than yourself that the amount of cut and distance that you will get on your ball will depend on how much and how fast you send your brushing motion through the ball: in other words, on how you decrease the angle at which the face of the club moves across the intended line of flight and how fast you strike the ball.... [This] is the shot that was mainly responsible for J.H. Taylor's wonderful position in the world of golf, for his cut mashie approaches to the pin are still regarded as the last word in this invaluable and not too well understood branch of the game.

When one has acquired the simple art of cutting, or playing across the line of flight, one can go "all out" at the ball, get a tremendous amount of spin, and yet merely propel the ball a few yards. Perhaps the extreme illustration of this may be seen in the well-known trick of cutting clean under a ball with the niblick, sending it vertically into the air, and catching it in the hand as it comes down.

This stroke produces more of what is commonly called backspin than cut, and comparatively little of that, for it is in effect an illustration of the first step in my lesson on how to cut. It shows how hard one can hit *across a ball* and at the same time move it forward very little.

From *The Short Game*, by P.A. Vaile. Copyright 1928, 1929, Beckley-Ralston Co., Chicago, Illinois. Reissued in 1936 by Duckworth, London, England.

Stopping the Ball

1957 • Cary Middlecoff

As a teenage sensation, Cary Middlecoff already was playing in big tournaments, but he opted for college over golf, earned a dentistry degree, and then filled several thousand teeth in the Army before returning to civilian life as a pro golfer, and, until 1948, a part-time dentist. A slow player with a distinct pause at the top of his backswing, he had the skill to earn 40 PGA wins between 1945 and 1961, including two U.S. Opens and a Masters victory that included an 82-foot eagle putt in the final round. In this excerpt from his first book *Advanced Golf*—he would write *The Golf Swing* after his retirement—the "Doc" conducted a master class on specialty shots around the green, including an updated version of the high cut that was described by P.A. Vaile. Of special note is his advice on how to add deadly backspin.

Consider…a shot from about 20 yards out, under these conditions: the green is guarded by a deep trap that makes it impracticable, if not impossible, to get your ball on the green in any other way than making it land there on the fly; the pin is positioned about 15 feet from the edge of the green nearest you; and the green slopes slightly away from your side.

A tough situation surely, and the only way you can get close to the hole is to strike the ball in such a way that it will land on the green and stop quickly after it hits. What I am leading up to then is my answer to the often asked question: how do I get backspin on the ball?

The first consideration is to have a deeply lofted club…. The scoring [or grooves] should be entirely free of all foreign matter—dirt, grass, sand, and the like—when you make the shot. A wooden tee can be used to clean the grooves before the shot.

The maximum under-spin (or backspin) on a golf ball is obtained in much the same way as the maximum reverse English on a billiard ball is obtained—by a downward blow that first comes in contact with the ball at the lowest practicable point.…

Cary Middlecoff earned 40 PGA wins between 1945 and 1961, including two U.S. Opens and a Masters. Middlecoff stressed that maximum backspin is obtained by hitting down sharply, contacting the ball at the lowest point possible. (Bob Thomas/Getty Images)

To go back to our shot, and to the original proposition of stopping the ball quickly after it hits, we will find another factor besides under-spin is involved—loft, or the angle of descent. A pitching wedge or a sand wedge (the pitching wedge is preferable if the lie is a close one in grass, because the bigger flange on the sand club may hinder it getting under the ball) will provide the needed loft in nearly all instances. Some extra loft may be obtained by opening the clubface and positioning the ball about even with the left toe....

Take a slightly open stance with feet close together, a slightly choked grip, a relaxed and fairly erect posture permitting full extension of the arms, and fix your eyes on the ball, which should be positioned a little forward of the left heel. Concentrate on bringing the clubhead into contact with the underside of

- Use a wedge with a minimum of bounce for tight lies.
- Clean the grooves on the clubface first; that's essential to imparting backspin.
- Fix the eyes on the ball.
- Hit down sharply, contacting the ball at the lowest point possible.

the ball. The swing characteristics advocated for the chip shot…are applicable here—the firmness, crispness, smoothness.…

All golf shots from whatever position call for a firm and definite decision in advance as to what exactly will be attempted; but on none—unless it be the putt—is this factor as important as on this delicate pitch over intervening trouble where stopping the ball quickly is paramount.

From *Advanced Golf*, by Cary Middlecoff. Reprinted with the permission of Simon & Schuster Adult Publishing Group. Copyright © 1957 by Prentice-Hall, Inc.

Shotmaking: The Fun Begins

1987 • Nancy Lopez with Don Wade

In 1978, Nancy Lopez, from Roswell, New Mexico, burst on the LPGA scene at age 21 by winning five straight tournaments and nine overall titles. That she had charisma to match her talent was the major reason that the gate at ladies events instantly tripled. And to prove she was no one-year wonder, the future Hall of Famer won eight times in 1979. The title of this excerpt from *Nancy Lopez's The Complete Golfer* seems appropriate because the tough shots that might drive other golfers up the wall actually contributed to Lopez's sunny disposition. She offered clear, useable advice, making advanced shots like the intentional draw or fade less intimidating. She concluded with a lesson on the "knockdown," or punch shot, a useful but often neglected approach that flies low and stops quickly on the green.

I 've always enjoyed learning to hit a wide variety of golf shots, and I really admire players who fit the shot they want to play to the shape of the hole and the playing conditions. Once you've mastered the fundamentals of the golf swing, this is an area where you can really improve if you are willing to put in some hard work. It's also an area that can help you save strokes when you are faced with difficult playing conditions such as strong winds or tricky pin positions....

The key to this sort of versatility is understanding some fundamentals about the swing and about what makes balls fly the way they do when hit in a certain manner. Experienced players do this almost by instinct. It's almost as though their eyes see a certain situation, their brain programs the proper shot, and their muscles produce the shot.

In this chapter, I want to give you the fundamentals of shotmaking that will allow your muscles to hit the shots required by the course and playing conditions. When you can do that, you'll have taken a giant step closer to becoming a complete golfer.

DRAW VERSUS FADE: WHICH IS BEST FOR YOU?

I like to draw the ball, or hit it slightly from the right to left, for the majority of the shots I play. I think the draw is a stronger, more aggressive shot, and it's the swing and the ball flight I feel most comfortable with.

There are times, however, when I need to fade the ball, or hit it slightly from left to right. For one thing, a fade will not run as far as a draw because it doesn't have as much over-spin. This makes it a better shot if you are trying to drive the ball into a narrow fairway landing area. It's also a better shot to hit to a tight pin placement because it will stop more quickly on the green....

To draw the ball, or hit it from right to left, I want to make sure that I hit the ball with the clubhead moving from inside the target line, to square at impact, to back inside the target line.

The best way I know to ensure this inside swing path is to address the ball with a slightly closed stance. I address the ball with [a] square stance...and then simply drop my right foot back off the target line. In other words, if you drew a line from my right toe to my left toe, that line would point to the right of the target if I was playing from a closed stance. By doing this, I make it possible to strike the ball from the inside, and give it a right-to-left spin....

Feel is a very important factor in playing golf, and that's especially true when it comes to shotmaking.

Hall of Famer Nancy Lopez suggested hitting a low, piercing "knockdown shot" in windy conditions—urging golfers to play the ball back in their stance, take a three-quarter backswing, then punch down on the ball and hold the follow-through. (AP Images)

To put a right-to-left spin on the ball, you want the toe of the clubhead to come into the ball ahead of the heel. In other words, you want to have the clubface closing down at impact. To do this, your right hand must pass over the left at impact. The more the clubface closes down at impact, the more spin you'll be able to put on the ball and the more the shot will fly from right to left. To get this kind of hand action in the swing, it helps if you think of being very "wristy" at address. As you waggle the clubhead at address, let your hands and wrists feel very loose, and make sure you have a nice light grip pressure on the club.

NANCY LOPEZ'S STROKESAVERS:

- Focus on the back left-hand quarter of the ball to hit a draw.
- Move the ball forward and hold the clubface open at impact for a fade.
- For a knockdown shot, put the ball back and take a three-quarter backswing—then punch down on the ball and hold the follow-through.

In terms of actually hitting the shot, you want to try to take the clubhead away from the ball farther inside the target line than you would for a normal shot. Don't hurry the swing, which is a natural tendency, but let your hands release fully at impact. Again, you want them to feel very loose. It will also help if you look at a spot on the back left-hand quarter of the ball and try to hit the ball on that spot. In fact, if you are hitting a tee shot or are on the practice tee, you might try putting the trademark in that position and then try hitting the ball squarely on the trademark. This will help you swing into the ball from the inside.

As in all shots, it helps if you visualize the flight of the ball as you address the shot. Burn the image into your mind, and when you make your practice swing, get a feel for how the swing you need to make will feel—and for a draw or hook, it should feel very loose and relaxed.

One final thought: a ball hit from right to left will run, and the more spin you put on it, the farther it will run. Take that into account when you study the shot. It doesn't help to crack a big draw off the tee, only to watch it bound through the fairway and into trouble. It will also fly somewhat lower, which makes it a good shot when you need to drive the ball into the wind.

HITTING A FADE

Occasionally logic and common sense really do come into play in golf, and this is one of those times. To fade or slice the ball, you do just the opposite of what you do to bring it from right to left. Let's run through the important points one by one, comparing them to the previous section on hitting a draw or hook.

Stance: Again, this is the most important alteration I make when I hit the ball from left to right. I play this shot from an open stance. My feet, knees, and shoulders are all aligned to a point well left of my target. This allows me to strike the ball with an outside to on-the-line to inside swing path. This path sets the clubface open at impact and produces a left-to-right spin on the ball.

Grip: While I don't change my grip, I do alter my grip pressure slightly. I grip the club a little more tightly in my left hand. This will keep my left hand from breaking down at impact and will help keep the clubface slightly open at impact. The more open the clubface is at impact, the greater the amount of spin put on the ball.

Ball Position: To hit a fade, I move the ball slightly forward in my stance.... Just as in other shots, you have to experiment to find out which position works best for your swing.

The Swing: As I've said, the key to this shot is keeping the clubface open at impact. To do this, I take the club away from the ball, trying to move it outside the target line. This will cause me actually to swing on a slightly more upright plane and will help me cut across the ball with an open clubface at impact. You must consciously keep a firm grip with your left hand, not letting the right hand cross over the left until well after impact.

If you are having difficulty visualizing how this swing should look, my suggestion is to watch Lee Trevino play sometime. Actually, he doesn't fade the ball as much as people think, but his swing is designed to fade the ball at will. He takes the club back outside the line, then drives down and through the ball while keeping a firm left wrist. The ball comes out nice and high and lands softly. The beauty of his game is that he takes virtually all the trouble on the left side out of any hole he plays. That's a big edge.

Keep in mind that a fade or slice will fly higher than other shots and will run less. That's important to remember when planning a shot, because you may need to take one more club to reach your target if you plan to hit a fade.

HITTING IT LOW: THE "KNOCKDOWN" SHOT

There are a lot of times in the course of a round when being able to knock the ball down is a valuable shot to have. It's good in the wind, because the ball will drive lower and be less influenced by it. When you study players from Texas or the British Isles, where the wind is a big factor in the game, you quickly see that they are all good at hitting the ball low and out of the wind.

It's also a good shot if you've hit the ball into trouble and have to hit a low shot under branches and limbs. And it's the shot to play if you find your ball sitting in a divot mark....

The ball should be positioned back in your stance, at least to the middle of your stance and possibly even more than that. Keep in mind, however, that the more you move the ball back in your stance, the more you deloft the club you plan to hit.

With the ball back in your stance, you will...find that your hands are set well ahead of the ball. This is where you want them to be at impact as well, and you'll find this is an easier shot to hit if you have a slightly firmer grip pressure, since it's essentially a "hit and hold" shot.

Take the club back straight away from the ball, and remember that this is a three-quarter swing. You just want to set the club at the top of your back-swing—your hands should be about shoulder height—and then drive down on the ball with a descending blow, with your hands leading the clubhead into the hitting area. All you are doing is "punching" down on the ball. Your left wrist doesn't collapse, and your hands don't release. Just punch down on the ball and hold your follow-through.

The mistake most people make with this shot is trying to hit it too hard. Remember that the harder you hit the shot, the more spin you'll put on the ball, and you'll actually cause the ball to fly higher than you want. It's a three-quarter shot, played with a three-quarter swing at three-quarter speed—and it will run, so make sure to take that into account when you plan the shot.

Cut It Out—Here's How Ben Hogan Taught Me the All-Important Cut Shot

1991 • Ken Venturi

Silver-haired Ken Venturi retired from CBS Sports in 2002 after 35 years as a distinguished golf commentator and frequent contributor of instruction tips—though he still shows up for occasional guest spots. Before that he was a top-ranked professional who lost two Masters at the tape and won the 1964 U.S. Open at Congressional in one of the game's most dramatic finals. Playing in temperatures over 100 degrees, and suffering from heat prostration, Venturi staggered to the finish accompanied by his caddy *and* a doctor. In this piece from *Golf* magazine, he described a nifty, more modern and practical version of the cut shot Vaile relished. Having learned the technique from his frequent practice partner Ben Hogan, Venturi insisted that even hackers can master it with a minimum of practice time. Plus they can execute it under pressure because they will swing with the arms, rather than relying on the more twitchy-prone hands.

The short cut—a high shot that flies slightly from left to right and lands softly on the green—is one of the most versatile shots in golf. I use it often: to hit over a trap to a tight pin placement, over a bank to a hole cut on the top tier of a green, from a grass bunker, or from deep fringe to a quick or downhill putting surface.

Some golfers play the cut by manipulating the club on an outside-to-inside path with their hands controlling the action. There's nothing wrong with this technique provided you have exceptional feel and hours to practice. Years ago, the great Ben Hogan taught me an easier and more consistent way to swing from out to in and cut across the ball. This technique uses the arms more than the hands, which gives you more control.

Check out this simple method from the master and play a greenside shot that's a "cut" above the rest.

OPEN THE SETUP

To promote the proper outside-to-inside swing motion, stand open with your feet, hips, knees, and shoulders aiming left of the target. For most shots, play the ball a little forward in your stance with your hands in line with it. If you need extra height, set your hands slightly behind to help you slide the clubface under the ball.

KEN VENTURI'S STROKESAVERS:

- Play the cut shot mostly with the arms; the wrists stay firm.
- Set the ball forward, and open the clubface and stance.
- Place the hands even with, or behind, the ball.
- Use an extremely weak right-hand grip, the V pointing to the chin.
- Make sure the clubhead points to the sky after impact.

OPEN THE FACE

Use your pitching wedge or, if the lie allows, your sand wedge. (There must be enough cushion beneath the ball that you can slip the deep flange of the sand wedge underneath it.) Always open the face for a cut shot; this creates the high trajectory and causes the left-to-right flight.

Lefty Phil Mickelson is a short game artist who uses a variety of sophisticated shots around the green to recover from his sometimes errant ways. When the ball is sitting in high grass and the pin is cut close, Mickelson explained in *Golf Digest*, he opens the blade on his lob wedge, aims for a spot a few inches behind the ball, and makes a very handsy swing. The ball comes out high and lands softly. Walter Hagen used a similar method decades ago, letting the weight of the clubhead drop naturally under the ball; British champion Laura Davies said in *Today's Golfer* that she can stop her ball on a "sixpence" using the same technique.

THE GRIP AND SWING

Hogan's secret to a soft cut shot is an extremely weak right-hand grip. Exaggerate the turn of your right hand on top of the club so that the V formed by the thumb and forefinger points at your chin.

A weak grip forces your right arm to extend and rise slightly above the left arm at address. From this position, the only natural motion is an abbreviated out-to-in, upright backswing. Once you start the motion, shift your weight to the right foot; on the downswing, the weight should move back to your left side.

A weak grip also encourages keeping the left hand and wrist firm in the hitting area. Note [that] the clubface points to the sky after impact. This is essential for maintaining the high trajectory of the shot.

From *Golf* magazine (October 1991), by Ken Venturi. Copyright ©1991–2005, Time4Media, Inc. Reprinted with permission of *Golf* magazine.

How to Control and Work the Ball
and How to Play the Bump and Run

1993 • Tom Watson with Nick Seitz

Tom Watson's mastery of British Open courses and his conquest of the Pebble Beach links in 1982–when he snatched the U.S. Open from Jack Nicklaus on the 71st hole–are testaments to his extraordinary ability to both "work" the ball and play that most un-American of shots, the bump-and-run. The latter, usually associated with British and European stars–since most Yanks play "target" golf–has been a potent tool for Watson throughout his marvelous career. In this excerpt from *Tom Watson's Strategic Golf*, an often overlooked but highly valuable book, Watson provided a thorough examination of the bump-and-run from the American perspective, and offered lucid instruction on how to shape a variety of shots high, low, and around obstacles with hook and slice spin. Watson is hacker-friendly because he doesn't believe in overly sophisticated techniques–even when hitting truly masterful shots.

HOW TO CONTROL AND WORK THE BALL

Good strategy demands good control of the ball.

Different players and teachers use different methods for maneuvering the ball. My basic method is based on simplicity.

You don't have to be a low handicapper to hit a low hook or a high slice. I'll ask you to make no adjustments in your swing. I rarely make them myself. I don't change my grip except for exaggerated instances.

The benefits of knowing how to shape your shots are several.... You can avoid an obstacle like a tree; you can play a dogleg hole the way the architect designed it; you can get the ball closer to a tight pin position....

I try to make every shot fall left or fall right—a straight shot's an accident....

To curve the ball, I align my body well away from the target, aim the clubface at the target, and make a normal swing along my stance line. I align my body before I aim the clubface. Once my body is aligned away from the target, I rest the club on the ground (assuming I'm not in a hazard), square the clubface to the target, and take a normal grip. Your ball position should be normal, even though changing your stance may make it appear to change. The ball starts out along the stance line and then curves to the target.

HOW TO SLICE—ON PURPOSE

Most of you slice and don't want to, but at least this will help you understand why. To cut the ball, I align my body left of target and aim the clubface at the target, then swing to the left along my stance line.

The face, in effect, is open and cuts across the ball to impart slice spin. Do not let the toe of the club pass the heel through impact.

HOW TO HOOK

You pretty much can infer from the above slicing segment how I hook the ball. I align my body—shoulders, hips, knees, feet—to the right of the target, aim the clubface at the target, and swing out to the right.

I make a normal swing along my stance line and control the shape of the shot through the angle of the clubface. The face comes into the ball in a closed position and delivers hook spin.

If you're a chronic slicer, you may have to align your body farther to the right than you think to hit a hook. And you may have to aim at the left rough off the tee to get the ball in the fairway with your slice until you master this approach.

It also can help the chronic slicer to position the hands more ahead of the ball at address and think about making the toe of the club pass the heel through the impact area.

HOW TO HIT IT LOW

Hitting the ball low is primarily a matter of ball position. I move the ball back in my stance.

Moving the ball back reduces the effective loft of the club. Be aware that when you move the ball back you must square your clubface to the target, because your normal clubface position would now be open. I don't consciously adjust my weight distribution. This follows from the ball position.

For a low shot I try to finish my swing low.

A key point: play the ball an inch or so closer to your body on low and high shots or you'll hit the ball on the toe of the club. The correct path of the club comes from inside the target line to along the line to back inside, and when you move the ball forward or backward, the center of the clubface swings into the ball inside the line unless you adjust.

HOW TO HIT HIGH

I move the ball forward in my stance, adding loft to the clubface, to hit it higher. As with the low shot, I make sure I square the clubface to the target.

Moving the ball upward toward your front foot encourages a higher swing finish, and I strive to finish high with my arms. I also want to stay back with my upper body on the downswing.

Hitting the ball high, I select one more club than usual—a 6 iron instead of a 7 iron, for example—and more than that into the wind, because I'll lose distance. Of course, I still make sure I can clear any obstacle in my path.

Play the ball an inch closer to your body....

HOOK IT LOW

This is a comparatively easy shot. Just smother-hook it. Put the ball back in your stance, align your body to the right and your clubface at the target, and swing normally along your stance line.

Let the club release, making the toe of the club pass the heel through impact. Finish low.

Be sure you select a club with enough loft to get the ball airborne.

HOOK IT HIGH

This one's tougher. You really have to release the club and finish high.

Put the ball forward in your stance, align your body to the right, aim the clubface at the target, and swing out to the right. Keep your head behind the ball on the downswing, and feel that you are releasing the clubhead out and up.

An important aid to that kind of release and follow-through is to take the clubhead away from the ball quite low.

SLICE IT LOW

Another true tester. The difficulty is keeping the ball down. I'll put the ball back a bit in my stance to keep from hitting it too high. Gripping down on the club also helps.

Align your body left, aim the clubface at the target, and swing along your stance line. I "block it" hard with my hands—retaining the wrist break on the downswing and making sure the toe of the club does not—repeat, not—pass the heel through the ball.

Finish your swing very low and left, pulling your arms across your body and shutting off your follow-through.

SLICE IT HIGH

Most golfers would prefer to be rid of this shot, and maybe you already know too much about it. Just be sure to keep the clubface open going through the ball.

Position the ball forward and an inch closer to you than normal, with the same body and clubface position as for the low slice. Keep your head back. Finish high and left.

CHANGE YOUR GRIP FOR TROUBLE SHOTS

When I face a trouble shot where I have to slice or hook the ball a lot, I will change my grip. Actually it's probably the easiest way for most players to stop slicing and start to hook the ball. And changing your grip in practice is an excellent way to learn about spin and train yourself in trouble shots.

To hit a major slice, rotate your hands counterclockwise on the grip. To hit a large hook, rotate your hands clockwise. Do *not* rotate the clubhead as you rotate your hands. Many people will strengthen their grips to hit a hook—and set the club down behind the ball with the face rotated open. They defeat their purpose. Leave the club aimed where it was, then just relax your hands and rotate them the way you want to.

"No matter what kind of stroke you play or what sort of club you use, you need to make only minute adjustments for shotmaking."

—Greg Norman

The position of the left thumb is central here. If you want to slice the ball, your left thumb should be straight down the top of the club or even a little left of that, in a weak grip. To hook the ball, set your left thumb well over to the right and more under the club. That's an extra strong grip.

Make some swings both ways. It will probably feel terribly awkward. But try to make contact and see what the ball does. When your hands are in a very weak position, the ball will go short, high, and to the right. When your hands are in a very strong position, the ball will go lower, longer, and left. This happens almost regardless of your swing path. (Normally I'd rather see most of you use a fairly strong grip than a weak one.)

TOM WATSON'S STROKESAVERS:

- Play the ball an inch or so closer to the body on high and low shots.
- Don't change the grip except for exaggerated slices and hooks.
- Set the left thumb straight down the grip for a big slice, but more under for a hook.
- Use a basic chipping stroke for the bump and run.
- Aim to land the ball on a flat spot, avoiding side-slopes at all costs.
- Don't try the bump and run in lush, long grass. It's ideal for dry, firm conditions.

HOW TO PLAY THE BUMP AND RUN

I love the British Open for the bump-and-run shots you play.... Chipping and running the ball is a style of play I didn't like at first, because I thought too much luck was involved, but I've come to consider it the ultimate.

On our Tour we play soft courses that force you to fly the ball onto the green. In Britain they play firmer courses that call for more inventive shotmaking into and around the green, which often is open in front. The ground is hard and you want to bounce and roll the ball onto the green in many cases.

Bump-and-run golf is often the way you should play when the weather is poor. For example, downwind with the pin cut close to the front of an open green behind a mound, you probably can't get the ball close unless you run it....

Americans rely far too little on the bump and run. On dry courses with a lot of rough, the average weekend player would improve his up-and-down percentage by trying more ground shots and fewer finesse wedges. I will play a bump-and-run shot any time I have the opening and don't think I have enough room to land the ball on the green and stop it within 25 feet of the hole....

AVOID LANDING ON SLOPES

Slope is a major factor playing the bump and run. I always prefer to land the ball on a flat area for greater control. I avoid side-slopes like wild animals, because you never can be sure how the ball will kick.

Up-slopes and down-slopes you can handle more easily. Take a less lofted club into an up-slope and a more lofted club into a down-slope. Wind is another factor. You may well need less club than you think going downwind and more club upwind.

The big key to the bump and run: pick the spot where you want to land the ball and then pick the club that will carry it to that spot and bounce and run it to your target.

Don't try a bump-and-run shot through lush, long grass. But under dry, firm conditions, the bump and run often is your smartest choice.

This is the most common bump-and-run situation. I'm short of the green, and the pin is near the front edge. I want to bounce and roll the ball over a mound and be able to stop it near the hole. Using a basic chipping stroke, I land the ball in a flat "valley" so the ball will have the forward momentum to get up

GETTING PAST (PAST) MISTAKES

Dr. Bob Rotella, golf's preeminent psychologist, says players at all levels must expect to make bad shots and not dwell on them. That concept echoes Hall of Famer Walter Hagen's famous philosophy, and was more recently put into play by veteran Darren Clarke and rookie Keegan Bradley, the respective winners of the 2011 British Open and PGA championships. During post-tournament remarks, both men thanked Rotella for his help. In his aptly titled bestseller, *Golf Is Not a Game of Perfect* (1995), written with Bob Cullen, Rotella says, "Golf is indeed about recovering from bad shots." He advises, "On the first tee, you should have two immediate goals. One is to have fun. The other involves the process of playing, not the results. This goal is to get your mind where it's supposed to be on every shot.... When a shot is done, it's done. The only constructive thing you can do about it is to hit the next shot as well as you can." Bradley obviously followed his doctor's advice, coming back to win the PGA in a playoff despite a triple bogey on the 69th hole.

the slope. Usually I try to bounce the ball twice before it gets to the green. The first bounce takes the steam off the shot, the second bounce gets the ball rolling. I want the ball rolling smoothly down the slope like a putt.

From *Tom Watson's Strategic Golf*, by Tom Watson with Nick Seitz. Copyright © 1993 by Tom Watson. Reprinted with the permission of Pocket Books, an imprint of Simon & Schuster Adult Publishing Group.

I Dare You: Try My Killer 2 Iron

2000 • Tiger Woods with Pete McDaniel

After taking the 1997 Masters by a record 12 strokes for his first major title, Tiger Woods refused to coast. Under the tutelage of Butch Harmon, he retooled his swing and added new shots to his arsenal, eyeing what lay ahead in 2000 – coping with the windy, tight links of Pebble Beach and St. Andrews, the sites of the U.S. and British Opens, respectively. By the end of that year, Woods had become only the fifth man – and the youngest – to capture a career Grand Slam. In this short piece from *Golf Digest*, Woods described one of the new shots he rode to victory – the knockdown 2 iron, a "wind-cheater" first made famous 100 years before by J.H. Taylor. As Tiger said, the shot takes both finesse and very strong hands, but for the advanced golfer, he offered the formula for giving it a go.

This knockdown 2 iron off the tee is a shot I've developed in the past two years with my [former] coach, Butch Harmon. I use it to keep the ball in play when I'm facing a tight fairway, especially down the stretch in a tournament or in the wind. I used it a lot this year when I won the Mercedes Championships in Kapalua, Hawaii. A low shot, it carries about 220 yards, about 30 yards shorter than my full-release 2 iron. It's designed for accuracy, not length, though on a hard fairway it can run up to 80 yards.

What's different about this shot is that I have very quiet feet, a bowed left wrist at impact, and an abbreviated follow-through. I've done a lot of strength

TIGER WOODS' STROKESAVERS:

- Tee the ball low and back in the stance, with the hands ahead.
- Take a full backswing, but don't hurry the action.
- Keep the feet quiet and firmly planted.
- Hold the left wrist bowed at impact, and abbreviate the follow-through.

training in the last two years just for this type of shot. I had to be stronger to hit the ball with a bowed wrist and to hold my follow-through like this. If my feet were more active or my arms weaker, I'd be forced to release the club, and the ball would go higher.

To hit the knockdown 2 iron, I tee the ball low and play it back in my stance, with my hands ahead of it. I also sit a little lower in my setup to get my center of gravity down, and I make a full backswing turn. Average players often try to hit this shot too hard; they end up rushing, restricting their backswing, and coming down too steep, so the ball spins too much and balloons. I'm still working to perfect this shot. I want to be able to hit it the exact same trajectory every time—which means, of course, I can never really perfect it.

From *Golf Digest* (April 2000), by Tiger Woods with Pete McDaniel. Reprinted with permission from *Golf Digest* ®. Copyright © 2005 The Golf Digest Companies. All Rights Reserved. Golf Digest is a Registered Trademark of the Golf Digest Companies, which is a subsidiary of Advance Magazine Publishers, Inc.